CAMBRIDGE SOUTH ASIAN STUDIES

THE
MUTINY OUTBREAK
AT MEERUT IN
1857

CAMBRIDGE SOUTH ASIAN STUDIES

These monographs are published by the Syndics of Cambridge University Press in association with the Cambridge University Centre for South Asian Studies. The following books have been published in this series:

GOPAL, S., *British Policy in India, 1858–1905.*
PALMER, J. A. B., *The Mutiny Outbreak at Meerut in 1857.*

THE
MUTINY OUTBREAK
AT MEERUT IN
1857

BY

J. A. B. PALMER

CAMBRIDGE
AT THE UNIVERSITY PRESS
1966

PUBLISHED BY

THE SYNDICS OF THE CAMBRIDGE UNIVERSITY PRESS

Bentley House, 200 Euston Road, London, N.W. 1
American Branch: 32 East 57th Street, New York, 22, N.Y. 10022
West African Office: P.M.B. 5181, Ibadan, Nigeria

©

CAMBRIDGE UNIVERSITY PRESS

1966

Printed in Great Britain at the University Printing House, Cambridge
(Brooke Crutchley, University Printer)

LIBRARY OF CONGRESS CATALOGUE
CARD NUMBER: 65–20790

To
M.O.T.L.

CONTENTS

Introduction   *page*   ix

1   CHAPĀTĪS   1

2   GREASED CARTRIDGES   8

3   THE PRESIDENCY DIVISION, FEBRUARY TO MAY   21

4   REGIMENTS AND OFFICERS AT MEERUT   34

5   MEERUT CANTONMENT IN 1857   47

6   THE FIRING PARADE OF 24 APRIL AND ITS
    SEQUEL   58

7   THE OUTBREAK: (a) The Native Infantry Lines   70

8   THE OUTBREAK: (b) The Native Cavalry Lines   80

9   THE OUTBREAK: (c) The Bazar Mobs   88

10 THE OUTBREAK: (d) The European Troop Move-
    ments and the European Lines   97

11 THE HANDLING OF THE EUROPEAN TROOPS   106

12 TO DELHI   119

13 CONCLUSIONS   129

Notes and References   138

Index   167

Plan of Meerut Cantonment in 1857   *at end of book*

INTRODUCTION

On the evening of Sunday 10 May 1857 there occurred at Meerut, about 40 miles north-east of Delhi, the outbreak of the native regiments which marked the real beginning of the Indian Mutiny. This outbreak at Meerut is the true subject of the present volume and I should like at the outset to define as exactly as possible the scope and intention of the work, so as to avoid misunderstanding on the part of any reader. This is *not* a full study of the origins of the Mutiny, such as is to be found in the classic work of Sir John Kaye or the more recent but no less admirable work of S. N. Sen. To those works the reader is referred for the full prolegomena to the history of the actual Mutiny itself: he may, if he wishes, push his examination further into the collections of the papers of former Viceroys or Presidents of the Board of Control now surviving in the India Office Library but either not available to, or not fully examined by, the distinguished historians just mentioned. Except to the extent which is specified below, the general subject of the origins or causes of the Mutiny falls beyond the scope of the present work.

It may be remarked that for the purposes of the following pages such unexamined or imperfectly examined collections of papers of former Viceroys or other exalted personages would only be of use if containing an unknown contemporary eyewitness account of the events at Meerut (or at Delhi next morning) which I am about to attempt to describe. The presence, however, of any account of that kind in any of those collections is most unlikely. The Viceroy at the time, Lord Canning, was 900 miles away in Calcutta, the Board of Control some 6000 miles away in London: Lord Canning got such information as he had in a confused form either from Mr John Colvin, Lieutenant-Governor of the North-West Provinces, at Agra, or through the Viceroy's Military Secretary from the officer commanding at Meerut. How difficult it was even for the Viceroy in these circumstances to obtain any clear account of what happened at Meerut is manifest to anyone who refers to the useful printed collection of Mutiny papers prepared by Sir George Forrest: how utterly garbled any private Calcutta narrative of those events could become may be discovered by any reader

Introduction

of Malleson's *Red Pamphlet*, at the contents of which the distinguished writer must have in after years often blushed.

What this work does primarily seek to provide is a clear and accurate narrative of the events at Meerut on the evening of 10 May 1857 and at Delhi on the morning of 11 May 1857 based on the accessible sources containing eyewitness accounts or reminiscences or statements, and reports or despatches composed immediately or quite shortly afterwards. The accessible sources of this kind are nearly all printed but it is always possible that there may lurk among journals or letters in private hands unrecorded eyewitness accounts of the sort in question. My principal aim has been to combine the facts in the now accessible sources into a connected narrative and to give the story of the evening at Meerut, and to a lesser extent the story of the next morning at Delhi, in a form more accurate than do the standard writers such as Kaye and Sen: the attempt seems worth making particularly as to the outbreak at Meerut, because on that subject the standard historians provide only an account which at its best is highly compressed and at its worst is positively inaccurate.

Even though the accessible sources of the present work, indicated in the notes, are for much the greater part printed sources, they are none the less original sources. Secondary sources have been used as sparingly as possible: technical works in the case of chapter 2 are an instance of where they are indispensable. A comparatively small quantity of unprinted material has been drawn upon—a few letters gleaned from Sir John Kaye's Mutiny papers in the India Office Library, a few despatches from other series in the same library, and (for one suggestive but otherwise quite unknown incident) the unpublished diary of William Waterfield, B.C.S.; for permission to quote from this diary I am greatly indebted to Miss Waterfield.

So much for the sources: now for the events. The outbreak at Meerut arose from the affair of the greased cartridges, and that affair grew to its actual proportions because of suspicions about the policy of the British rulers in relation to the religion of the Hindus and of the Muhammadans. Of these suspicions there is ample proof in contemporary writings but of their very shadow skimming the fields and villages of northern India one may only perhaps catch a glimpse in the curious episode of the chapātīs. The first chapter will therefore be taken up by this episode and the

Introduction

next chapter will go into the question of greased cartridges, a matter which to a present day reader takes a little explain-ing. Chapter 3 will then run over the incidents occurring at or near Calcutta between February and May 1857, because these in-cidents arose, like the Meerut outbreak, from the affair of the greased cartridges and because they yield on examination both remarkable resemblances to the Meerut outbreak and also signi-ficant differences therefrom. After these three initial chapters, the story will shift entirely to Meerut—the character of prominent officers there, the local topography, the actual events of 10 May—and eventually to Delhi on the following morning.

Like every worker in this field I have to express my great grati-tude to the Librarian of the India Office Library and his staff, and the staff of the Indian Records Department, at the Commonwealth Relations Office, for their unfailing help and kindness in giving access to or tracing documents in their care.

This is not a philological work and it is my opinion that in such a case transliteration according to an exact and universal system is more a hindrance than a help: I regard Malleson's continuation of Kaye's work as an awful warning in this regard. Where there is a well-established transliteration, as in the case of Meerut itself, I use it. Otherwise I frequently use the spelling of the original source for facility of reference. In what I think is a minority of cases I adopt the standard system used by orientalists in Great Britain but without indicating the Arabic 'ain or hamza and with-out diacritical marks beneath consonants which in Hindustani are assimilated to each other. Sometimes I follow the Hindustani pronunciation (e.g. z for dh) and I use the long mark (–) above a vowel only where I think it may help a reader to get the pronuncia-tion more or less right.

I have tried to give the translation of any Hindustani word after it in brackets on its first occurrence.

CHAPTER I

CHAPĀTĪS

George Harvey, B.C.S., Commissioner of the Agra Division, writes:

In the commencement of 1857 while marching through the Mynpoorie district, my attention was drawn by Zumindars in villages adjoining the road to a mysterious distribution of chuppattees, (or small wheaten cakes), with astonishing rapidity through the country. The bearers knew apparently no more than those from whom they last received the cakes what the purport of the injunction was which directed the preparation of five cakes to be carried on to the villages in advance. 'They would be called for', it was stated, and in this way chuppattees or their counterparts travelled often over 160 or 200 miles in a night. Those I saw had been delivered on the Etawah side of Mynpoorie: yet on the following day I heard of them at the extremity of Etah and Allyghur.... The course taken suggested a probable starting point in Bundelkund or Nagpoor.[1]

The chapātīs are reported in the Muttra District, in the Meerut Division, in Gurgaon and the neighbourhood of Delhi, and are said to have reached the borders of the Punjab: north of the Ganges, they appeared in Rohilkhand and in Oudh. In the whole area, they seem to have travelled from south-east to north-west, or perhaps from east to west, moving as Harvey describes up the Doab, crossing the Jumna into the Delhi territory, entering the Badaon District in Rohilkhand from the Shahjahanpur District to the east. South of the Jumna, reports of them are less precise: they are said to have spread over the whole of what were then known as the Saugor and Nerbudda Territories, and their arrival is specifically attested in Nimar far away on the Nerbudda, at Bajenghur (Bajrangarh near Guna), and at Nimach on the edge of Rajputana, occurrences which seem to indicate in general the same east–west transit.[2]

The 'bearers', who are mentioned but not named by Harvey, were the village *chaukidārs* or watchmen. One of their ancillary duties was to act as guides from village to village and to this extent their employment is easy to understand, but it carries implications to which further reference will be made. Generally the number five seems to prevail in the distribution: the carrying chaukidār hands the chapātī to the receiving chaukidār with instructions to make five more and distribute them to the five nearest villages in the desired direction. There are however cases of two chapātīs delivered and ten to be made and passed on or two of that new supply to be kept and the rest sent forward; and there are references to six or four. Harvey perhaps exaggerates the speed of distribution; *dāk*-runners with the mails covered about 100 miles in 24 hours and maybe the chapātīs moved at about the same rate.

The great majority of contemporary observers came to the conclusion, after the outbreak of the Indian Mutiny, that the chapātī distribution had some connection with it. A few only at that time advanced the idea that the distribution was some form of magical practice, recalling a 'scapegoat', for the expulsion of epidemic disease, particularly cholera. That explanation is untenable. There was no epidemic of cholera at the time in question, that is in about January to March 1857: at the most, there may have been small, purely local occurrences, due to the brief winter rains or lingering as traces of the previous year's epidemic onset. Not one observer (except only in the report from Nimar) records a synchronous outbreak of cholera or other disease together with a particular case of chapātī distribution. In the hot weather and rains of the preceding year, that is to say between May and October 1856, there was a severe though not catastrophic outbreak of cholera, about which we possess reports for the Meerut and Rohilkhand Divisions, through which the chapātīs passed a few months later. These reports contain no reference to a chapātī distribution for the expulsion of the sickness: if that was really the reason for the distribution, it is impossible to believe that such a thing did not occur in 1856 in the midst of the epidemic but did occur in 1857 when the epidemic had passed. It is equally impossible to believe that, if there had been a distribution connected with the epidemic in 1856, that would not have been remembered by the officials who puzzled over the chapātīs in 1857: but not even those who do propose the 'scapegoat' theory aver that any chapātīs were noticed in 1856. The epidemic reports for 1856 do contain one or two references to the use of a 'scape-buffalo' to push the disease over the boundaries into the next village, and it is mentioned that in one such case an affray resulted, the inhabitants of the next village naturally objecting to the buffalo being driven within their bounds: if the chapātīs of 1857 had had this object, the whole area north of the Jumna would have been covered with village fights, but not one is recalled at that time.[3]

It is easy thus to demonstrate that the chapātīs had nothing to do with expulsion of epidemic disease. It is less easy to say what their real purpose was. In that regard, the great difficulty is that the inhabitants themselves were in doubt about them. If they had a message to convey, its purport was not clear. Some witnesses regard them as a propitiatory observance to avert an impending calamity, others suggest that they were circulated by Government to indicate that the people would be compelled to eat the same food as Christians, or that their purpose was to give warning of the intention of Government to force Christianity upon the people and to serve as a call to resist this. One Muhammadan of Delhi recalls how his father had told him that 'in the downfall of the Mahratta power, a sprig of *chīnā* (or millet) and a morsel of bread was passed from village to village': the reference is probably to the wars of 1803–5 and, since evidently the English could not have set such a thing in motion, it can best be explained as a warning signal which preceded Holkar's campaign of 1804. This seems to be a trace of something comparable to the chapātī distribution of 1857.[4]

It must seem odd to us that anyone should think the chapātīs were circulated by Government. The explanation lies in the organ of distribution. The chaukidārs were village servants, whose prime duty was watch and ward, in the village itself more than in the fields: but they were also links in the still rudimentary police organisation. They had to report weekly at the police *thāna* of the circle containing their village with information of anything criminal or suspicious in their village: during the 1856 epidemic they received on these visits cholera pills for distribution. It is clear that anything passed along through them could readily be thought to come from Government: it is also clear that the distribution was never intended to be clandestine, since the one agency was chosen which was bound to report it to the authorities and which did in fact so report it, as is definitely known in several cases.[5]

The chapātī distribution has hitherto stood as an isolated, though widespread, phenomenon, without any parallel contemporary with

3

it. However, a passage in the unpublished diary of William Waterfield, B.C.S., provides a contemporary parallel in the area of Bengal around Murshidabad. Waterfield was stationed on Revenue Survey duties at Berhampore, the civil station and cantonment for Murshidabad, and an entry in his diary (kept apparently for his wife) dated 15 January 1858 reads as follows:

I do not know whether I ever told you of a curious circumstance that occurred here last year. When the Survey went out, they found spinning wheels floating down all the rivers; and it was discovered that chuprassies had been round the villages the year before, telling the people that Government were going to introduce iron ones, and only a certain number were to be allowed in each village. So when the Survey came, they thought it was to inquire into the matter, and broke and threw theirs away for fear of a fine. This looks more like a plot to excite previous discontent in the country than anything I have yet heard.

Waterfield, writing in 1858, is referring to the Survey going out the previous year, which would have been in about January or February 1857. The mission of the chaprāsīs is placed in 1856, probably after the rains. The affair was thus at about the same date as the chapātī distribution. Chaprāsīs are messengers wearing a badge of office. They might have been actual Government chaprāsīs deceived, suborned, or bribed into performing this mission; or they might have been messengers wearing a false badge to suggest official status. In either case, their employment is a parallel to the employment of the chaukidārs in the chapātī distribution.

The message about the spinning wheels was clear and precise: it only needed the appearance of a Government party, in the shape of the Survey party, to produce the intended effect, which however was restricted in scope and area. The message of the chapātīs was at the worst ominous but its purport was so uncertain that the effect may not have been great; yet just how great or how slight the effect may have been in hundreds and hundreds of villages over the large area involved, it would be difficult to say. The testimony is limited and does not rule out the possibility that some degree of alarm and consternation in the villages followed the distribution. That such was the object of the chapātī distribution can hardly be doubted, particularly in the light of Waterfield's remarkable story.

4

It can readily be seen that a message of such vague import as that intended to be conveyed by the chapātīs could only hope to be effectual in the way intended, if there was an atmosphere propitious to it. That would be an atmosphere of discontent, uneasiness or suspicion spread about through the villages in the affected area.

The point which is particularly relevant to this study is the undoubted existence in the Ganges–Jumna Doab, Oudh and Rohilkhand of widespread suspicion and uneasiness in regard to the intentions of the Government concerning religion. This has a double relevance, first because it was the factor which the distributors of the chapātīs sought to exploit, secondly because it was the condition which aggravated the question of the greased cartridges to the intensity which caused an explosion. Both Hindus and Muhammadans had become widely convinced that the object of the Government was to draw them away from their inherited religions and convert them to Christianity and that the achievement of this object was being covertly matured by Government. Such fears seemed to the most religious of the English officials and officers entirely groundless and they continually assured their subjects that Christianity neither sought, nor tolerated, forced, feigned, or insincere conversion. The Hindus and Muhammadans, however, had seen plenty of cases of such conversion under previous rulers. They observed the introduction of reforms which disturbed them. Such a measure as the abolition of *satī* aroused no great feeling: laws permitting the remarriage of Hindu widows and preserving the property rights of converts to Christianity had much stronger effects on the minds of Indians. Common messing in jails seemed to betray the dreaded policy: so did orphanages where the waifs were brought up as Christians. Education in the form of village schools, and above all where applied to females, was strongly suspected or disliked. The spread of Protestant missionary activity since the Charter of 1813, the outdoor preaching and the village perambulations, the proselytising interests or even zeal of not a few officials and officers induced a widely held conviction that mission work was directly supported, subsidised, and protected by Government. There is irrefutable evidence from at least two, if not three, contemporary Indian sources of a general fear about religion which at times reached panic pitch. The activities which engendered this fear were mainly those of missionaries and laymen of the Evangelical persuasions but there was an odd community of aims between them (who worked for 'improvement' on religious grounds) and laymen who had adopted the tenets of Utilitarianism (and who worked for 'improvement' on what they regarded as rationalistic grounds). Both groups were working in the end to upset the long-established customs and beliefs of Hindus and Muhammadans in the matter of religion and it was impossible to dissuade the Indian population that these activities were supported by Government.[6]

The soldiers of the Bengal Army were only an extract from the population of the North-West Provinces and Oudh. This very simple fact is seldom emphasised enough: the Mutiny is, as it seemed to the English at the time, incomprehensible, if this fact is not grasped. The grievances and suspicions prevalent over that area worked continually in the minds of the sepoys and sowars. They were, in the vast majority, of Brahmin or Rajput caste when Hindus, of good class Muhammadan families when of that religion. They did not shed their religion, their caste, or their family ties when they enlisted: far from it; intercourse with their homes was ceaseless, social status all-important to them. A dread which pervaded their villages and families pervaded them. When they express their fears about the greased cartridges it is not in the form that 'this unholy object will pollute *me*': it is in the form that 'if I handle this polluting object, I shall become *badnām*' (of ill-repute), 'my social good-standing will be destroyed, my comrades will have nothing to do with me, my family and my home will turn me away, my caste *panchāyat* will exact expiation'. It is not the personal defilement but the social ostracism which makes the use of the cartridges intolerable. The acuteness of the feeling about the cartridges depends on the pervading sentiment in family, village and caste; this sentiment in turn arises from the suspicions and grievances in matters of religion described above.

These lines on the subject of religion are justified within the limits I have set myself by the double relevance of the matter to the chapātī episode and to the greased cartridge agitation. I wish to stray no further but only to mention that I am well aware of such other factors as the poor state of discipline in the Bengal Army and the civil discontents aroused by the land revenue settlement and the introduction of the English procedure for sale of land in the case of default of revenue payments as at the suit

6

of a mortgagee. I leave the reader to pursue these subjects elsewhere.[7]

It is relevant also to the conclusions reached below to note that there was a very strong cohesion among the men within each regiment itself: a native officer and a sowar who brought the young Hugh Gough safe to the European lines at Meerut on 10 May 1857 then returned to their mutinous regiment because in their view duty, or rather honour, required them to join their comrades. This sentiment within the regiment was based not only on the unity of the regiment as a body of men but on the innumerable family relationships, village connections, and bonds of caste or community existing among the men. There was likewise a close cohesion among the regiments of the Bengal Army as a whole, or, to be more exact, among the Pūrbiya regiments—roughly speaking those recruited east of the Jumna or at any rate east of the Sutlej. Here again the same relationships, connections, and bonds, spread through the army as a whole, operated in addition to the bond of common service, history, and traditions. There was what Martin Gubbins calls the *Faujki Bheera,* which he translates as the common feeling of the army apparent, almost instinctively, to the whole mass, and to that feeling each regiment tended to conform.

But for the intensity of the prevailing grievances and suspicions about religion in the North-West Provinces and Oudh, shared by the soldiers drawn from among the population of that part of India, the agitation about the greased cartridges would not have risen to the pitch which it did, and the Enfield cartridges would not have brought about, as the current couplets had it, what neither the Crimean nor Persian Wars, what neither Tsar nor Shah had accomplished.

> Na Iran ne kiya, na Shah Russ ne —
> Angrez ko tabah kiya kartoosh ne.[8]

CHAPTER 2

GREASED CARTRIDGES

'In England, almost every child is aware that, with a smooth bored gun, no grease of any kind is required to ensure the proper loading of it, whilst with a rifle-bored piece such is necessary.' So writes Mrs Peile, one of those who escaped from Delhi on 11 May 1857.[1] The statement, if lacking in precision, may have been true as to the common information or belief in 1857, but at the present time there may probably be few readers of these pages who could explain thus, or with more exactitude, why a cartridge in those times had to be greased, and why or how, if greased, it required to be bitten. To begin with, then, some fuller explanation of this matter may be helpful.[2]

Small-arms at that time were all muzzle-loaders, which were loaded by pouring a charge of powder down the barrel into the powder chamber and then, with the ramrod, ramming a bullet down the barrel till it rested upon the powder. By origin, a cartridge is a container, usually of paper, designed to hold enough powder for one discharge of the weapon. A cartridge of this kind, containing powder and nothing more, is often specified as an 'unballed cartridge'. It is however also possible to enclose within the paper container the bullet as well as the powder and the cartridge then becomes a 'balled cartridge'.

Whether the cartridge was unballed or balled, it was necessary, in loading a muzzle-loader, to open the end of the cartridge. This was supposed to be done, in drill or in battle, with the teeth: it may in fact very often have been done by tearing with the hand, but the drill prescribed was to bring the cartridge to the mouth and bite it, tearing the end off with the teeth. Then, the charge of powder was poured from the cartridge down the barrel. Next, if the cartridge was unballed, the container was simply dropped and the bullet, separately carried, was taken from the pouch and inserted in the barrel. If, however, the cartridge was balled, then the fag-end of the container was reversed (after the powder had been emptied), inserted in the barrel with the bullet which it contained, and so rammed home.

8

Greased Cartridges

A bullet must fit pretty neatly or otherwise the gases of the explosion escape round it at the discharge and the propelling force is reduced. It must not be too tight or there is difficulty in ramming it home, and this becomes more the case when the barrel is fouled with firing. This particular difficulty also becomes accentuated when, instead of a smooth bore, the weapon has a rifled bore, that is to say has grooves cut in the interior surface of the barrel which assist the flight of the bullet.

To make easier, therefore, the passage of the bullet down the barrel in loading, a device known as a 'patch' can be, and was, used. This was a small piece of textile material soaked in a greasy composition which was wrapped round the bullet at the moment of loading, and lubricated its passage down the barrel. A patch was useful when the ammunition consisted of an unballed cartridge and a separate bullet. In the case of a balled cartridge, this particular problem could be differently solved. The fag-end of the cartridge, containing the bullet, could be *greased*. When the opposite end or tip of the cartridge had been bitten off and the powder emptied from it down the barrel, the fag-end containing the bullet was reversed, inserted in the barrel, and rammed home; the casing, if greased, served in place of a patch. This is how it came about that balled cartridges were bitten at the tip and greased at the base containing the bullet.

The discharge of the weapon requires the use of some form of igniter for the charge of powder. Once, this had been a slow-match, a piece of stuff soaked in a slow-burning fluid: weapons so discharged were matchlocks. Roughly in the eighteenth century, the match was replaced by a flint which, brought down by a firing mechanism, struck sparks to ignite the powder: weapons so constructed were flintlocks or firelocks. At the beginning of the nineteenth century, substances known as chemical fulminants came into use as igniters: these are substances which explode when struck. A small quantity of a fulminant, enclosed in a thin metal envelope, is a percussion cap. This, placed on a nipple, was exploded by being struck by the firing mechanism, and in its turn exploded the charge of powder. Needless to say, a weapon constructed for discharge by this method could be made useless if its owner was deprived of percussion caps with which to discharge it, and there were occasions during the Mutiny when the attempt was made to disarm native regiments by impounding the supply of percussion caps.

9

The East India Company maintained arsenals and magazines for the manufacture and storage of weapons and ammunition. There were, for the various divisional commands, storage magazines where the heavy stocks of powder were kept and expense magazines from which weapons and the components of ammunition were issued to the units. Powder and bullets, and apparently cartridge paper also, were issued to each regiment from the expense magazine and they were each made up, by a staff of workmen attached to the regiment in the regimental magazine, into cartridges for the weapon or weapons in use by the regiment.[3]

There appear, in 1857, to have been four firearms in use by the native infantry or cavalry regiments of the Bengal Army. First, there was a smooth-bore musket, with no rifling, which was the weapon in general use in the infantry regiments. This was in fact the same weapon as had been in use in the British Army during the Napoleonic and Peninsular Wars and to which the name 'Brown Bess' had become attached: the weapon had since been modified only by the substitution of the percussion cap in lieu of the flint as the igniter. Secondly, there was a rifled weapon, used by 'rifle companies' which existed in all, or some, of the native infantry regiments.[4] The weapon in question was one which was known as the Brunswick rifle, because it had been developed on the suggestion of a Captain Berners, an officer of a Jäger Regiment in the Brunswick Army: it had two grooves of rifling and it is therefore often referred to as 'the two-grooved rifle'.[5] Later in adoption and strictly confined in use was the Minié rifle. This was the invention of a French officer, Captain Minié: its special peculiarity was the structure of its bullet, which will be described below. This weapon had been used to some extent by the British troops in the Crimean War but never became a general issue in the British Army. In India, it had been issued to some of the native troops on the Peshawar Frontier, which of course was only reached after the Second Sikh War in 1849.[6] Lastly, the cavalry employed a shortened musket, which was known as a carbine. It is difficult to ascertain whether this was rifled or unrifled and what models were in use. A stray reference reveals that there was a Minié carbine among them: but this may not have been general. The weapon was used in each of the Light Cavalry regiments by a body of men known as skirmishers, ninety in number and drawn fifteen from each troop.[7]

Rifling of the bore improved the range and accuracy but it aggravated the problem of confining the escape of the gases at the moment of discharge, since these could find their way up the grooves. The Brunswick and the Minié rifle both represented experiments aimed at overcoming this defect. The Brunswick had a belted bullet which engaged in the grooves but it was unbalanced in flight. The Minié bullet had a metal thimble in its base which expanded at the discharge, thus causing the missile to seal the bore: the trouble was that the metal thimble was apt to drive through the bullet.[8] The British military authorities conducted further experiments at Enfield and eventually in 1853 they evolved an improved form of bullet for use with a rifled weapon which came to be known as the Enfield rifle or the Enfield–Pritchett rifle (Pritchett being the inventor of the bullet). The ammunition for this was balled and was heavily greased at the base, since it was considered that the grease must retain its properties in store for a period up to three years. A consignment of this ammunition was sent out to India in 1853 to test its keeping qualities (not for firing purposes): the grease made at Enfield was composed of tallow from beef and pork fat. Cartridges from this consignment were handled by sepoys, by keeping them in pouch in the course of the test: its composition did not become known to them. The grease was found to stand up to the Indian climate and the consignment was returned to England in 1855 with a report that it had survived the test.[9]

It is less easy to state with clearness and certainty the types of ammunition in use in the Bengal Army immediately prior to the Mutiny than it has been to state the types of weapon. There is, rather surprisingly, no comprehensive note discoverable on the subject, and nothing beyond sparse and scattered papers in the India Office Records. The reader of Kaye can see that even he, with all the facilities at his disposal, was compelled to fashion an account out of just this unsatisfactory material, supplemented by some personal enquiries from officers who should have known what they were talking about. We are in no better case today. Yet there are reasons for regarding Kaye's account as unsatisfactory in certain particulars.[10] A serious defect is that Kaye fails to bring out the distinction between *unballed* cartridges, with a bullet loaded with a patch, and *balled* cartridges which might be (but were not always) greased at the base. But one must add that there are passages in the Parliamentary Papers, which he was using, where likewise it is difficult to observe this distinction clearly.

In 1847 the ammunition used with the Brunswick or two-grooved rifle was unballed and the bullet was loaded with a patch. Kaye so stated in his text and after he had completed this he discovered and printed in an appendix a memorandum of the Military Board in that year, prescribing that for this weapon the cartridges were to be prepared as blank in bundles of ten, the balls separately in strings of five, and the patches to be made from calico lubricated according to further instructions which, when issued, provided for a lubricating mixture composed of linseed oil and beeswax. Observe that these instructions apply to the greasing of patches, not of cartridges.[11]

One can assume that, if in 1847 the rifle cartridges were unballed, then so at that date were the cartridges for the unrifled muskets. By 1855, however, balled cartridges were being manufactured, and therefore no doubt used, in the Bengal Army: this important fact is stated *en passant* in the document of 1855, mentioned above (see note 9) which refers to the return to England of the consignment of Enfield ammunition.[12] It is not clear whether all small-arms ammunition was in 1855 balled or only that for certain weapons. It would be somewhat inconvenient to use balled cartridges with some weapons and unballed cartridges with others, because the loading drill is necessarily quite different, as can be seen from the description of the methods of loading given above. It would mean that troops would have to learn two loading drills and that the manual, known as the Platoon Exercise, which contained the loading drill, would have to be in two editions or would have to contain alternative sections for different types of weapon or ammunition.

One would greatly wish to see a series of the Platoon Exercise manuals from 1847 to 1857; that would clear up the question of the changeover from unballed to balled cartridges, but no such series, nor (with one exception) any isolated copies, are traceable in the India Office Records. The one exception is a copy of the Platoon Exercise which was issued, with one special revision, at the end of March 1857 as the final attempt of Government to allay the suspicions of the sepoys about the cartridges. The revision, of which the wording will be given exactly below, was the substitution of a motion of tearing off the end of the cartridge with the fingers in place of biting it. In all other respects the Platoon Exercise in this edition was apparently unaltered, and there is nothing which suggests that in its form immediately before this revision it had only been issued in the early part of 1857. One is entitled to think that, in that form, it had been in force earlier—in 1856, 1855, or before. Now, this edition of the Platoon Exercise is expressly stated to be applicable both to the ordinary musket and to the rifle-musket: it was also applicable to the carbine, because the trouble at Meerut started through an attempt to introduce the 'tearing' revision to the skirmishers of the 3rd Light Cavalry. We have then a Platoon Exercise applicable to all weapons and in this Platoon Exercise the loading drill is for balled cartridges and only balled cartridges. Here are, then, strong grounds for supposing that between 1847 and 1857 there had been a general changeover in the Bengal Army from unballed cartridges to balled cartridges.[13]

However, against that view are to be set two references in the correspondence of the month of January 1857 over the cartridge problem: they are perhaps not quite conclusive but they can both be taken as indicating that patches were still in use, and therefore unballed cartridges.[14] Both observations come from the Inspector-General of Ordnance, who was Colonel Augustus Abbott, and from whom Kaye claimed to have obtained personal confirmation that the 'patches' instructions of 1847 had not been varied down to 1857. But if Kaye simply asked Abbot whether the mixture used under those instructions was unchanged down to 1857, a negative answer would have been true, but relevant only so far as patches were still being used.[15]

Until it is established that in the first quarter of 1857 or earlier the Platoon Exercise allowed for alternative loading drill, it seems to me that one must suppose a general changeover between 1847 and 1857 (or more probably 1855) from unballed to balled cartridges. Were, then, these balled cartridges greased? Observe in that connection that, while service cartridges were balled, practice cartridges for loading and firing drill only were blank, which is to say unballed.[16] When the balled cartridge loading drill, with reversal of the fag-end, was applied to a blank cartridge, greasing would be unnecessary, for there was no ball within the paper to obstruct the passage down the barrel. Blank practice ammunition of this kind therefore remained without grease. That is confirmed by the evidence at the Courts of Inquiry in February and

April 1857 into the suspicions of the 2nd N.I. (Grenadiers) at Barrackpore and the refusal of the 3rd L.C. skirmishers at Meerut: these all reveal suspicion of the paper, not grease.[17]

The service ammunition, however, was greased. The greasing composition was apparently mutton fat. This explains a statement of the Adjutant-General that for some years greased rifle ammunition had been used by native troops to whom Minié rifles had been issued on the Peshawar frontier and also by the rifle companies.[18] Kaye doubted, and indeed disbelieved, this statement: but that was because he thought the whole question of cartridge-greasing before the appearance of the Enfield rifle was governed by the instructions of 1847.[19] That opinion is not really tenable because it confuses greasing of patches with greasing of cartridges; so, in spite of Kaye's doubts, the Adjutant-General's statement that cartridges had been greased with mutton fat ought to be accepted. It applied to balled service cartridges, which would be used, of course, also for target practice.

It was the appearance in India of the Enfield rifle, and the re-appearance of its ammunition for actual use, which precipitated a crisis. The British authorities officially adopted the Enfield rifle, but in the first place it was issued to the rifle regiments. The 1st Battalion of the 60th Queens Royal Rifles, stationed at Meerut (as it happened), which had used the Brunswick rifle since 1 January 1841, was issued with the Enfield rifle on 1 January 1857.[20] The Indian military authorities also decided to introduce the Enfield rifle as a general issue. In the first place they obtained enough pieces for use in training at the Musketry Depots at Dum-Dum, Ambala and Sialkot. From the latter part of 1856 or early in 1857, detachments of five men at a time from native infantry regiments began to pass through these depots for training in the new weapon. Detachments from forty-four regiments went through the Ambala depot in the first quarter of the year.[21] Apparently, training was also given at the Artillery School of Instruction at Meerut, but this was presumably only to recruits for the Bengal Artillery. The parties under instruction at that stage only learnt the mechanism and care of the weapon covered by the Manual Exercise: they did not proceed to the firing motions in the Platoon Exercise and so, at first, they did not handle, and still less were they called on to fire, the cartridges. The cartridges were used at Ambala for the first time on 17 April; they were issued ungreased and the men greased them with a composition of clarified butter.[22]

At Meerut, when the Enfield rifle was issued to the 60th, no ammunition was issued with it. Protest was made against this and thereupon ten rounds per man were issued.[23] This was apparently service (balled) ammunition and it had been greased at the time of manufacture: it was the only issue of such ammunition in India known to have been made prior to the evening of 10 May, apart from the small quantity issued at the Musketry Depot at Ambala on 17 April as just mentioned. It was supplied from Calcutta: there was a considerable quantity of it sent up to Meerut for the 60th and the manufacture went on at the arsenal at Dum-Dum.[24]

Somewhere about the end of the third week in January 1857, a *khalāsi,* that is to say a labourer, at the Dum-Dum arsenal accosted a high caste Brahmin sepoy and asked for a drink of water from his *lotah* (water-pot). The Brahmin refused on the score of caste. The khalāsi then said 'You will soon lose your caste, as ere long you will have to bite cartridges covered with the fat of pigs and cows', or, it is added, 'words to that effect'. This is the form of the khalāsi's words as originally reported by Captain Wright, commanding the Rifle Instruction Depot.[25] Slightly later Major-General J. B. Hearsey, the officer commanding the Presidency Division, gives a version which perhaps has a rather different sense, namely 'the saheb-logue (Europeans) will make you bite cartridges *soaked* [my italics] in cow and pork fat, and then where will your caste be?'[26]

It was the report by Captain Wright of this incident which awoke the military authorities and the Government of India to the state of suspicion and fear which was permeating the Bengal Army. It will make for clarity if the incidents which marked the spread of that state of mind are described in a separate chapter and if we now complete this chapter only by noticing the various steps taken to revise the mode of preparing the ammunition or the drill motions in order to obviate the sepoys' objections.

Wright's report was passed to Major J. Bontein commanding the Musketry Depot, who passed it on to General Hearsey. He in turn transmitted it, through channels, to the Government of India, with the suggestion that authority be given to obtain greasing materials from the bazar and the men at the depot be allowed to make up the grease themselves. The papers passed through the hands of the Inspector-General of Ordnance, Colonel Abbott; he observed that tallow grease must be used and the patches composition of coconut (Kaye says linseed) oil and beeswax was unsuitable because it dried in store. He suggested a committee to decide on the grease to be used and that meanwhile practice cartridges be issued ungreased and the men allowed to see that no objectionable grease was used.[27]

The circulation of these papers was delayed by an intervening weekend, but it may be doubted whether this, as Kaye thought, made matters much more difficult: for it will be seen in the next chapter that the sepoys' fears had most probably begun to arise before the incident of the khalāsi. Eventually on 27 January Government gave orders that the men at all the instruction depots were to be allowed to grease their own cartridges. The orders were sent to Hearsey for Dum-Dum, and they were telegraphed by Government direct to Ambala and Sialkot and to the Adjutant-General, Colonel Chester, who was at Meerut. The latter telegraphed back on the 28th, referring (as mentioned above) to the previous use of cartridges greased with mutton fat and questioning the expediency of the new order because it might throw suspicion on the fat in use for some years past. Government replied on the 29th that the existing practice might continue, if the materials were mutton fat and wax.[28]

So far as concerns the greasing materials, the matter rested there. However, as will become apparent in the following chapter, this concession had no effect on the state of mind in the Army. Just over a month later, on 2 March, Major Bontein of the Dum-Dum Musketry Depot propounded what at the time seemed no doubt a more radical remedy. His suggestion was for a revision of the loading drill, so as to eliminate the biting of the cartridge. In his letter containing this suggestion, he quotes as follows the existing, unrevised form of the drill:

6. Permit me to quote the regulation as it now stands—the firelock being at the word '*Prepare to load*' placed on the ground six inches in front of the body, and held *at the full extent of the left arm*, the recruit receives the order '*Load*' upon which the regulation says—

> 1st—Bring the cartridge to the mouth, holding it between the forefinger and the thumb with the ball in the hand, and bite off the top; elbow close to the body.

Note first the words 'with the ball in the hand': this, the exist-ing regulation, is a form of drill for *balled* cartridges. Then Bontein suggested that this practice was a mere remnant of the Platoon Exercise of flintlock days 'when the musket being brought to the right side with the left hand, for the purpose of *priming*, it was almost impossible to use the cartridge without the aid of the teeth'. He further said that according to his information the *form* of biting had always been observed but the *practice* had been to tear it immediately afterwards with the left hand. He therefore sug-gested a modified motion in which the left hand would at this point be slipped up the barrel to meet the right hand and tear off the end of the cartridge. This letter was passed on to Hearsey and by him, on 5 March, to Government. Its further course of circulation is not traceable but it must have been passed on to the Commander-in-Chief, the Hon. George Anson.[29]

Anson was up-country and after visiting Meerut went on to Ambala. The 36th N.I. was marching as his escort. There was a detachment of this regiment among those at the Ambala Musketry Depot. Two native officers from that detachment visited the regimental camp, were taunted with having become Christians, and complained to Captain Martineau, commanding the Musketry Depot, who reported the incident, and the state of mind at the Musketry Depot, to the First Assistant Adjutant-General, Captain Septimus Harding Becher. The Commander-in-Chief then addressed personally the native officers at the depot: they pro-fessed themselves personally satisfied with his explanations but maintained that among their comrades and their families the suspicions would not be allayed and they would remain subject to contempt and to ostracism. Anson decided that for the moment firing practice must be suspended and on 23 March he issued an order to that effect, apparently to all three Musketry Depots. The suspension was to continue until receipt of a special report, which he called for from Meerut, on the *paper*: but in writing to Canning on the same day, 23 March, he said that he had been impressed by the great quantity of *grease* on the Enfield cartridges.[30]

Nothing more is to be learnt about the special report which was to be furnished from Meerut. Meanwhile, Bontein's suggestion had been adopted, exactly when is not clear. The revised Platoon Exercise, containing the altered loading drill, was ready in April. Kaye does not mention this interesting document and its actual wording has not previously been published by any of the Mutiny historians. It will therefore be of interest to give the relevant passages for comparison with Bontein's quotation of the unrevised (and now undiscoverable) Platoon Exercise which it displaced:

Prepare to load...

> 4th—Raise the left hand smartly to the upper brass of the stock: seize the piece between the hollow of the hand, and the second, third and fourth fingers, thumb and forefinger (to the second joint) in *front* of the barrel ready to receive the top of the cartridge.

Load

> 1st—Bring the cartridge to the left hand, bullet resting on the palm of the right, right elbow slightly raised, tear off the top of the cartridge by the action of dropping the elbow.[31]

In this despatch of 8 April, the Government informed the Court of Directors, with reference to the ill-feeling about the cartridges for the new Enfield rifle already reported, that the chief objection was to the biting and that, as it was doubtful whether any composition such as wax and oil would answer the required purpose, they had adopted a suggestion of Major Bontein to abolish the practice of biting. Government went on to say that the Commander-in-Chief had recommended that the altered mode of loading should be applicable to the ordinary percussion musket as well as to the rifle musket and this had been authorised: from which it must follow that for *all* weapons now *balled* cartridges were in use, and *patches* were obsolete. Government further went on to say that they were instructing the Governments of Madras and Bombay to introduce the revised practice in those Presidency Armies, but they were unable to extend it to the Queen's regiments in India: for this reason, they sent home these six copies of the new Platoon Exercise, requesting that they be submitted to the Horse Guards with a view to the adoption of the modified drill by the Queen's troops in India so as to secure uniformity.

The revised manuals were doubtless sent up-country very early in April. Meanwhile, Lord Canning had written to the Commander-in-Chief, disagreeing with his decision to postpone firing drill as likely to do more harm than good, and urging its revision.[32] On 13 April the Adjutant-General, Colonel Chester, sent out a direction that the musketry course should now be completed and target practice commenced. The letter does not allude to the Governor-General's views, naturally enough: it does expressly mention that the revision of the drill had removed any reasonable objection.[33] Hence, the revised manuals had reached the Upper Provinces before 13 April. Firing practice, according to the new drill, was first carried out at Ambala on 17 April.[34]

The letter of 13 April directed that target practice should be commenced as soon as possible after the Governor-General's order disbanding the 19th N.I. had been read to the troops at the station. The genesis of this order will appear in the next chapter. The object of this was to make a watertight case of disobedience, if there was any further refusal. No man who had heard that order read, with its express warning of consequences, could plead ignorance or reasonable uncertainty, and no court-martial could let him off. That may be fairly described as a Judge Advocate-General's view: but after a refusal, after a court-martial—what then? Meerut was to show.

It was not anticipated by Chester, so he states in the letter of 13 April, that the men would refuse target practice; if they did, officers were to reason with them and explain that the grease and paper had been proved harmless, and that anyone who molested or taunted them would be severely punished: individuals who showed disinclination to use the cartridges were to be warned that they were guilty of disobedience, and if they persisted they were to be arrested and court-martialled. These prescriptions are concluded by one further direction which betrays at last the innermost, but carefully masked, apprehension which was developing even at the highest level. If the entire depot refused to fire— *which is very improbable* (my italics)—all native officers were to be placed in arrest, N.C.Os. and sepoys were to be disarmed, paid up and discharged, and ringleaders arrested and court-martialled.

Even in this last direction, nothing more is envisaged than a general refusal by the detachments at a Musketry Depot. Whether and how target practice was resumed at Dum-Dum or Sialkot, we have no record. It is recorded that it was commenced at Ambala on 17 April, which must have been upon receipt of this letter of 13 April.

With that, we conclude the examination of the cartridge question in itself—the mechanism and ingredients which caused it to arise, and the measures by which the military authorities or the Government sought to solve it, as a general problem. Before we can investigate the circumstances at Meerut in April, which demonstrated that the problem had not been solved as the authorities hoped, it is necessary to learn something of the preliminary occasions on which the agitation broke out visibly in the Lower Provinces, at or near Calcutta, during February and March.

CHAPTER 3

THE PRESIDENCY DIVISION
FEBRUARY TO MAY

The earliest reactions to the affair of the greased cartridges occurred swiftly both at Barrackpore, the cantonment which was the headquarters of the Presidency Division of the Army near Calcutta, and also at other stations in that Division.[1] Historians of the Mutiny have discussed at some length whether it is true that cartridges were manufactured at Dum-Dum or elsewhere in India with the use of grease made from the fat of cows or pigs. Kaye answered the question in the affirmative and Holmes could not quite get away from the fact, though he insisted that it was not proved.[2] It really does not matter much: here, if ever, is a case where what matters is not reality but appearance, not truth but opinion, not even fire but only smoke—and in the end possibly paper more than grease.

As described in the previous chapter, the khalāsi incident was reported to Government by Major-General Hearsey commanding the Presidency Division and the problem of the grease was considered by Colonel Abbot, the Inspector-General of Ordnance.[3] On Government's orders, Hearsey issued instructions for Dum-Dum on 28 January, directing that the greasing materials should be bought in the bazar and made up by the men.[4]

On 28 January also, Hearsey further reported to Government an ill-feeling in the minds of the sepoys at Barrackpore: he attributed it to agents of the 'religious Hindu party in Calcutta (I believe it is called the *Dhurma Sabha*)', who were telling the sepoys that they would be forced to embrace the Christian faith. He reported in the letter several incendiary fires at Raniganj, in which a sergeant's bungalow and the telegraph office had been destroyed. This place was 120 miles from Calcutta but with railway communication (as well as telegraph): it was at that moment the railhead, and the troops stationed there were a wing of the 2nd N.I. (Grenadiers), of which the other wing or main body was stationed at Barrackpore itself.[5] One Indian witness to these events, albeit from Delhi, avers that the burning of the Raniganj telegraph office was

21

deliberately carried out as a signal, on the calculation that such an event would be immediately communicated along the line from Calcutta to the Punjab.[6] On 5 February Hearsey suggested moving the 2nd N.I. back from Raniganj to Barrackpore and replacing them by a detachment of the 63rd from Suri not far to the north.[7]

Meanwhile, Hearsey had ordered a Court of Inquiry to be held into the objections of the sepoys of the 2nd N.I. to the *paper* of which the new rifle cartridges are composed. Thus, it is apparent that, even so early as this, it was no longer a question of *grease* applied externally but also of *paper* and impregnating substances. The Court assembled on 6 February and its findings were forwarded the next day. It heard ten witnesses, native officers, native N.C.Os. and sepoys of the 2nd N.I. Enfield cartridges, powder and bullets were produced on the table: and they had already been shown at a parade on the evening of 4 February. One of Hearsey's sons, Lieutenant J. Hearsey, who had passed the Enfield School of Practice, attended with an Enfield rifle to give explanations. It seems that the cartridges produced at the Court or on the parade were *not* greased. No witness refers to grease, but only to paper, powder and bullet. All witnesses said they objected to, or were suspicious of, the paper, because it had a glazed, shiny or waxed appearance, a stiffness, a difference from the old paper, and because there was a report that it was impregnated with grease. One witness attributes the origin of this report to the magazine khalāsis at Dum-Dum.[8]

On the evening of that day, 6 February, an officer of another of the regiments at Barrackpore (the 34th N.I.) was approached by a sepoy of his regiment, who told him that there was a plot among the men of the four regiments at Barrackpore, that as they were afraid of being forced to give up their caste and become Christians they were going to rise against their officers, and that a meeting was to be held that evening at a large tree near the station magazine. The officer, Lieutenant Allen, reported to his commanding officer, Lt.-Col. S. G. Wheeler,[9] and the latter to Brigadier Grant, the station commander. Allen was ordered to ride round and see, but found nothing. Yet, on the 10th, a jemadār of the 34th came forward to depose that a meeting had taken place on the 5th soon after 8 p.m., that is to say twenty-four hours earlier than Allen was warned, and there was talk of rising for the sake of religion on the evening of the 6th. This incident remains mysterious: possibly, it represents an attempt to test the nerves of the officers and the military authorities.[10]

On 9 February, Hearsey paraded the whole brigade at Barrack-pore and addressed them in Hindustani, assuring them that there was no intention of forcing them to become Christians and that forced conversion would be contrary to the tenets of Christianity itself. He believed that this address had a good effect and Government shared his hope.[11]

However, the uneasiness which in January had run 120 miles north-west up the railway to Raniganj now travelled about the same distance north up the Ganges to the cantonment of Berhampore, close by the old capital of the Nawabs at Murshidabad and the Company's old factory at Kasimbazar. The troops then at Berhampore were the 19th N.I., the 11th Irregular Cavalry, and a company of the Bengal Artillery.[12]

On 11 February, a consignment of magazine stores from Dum-Dum was delivered to the 19th N.I. at Berhampore: it included gunpowder but also some quantity of balled practice cartridges manufactured at Dum-Dum, and was accompanied by a guard stated to have been from the 65th N.I.[13] On 13 February, the authorities at Barrackpore seem to have received a report that the 2nd N.I. (Grenadiers) had sent a *cossid* to the 19th N.I. at Berhampore to ask for support in a rising, and they sent on the report to Lt.-Col. W. St L. Mitchell, the officer commanding the 19th N.I. (and the station) at Berhampore.[14] Mitchell called up his native commissioned and non-commissioned officers on 16 February and questioned them as to what reports they had received about the new cartridges: they replied that the report was that cartridges were being made up with beef fat and pork fat. Asked if they believed this, they said they did not believe that Government would serve out such cartridges, which would be contrary to their religious prejudices. Mitchell thought that if a cossid had been sent, there had been no effect on his men. He added however that about a fortnight earlier, that is in the first days of February, a Brahmin havildār (native N.C.O.) had asked him about this cartridge story: he had reassured the man.[15]

On 18 February, two days after Mitchell's talk with his native officers, a consignment of Government stallions passed through the station with an escort from the 34th N.I.[16] A week later, on 25 February, a party of European invalids also arrived in transit, again with a guard of the 34th N.I.[17] This guard camped on the 19th N.I. target practice ground, which was apparently on the edge of their parade ground alongside a tank.[18] The 19th N.I. and the 34th N.I. were regiments which had a recent acquaintance with each other and in rather significant circumstances: they had been stationed together at Lucknow at the time of the annexation of Oudh.[19]

Next day, 26 February, about 11 a.m., Mitchell issued an order for a parade to be held the following morning, 27 February, for firing exercise, and fifteen rounds of blank ammunition to be issued per man.[20] At about 4 p.m. this ammunition was brought down from the regimental magazine to the *kotes* or bells of arms.[21] It was the custom in this regiment, when a firing practice was to be held in the morning, to issue the percussion caps the evening before, apparently at the time of the sunset roll-call, which on this 26 February was at about 6 p.m. On the caps being served out that evening, the men refused to take them:[22] they did this because they intended to refuse to take the cartridges until the doubt about them was cleared up.[23] This was reported to the senior native commissioned officer, Subadār-Major Shaikh Murad Baksh: he pointed out that the rumours in circulation related to the new cartridges and these were old cartridges, but the men's answer was that there were two kinds of cartridge, and that, as stores had lately arrived from Calcutta, cartridges from there were likely to be used. The Subadār-Major sent for a bundle from one of the kotes and opened it but this produced no satisfaction. He then sent for all the native officers and told them to get the matter settled by eight o'clock roll-call.[24] It is possible that, in the interval between the two roll-calls, the men of the Light Company reinforced their determination by taking an oath not to receive the cartridges, sanctifying this oath by taking it in the tank near the target practice ground, mentioned above, which was held to contain Ganges water (the river itself was a mile away). The evidence for this incident was much shaken in cross-examination, and the facts are uncertain.[25] There was also apparently some idea that a small *panchāyat*, or meeting of ringleaders, had been held in order to concert resistance: several witnesses at the Court of Inquiry were asked whether this could have occurred without coming to the knowledge of the native officers and on balance they seem to have thought that it could.[26]

During this interval between the two roll-calls, the matter was

reported to the Adjutant, Lieutenant MacAndrew, and by him to
Lt.-Col. Mitchell: this was between 7 and 8 p.m.[27] Mitchell went
down to the lines and called up all the native commissioned officers.
He told them that the cartridges to be served out in the morning
had been made up by their predecessors in the station, the 7th
N.I., upwards of a year ago, and that they were to tell the men of
their companies that those who refused to take them were exposing
themselves to the severest punishment.[28] According to the Adjutant, he said the first man who refused his cartridges would be
court-martialled and according to two native officers he said that
those who did not take the cartridges would be sent to China or
Burma where they would perhaps die of privations.[29] It seems
that a number of the sepoys had gathered round while these
proceedings went on.[30] The native officers pacified the Colonel with
assurances that matters would be settled.[31] The Colonel then left
the lines and told his Adjutant to send orders to Captain W. C.
Alexander, commanding the 11th Irregular Cavalry, to have his
regiment on the parade ground of the 19th N.I. at 6 a.m. the next
morning, and also that the Adjutant should bring the post guns
down at the same time.[32] It can be supposed with certainty that
the issue of these orders, though private, was reported in the lines
and became known to the men.[33]

Between 10 and 11 p.m. that night, an uproar in the lines became
audible to the officers of the 19th N.I. in their bungalows. The
sepoys had rushed the kotes, forced the locks, and taken their
weapons: the roll of drums accompanied their movements.
Mitchell sent for his officers, went to Alexander and told him to
bring down the cavalry, and went to the artillery lines for the
artillery. He then went down to his own lines with the cavalry and
artillery. That took time. It was near midnight when these forces,
with Mitchell, reached the infantry parade ground. Mitchell
ordered the guns to load with grape and went down to his men,
though warned that this was risky. A colloquy followed, the
sepoys refusing to lodge their arms unless the artillery and cavalry
withdrew, and the native officers begging Mitchell to give way on
this. In the event, he did so. Thereupon the 19th lodged their
arms. Mitchell ordered a general parade for the next morning,
the 27th, but was again dissuaded from this by the native officers,
and ordered a regimental parade only. The few remaining hours
of the night passed in quiet. On the next morning's parade,

Mitchell sent for cartridges, both service and blank, left by the 7th and also balled cartridges received from Calcutta. The packets were opened and the sepoys alleged that two different kinds of paper were to be found among them. That night, on the 27th–28th, the men slept out round the kotes but did not force them again. Mitchell reported to Calcutta and ordered a Court of Inquiry which assembled, with Alexander as president, on the morning of the 27th. The sepoys drew up a petition, stressing the difference in the cartridge papers, their doubts about them, and their loyal past services, which Mitchell consented to forward to Calcutta.[34]

The sessions of the Court of Inquiry continued, though not daily, till 9 March. Witnesses stressed the violence of Mitchell's language to the native officers on the 26th and it was clearly brought out that he had eventually withdrawn the guns and the cavalry while the sepoys remained with arms in their hands: these were aspects of the events which forcibly struck the disciplinarians, his fellow Englishmen in the station, the military lawyers, and the majority of historians, and they earned Mitchell a bad mark and a change of employment. For the real history of the Mutiny they are of little importance: the truly interesting points which emerged at the Court of Inquiry are quite other.[35]

First of all, the witnesses were unanimous, or practically so, that the rumours about the cartridges had been circulating for at least two, or even two and a half, months.[36] Now, the khalāsi's taunt at Barrackpore had been uttered barely five weeks earlier; this taunt therefore was not the first source of the rumours but came as a terrifying confirmation of reports current since the last weeks of 1856.

Next, witnesses persistently declared that the cartridges at Berhampore had two different kinds of paper, one more shiny than the other, which reacted differently to burning. It seems to be the fact that the shinier sort was treated with some kind of size. But the sepoys suspected grease. Major Bontein admitted before a court-martial at Barrackpore that there were two sorts of paper, one thicker which was properly described as cartridge paper: though all the paper was manufactured at Serampore, that does not dispose of the fact that there was a difference of type. Moreover, there is reason to think that gelatine entered into their composition, and that is hardly better than grease.[37]

Finally, the only reason which was, or can be, given for the rush on the kotes late at night, long after the Colonel's harangue to the native officers, was a sudden panic fear that the guns and the cavalry were coming to attack and disarm the sepoys.[38] Beyond doubt, this must originate from Mitchell's privately given orders for the guns and cavalry to come down in the morning. Then, either that order became known in a garbled form or some person or group of persons in the regiment deliberately corrupted its true terms to provoke the nocturnal *émeute*. As has been noted above, there is some rather uncertain evidence of a small council or panchāyat having been held and if this is combined with the deduction that Mitchell's order to Alexander may have been deliberately corrupted, we seem to catch a glimpse of some concealed group of leading spirits who were the real, immediate authors of the events of that night.

The incident was of the most serious kind and was taken as such by the military authorities at Barrackpore and by the Government of India. They decided to punish the regiment by disbandment. To carry this out, they thought it necessary to bring the 19th down to Barrackpore where it would be outnumbered by other troops. Then the sentence would be carried out upon a parade accompanied with formalities. It took a little time to get the arrangements in motion and to collect transport for the regiment but on 21 March the 19th N.I. left Berhampore for the Presidency where it arrived on 31 March.[39]

The great interest of the Berhampore episode is that its pattern very closely resembles the pattern at Meerut some ten weeks later. At Berhampore, three causal factors appear; first suspicion about cartridges, secondly an order for a firing parade, and thirdly panic raised by a report of other troops coming to disarm the sepoys. The same three factors all appear in relation to the outbreak at Meerut.[40] For reasons which will emerge, there was at Meerut an interval of sixteen days between the outburst of suspicion with the order for the firing parade and the outbreak of violence following on the panic: at Berhampore, all three factors worked within about twenty-four hours. This difference in time intervals is inessential. Further, at Berhampore there is a story of an oath and at Meerut there certainly was one: and at both places there are signs of the existence of a small group who lead or sway the main body.[41]

Before all the consequences of the Berhampore incident could be known, further signs of uneasiness showed themselves at Barrackpore. A jemadār of the 70th N.I., which had only arrived in January, was accused early in March of declaring that he would not use the cartridges and of holding a meeting in his tent, which was a breach of regulations. The man, Saligram, tenaciously defended himself and his court-martial took up ten days: he was found guilty but sentenced only to be dismissed the service, a sentence which the Commander-in-Chief sent back for reconsideration but the court refused to alter.[42] Two sepoys of the 2nd N.I. (Grenadiers) were also court-martialled for an incident on the night of 10 March, when they were alleged to have tried to induce the subadār in command of the Mint Guard to march his men into the Fort to join in some mutinous movement: they received fourteen years' hard labour.[43]

On 18 March Major-General Hearsey repeated his previous measure of holding a general parade of all the troops at Barrackpore and addressing them himself in the vernacular. On this occasion, the burden of his address was to dispel the suspicion of the cartridge paper which was now so unmistakable: he produced for comparison with the suspected paper a ceremonial letter from Maharaja Gulab Singh of Jammu, written upon some kind of highly glazed paper, as evidence that paper of this kind was unobjectionable to a high caste Hindu, and offered to get leave for some of the men to visit the Serampore factory. He also told them that the 19th N.I. was being marched down and, if he received orders to disband it, the order would be executed in the presence of all the troops, but that no European troops would come to Barrackpore without his orders, of which he would give the native troops warning. Hearsey reported his address to the Governor-General but did not state, as on the previous occasion, that it was thought to have had a good effect: that may be taken as a sign that he and others could now hardly see any means to cope with the cartridge agitation, except possibly through Bontein's suggestion for a revision of drill which was at this moment under the consideration of Government.[44]

The Governor-General in Council minuted—and it is a very clear, able, and telling minute—on the case of the 19th N.I. on 27 and 28 March.[45] Their order, dated 27 March, was to disband the regiment in the presence of all troops within two days march of the station, the process of disbandment to be carried out in the same manner as at Meerut in 1844 in the case of the 34th N.I. (the predecessor of the regiment with that number then at Barrack-pore). It was directed that this order was to be read at the head of every regiment, troop and company.[46]

On 29 March two days after Government had thus delivered its decision in the case of the 19th N.I., a sepoy of the 34th N.I., named Mangal Pande, appeared about 4 p.m. at the regimental quarter-guard. He was in an excited, and apparently intoxicated, condition; inflamed, it is said with *bhang* (hemp); and he was armed with musket and sword. He tried to force a drummer to sound the assembly, and then moved to and fro in front of the quarter-guard, calling on his comrades to come out and help him for religion's sake, and abusing them for holding back when they had themselves got him to stand forward in this way. The guard did not interfere with him, and men gathered to watch: but none actually joined him. The regimental Sergeant-Major, Hewson, arrived on the scene and attempted unsuccessfully to disarm the man. Then the Adjutant, Lieutenant Baugh, appeared and closed with Mangal Pande, supported by Hewson and a Muhammadan non-commissioned officer. Both Baugh and Hewson were wounded in this encounter, and it seems that one or more of the guard attacked and injured them from behind. As these events proceeded, there was a turn-out in all the regiments in front of their bells of arms.[47]

Just after 5 p.m. a report was brought to Major-General Hearsey. He sent an order to Lt.-Col. Wheeler of the 34th N.I. to shoot the mutineer if he resisted arrest. He then mounted, and with his two sons rode down to the parade ground of the 34th N.I. Arrived there, after a few words with other officers standing by, and calling on the guard to follow him, he rode down on Mangal Pande himself, followed by his two sons: one of them called out that the man was taking aim and Hearsey told him to rush in and kill the man, if he (Hearsey) should fall. Mangal Pande, however, as the mounted officers bore down upon him, fell upon his own musket and tried unsuccessfully to kill himself.[48]

Hearsey's courage and the culprit's name made this incident famous: for the Brahmin surname Pande, thus made notorious, is the word 'pandy' (in its contemporary spelling) which English people adopted as the opprobrious term for the mutinous sepoys of the old Bengal Army. The real interest of the affair, however, resides in its failure and in its apparent background. It wears the air of an attempt to provoke an outbreak similar to that of the 19th N.I.

Mangal Pande called on his comrades to come to his aid for the sake of religion, as they would be forced to bite the cartridges, and he appears to have shouted that the Europeans were coming.[49] Thus, as at Berhampore, the general fear which permeated the army and the panic cry were raised. This time, however, there was no active response, only a hanging-back, an unwillingness to try and disarm a dangerously intoxicated man or to still an outburst which uttered the thoughts of all. Yet, in his hour of violence, Mangal Pande proclaimed that his comrades had sent him out and abused them because then they did not join him.[50] After he was wounded, it is true that he denied having been instructed by others and declared that he had acted on his own and under drugs.[51]

There is thus a strong suspicion once more of hidden persons in the background, who bring on the overt demonstration: the pattern is the same as at Berhampore. The failure on this occasion may be attributed to two factors. First of all, this was a faulty method of causing an explosion. It was broad daylight, only one obviously intoxicated man was used, the rumour of the approach of Europeans was not spread widely or mysteriously enough, there had not been enough previous consultation: the whole affair was ill-planned and ill-prepared. Secondly, the regiment was possibly not closely united enough. A Court of Inquiry, held on 15 April, heard the testimony of the officers and concluded that the Hindus of the regiment were not trustworthy, but the Muhammadans and Sikhs were.[52] The proportion of Hindus on the one side to Muhammadans and Sikhs together on the other side was just about three to one: this proportion applied in the regiment as a whole and also in that part which was on duty or off duty (excluding sick) at Barrackpore on 29 March. The Hindus were about equally divided between Brahmins, Khattris, and lower castes: there were three Muhammadans (nearly) for every Sikh, the latter being only seventy-four in a regiment of a thousand.[53] However, there is here some evidence that the regiment was more varied in composition than was usual. The story of Mangal Pande is that of a plan, if not a plot, which for these reasons miscarried.[54]

Early on the morning of 31 March the 19th N.I. was marched into Barrackpore, the troops in the station were paraded, the order for disbandment was read. The regiment then, in obedience to orders, piled arms, handed in belts and bayonets, and delivered its colours encased. They were not stripped of their uniforms, which was a relief to them, and they were told that Government would pay the transport expenses for themselves and their families from Berhampore. They were addressed by Hearsey, paid up, and sent off to Chinsurah, cheering Hearsey as they departed. The disbandment order was read to the other regiments; the 2nd, 43rd, and 70th N.I.[55] A special Court of Inquiry on Mitchell's conduct was ordered and found in the event that he should be transferred to other employment.[56]

Mangal Pande's self-inflicted wound was not fatal. He was court-martialled, condemned, and hanged on 6 April. The jemadār of the guard on that occasion, Issurī Pande, was also court-martialled and condemned. Owing to technicalities, there was a delay in confirming and executing the sentence, but he also was hanged on 21 April. The 34th N.I. was partially disbanded on 6 May: eleven named individuals were excepted, together with all non-commissioned (but not commissioned) native officers and sepoys whose absence from the lines on the evening of 29 March could be established, i.e. the large detachment absent at Chittagong, the sick in hospital and so on, and the actual number disbanded was 412 of all ranks.[57]

The Governor-General in Council, with the concurrence of the highest military authorities, had thus attempted to allay the cartridge agitation by two concessions and by one public example and threat—the order of 28 January directing the purchase of the greasing ingredients in the bazar and their mixing by the men, the revised drill based on Bontein's suggestion and prescribed shortly before 8 April, and the reading on parade to all formations of the order disbanding the 19th N.I. carried out on 31 March. It is probable that the order of 28 January was taken as proof that the use of objectionable grease had occurred or had been planned: the sepoys asked themselves, it seems, why such an order should have been issued if Government had not had some ill intention.[58] The reading of the 19th N.I. disbandment order had no deterrent or restraining effect: on the contrary, it infuriated and terrified the sepoys who regarded the 19th N.I. as martyrs for their faiths.[59] As for the new drill, it must have been practised at Ambala when firing practice was resumed there on 17 April, by when the new Platoon Exercise would have been received there. The letter of

13 April, directing the resumption of target practice, would have reached Barrackpore just about the day of Issurī Pande's execution, 21 April: we do not know to what extent the new drill was tried there, though surely Bontein, its originator, would have brought it into use at once if so ordered. The first recorded reaction to an attempt to introduce the new drill was at Meerut on 24 April.

Colonel Chester, the Adjutant-General, made it repeatedly clear in the letter of 13 April that, from the heights of Simla, the agitation over the cartridges seemed to be subsiding and all danger to be at an end.[60] These views were generally prevalent on the staff at Simla. Chester's next subordinate, the First Assistant Adjutant-General, Captain Septimus Harding Becher, maintained these views during a private correspondence that spring with Captain E. M. Martineau, who was commanding the Musketry Depot at Ambala.[61] Martineau closed that correspondence on 5 May with a letter of which he thought it worth while to preserve a copy so as to record his own deeper and more prescient understanding of the Army's condition. The following extracts from that letter give what is the truth indeed about the state of the sepoys' minds in the first week of May 1857:[62]

Feeling...is as bad as can be and matters have gone so far that I can hardly devise any suitable remedy. We make a grand mistake in supposing that because we dress, arm and drill Hindustani soldiers as Europeans, they become one bit European in their feelings and ideas. I see them on parade for say two hours daily, but what do I know of them for the other 22?

What do they talk about in their lines, what do they plot? For all I can tell I might as well be in Siberia.

I know that at the present moment an unusual agitation is pervading the ranks of the entire native army, but what it will exactly result in, I am afraid to say. I can detect the near approach of the storm, I can hear the moaning of the hurricane, but I can't say how, when, or where it will break forth.

Why, whence the danger, you say. Everywhere far and near, the army under some maddening impulse, are looking out with strained expectation for something, some unseen invisible agency has caused one common electric thrill to run thro' all.

I don't think they know themselves what they will do, or that they have any plan of action except of resistance to invasion of their religion and their faith.

But, good God! Here are all the elements of combustion at hand, 100,000 men, sullen, distrustful, fierce, with all their deepest and inmost sympathies, as well as worst passions, roused, and we thinking to cajole them into good humour by patting them on the back, saying what a fool you are for making such a fuss about nothing. They no longer believe us, they have passed out of restraint and will be off at a gallop before long.

If a flare-up from any cause takes place at one station, it will spread and become universal.

Unbeknown to Martineau, the cause of the flare-up had already occurred on 24 April, and the flare-up itself was to follow within a week, on 10 May at Meerut. Thither, to the personalities, the events, and the scene at that station, attention must now be turned, without pausing to consider in detail any other preliminary or peripheral episodes such as the disarming of the 7th Oude Irregular Infantry at Lucknow.

CHAPTER 4

REGIMENTS AND OFFICERS
AT MEERUT

The complement of foot and mounted troops at Meerut early in 1857 was a regiment of British infantry, a regiment of British cavalry, two regiments of native infantry and one regiment of native light cavalry. The station had recently become the head-quarters of the Bengal Artillery, and of this arm there were in station a troop of horse artillery with six guns, a company of foot artillery, a light field battery with six guns, and a number of recruits. The Bengal Artillery was manned by European gunners and Indian ranks known as *golandāz*.[1] This complement of troops was hardly ever complete during the period from 1 January to 1 May 1857.

The European infantry regiment present throughout these months was the 1st Battalion of the 60th Q.R.R. which had arrived on 31 December 1855 with a strength at that date of 18 officers and 814 other ranks. It suffered quite nastily from the cholera in August 1856, losing 29 men.[2] An observer on 10 May, O'Callaghan, gives its strength on that date as 901 officers and other ranks: it had presumably received a draft or drafts since the end of 1855.[3]

There was no British cavalry regiment until 11 March, on which date there arrived the 6th Dragoon Guards (the Carabiniers). They had been brought home from the Crimea unhorsed in May 1856, had taken a draft in England of 408 recruits, and had sailed for India with a strength of 33 officers and 704 other ranks. They were brought up from Calcutta to Allahabad in flats and then marched on foot to Meerut, arriving on 11 March. They were then mounted with 316 horses from Bengal light cavalry regiments and 305 (not fully broken) from the Government stud. O'Callaghan gives their strength on 10 May as 652 officers and men, which indicates a wastage of about 100 on the voyage from England, a possible figure. With the high proportions of recruits not passed drill and horses not broken, their effective strength on 10 May can hardly have exceeded 350 sabres, so that each of the troops would

34

have been about half-strength: and it was their first Indian hot weather.[4]

O'Callaghan puts the European artillery personnel at 225 on 10 May. Taking his three figures for European troops, their number was 1778 but this does not allow for the defective strength of the Carabiniers nor presumably for sickness, nor possibly leave on the date in question.[5]

At the beginning of 1857, the native cavalry regiment at Meerut was the 3rd Light Cavalry and this was, of course, the regiment in which the crucial act of disobedience was committed on 24 April: the regiment had been at Meerut before the First Sikh War and returned there in 1854. The two native infantry regiments at the station on 10 May were the 20th N.I. and the 11th N.I. The 20th had been at Peshawar in 1853, where it had taken part in a small outing against the Jowakis of the Kohat Pass.[6] The 11th had arrived at Meerut only on 1 May, after marching up from Allahabad: it was sent to replace the 15th N.I. which had been moved at the end of March from Meerut to Nasirabad.[7]

It is a curious fact, though probably of little significance, that there was a historical link between the 11th and the 20th N.I. Immediately before the re-organisation of 1824, under the two-battalion system which had existed from 1796, the 11th N.I. had been the 1/5th and the 20th N.I. had been the 2/5th. This link covered only the two-battalion period. It was noted at the time of the arrival of the 11th N.I. at Meerut that this historical link existed between the two regiments and hence the officers of the 20th had entertained those of the 11th on their arrival, and the sepoys were also going to exchange dinners. However, it cannot be shown that this historical connection between 1796 and 1824 was of any more than slight social importance in 1857. The evidence does not support the hypothesis of any deep collusion between the two regiments on 10 May; on the contrary, the 20th were the ringleaders while the 11th rather hung back.[8]

For the strength of the native regiments, we have only O'Callaghan's figures. These are 504 for the 3rd Light Cavalry, 950 for the 20th N.I. and 780 for the 11th N.I.: he gives the golandāz as 123 but these were embodied with the artillery. The three complete native regiments alone come to 2234, and they were seasoned troops: the two European regiments may have been less than 1778 men effective, though they had the guns.[9] It is a fact that man for man in assault, mounted or on foot, the Europeans were outnumbered. This is rather a different picture from that given by O'Callaghan, by Kaye or by Rice Holmes, of a European force inactive in face of an equal or inferior native force. There were the guns—but the event was a dusk or night engagement: by the mutineers' choice.

In Indian cantonments in those days all guard duties, in European or civil lines as well as in the native lines, were undertaken by the native troops: the Europeans did not share in them. Between the departure of the 15th N.I. and the arrival of the 11th N.I. (that is to say throughout April) there was only one native infantry regiment, the 20th, which could not supply all guards. Consequently, the 3rd L.C. was called on to do guard duty on foot, and for this reason its commanding officer discontinued riding school and firing parades.[10] For a month the 3rd L.C. and the 20th N.I. shared guard duties, which perhaps drew them in some ways closer together.[11]

Meerut was the headquarters of one of the Divisions of the Bengal Army, and in May 1857 the Major-General commanding the Meerut Division was Major-General William Henry Hewitt.[12] He was sixty-six or sixty-seven years of age, but Wheeler at Cawnpore was a year older and Hearsey at Barrackpore and Sage at Saugor only three years younger. He is said to have been fond of the pleasures of the table, and he had spent fifty years' service in India without once, so far as records show, taking furlough out of the country. His physical forces had certainly become impaired but he was not totally incapacitated: he moved about his division on inspection, visiting Moradabad, and at least intending to visit Delhi during the first quarter of 1857. His last experience of war had been in the First Burmese War in 1824. He had clung on to the ladder of seniority and at last got command at Multan in 1850 as Brigadier 2nd class, and then at Peshawar in November 1853 as Major-General, where he replaced an officer 69 years of age, Major-General Abraham Roberts, father of Lord Roberts. Perhaps it was as well that Hewitt should have been moved to Meerut in January 1855, rather than left at Peshawar until the Mutiny. He was a kindly and well-liked officer: it was noticed how deeply he was affected at the funeral of the victims of 10 May.[13]

The station commander, the senior regimental commanding officer, was Brigadier Archdale Wilson of the Bengal Artillery. He had arrived in India in 1821, and was now fifty-three years of age. His experience of active service was limited to the siege of Bhurtpore in 1826 and some minor engagements in the Jullundur Doab during the Second Sikh War. He was presently given command of the column sent from Meerut to join the Delhi Field Force. After two engagements with mutineer forces from Delhi at Ghaziuddinnagar, Wilson's column had to move up the Jumna to cross it by the bridge of boats at Baghput: it is difficult to understand why it was not directed by that route in the first instance. Sir Henry Barnard, who succeeded to the command of the Delhi Field Force on Anson's death at Karnal, himself succumbed to cholera on 5 July. The command was then assumed by Major-General Thomas Reed, another Queen's officer, who had been commander of the Peshawar Division. Actually senior to Barnard, he had stood down in favour of the latter, because of his own enfeebled health, which now compelled him to relinquish command and retire to the hills after ten days. Reed appointed Wilson as his successor, over the head of three senior officers present with the force.[14] Thus, by an extraordinary chance, the Meerut outbreak, which ended Hewitt's career, launched Wilson on the road to fame and fortune: he ended up with a G.C.B., a baronetcy, an Oxford D.C.L., a special pension of £1000 a year, and an article in the *D.N.B.*

He was, however, as Lord Roberts says, 'a soldier of moderate capacity', though (in Roberts' opinion) the best of the senior officers present at Delhi. He had some capability in regard to method and organisation, which the force at Delhi found an improvement on his predecessors. As an artillery man he was able to manage with his engineer officers the preparations for the assault. Neither the actions at Ghaziuddinnagar, bravely fought, nor the tactical plan for the assaulting forces within the walls at Delhi, heroically prosecuted, were models of military skill: but in each case the plan may not have been his. During the street fighting at Delhi, Wilson was several times on the point of giving the order to withdraw, and had to be stiffened by his staff officers and even, it seems, once by an opportune tot of brandy from a subaltern.[15] He was exhausted and ill, but so were others—Baird Smith, Chamberlain; and what happened with him at Delhi too much resembles what happened at Meerut. He was much criticised during his command at Delhi by the Europeans at Meerut— perhaps they knew him better than the Delhi officers and men.[16]

There is extant a letter from Wilson at Delhi to Hewitt at Meerut, in which Wilson calls upon Hewitt to contradict a report which he (Hewitt) was reported to have put about that Wilson had to be ordered out three times on the Ghaziuddinnagar road before he would start.[17]

Hewitt, or his friends, had reasons to grudge Wilson his surprising advancement. When Hewitt was hauled over the coals for the alleged mishandling of the European troops at Meerut on 10 May, his reply was that he had left the operations to Wilson: the latter was then called on to answer the charge and shuffled the responsibility back on to Hewitt by pleading that under army regulations the station commander had practically no authority when the divisional commander was present.[18] Now Hewitt's excuse may have been a poor one from the military point of view, but morally it was beyond doubt true. On that evening, Hewitt three times refused to give permission to an officer of the 11th N.I. to try and carry news to Delhi unless the officer first got Wilson's sanction.[19] If Hewitt would not even give such permission to a single officer of a regiment which had dissolved in mutiny unless Wilson's sanction was given, that is proof positive that Hewitt had withdrawn from intervention in the military plans and manoeuvres and had delegated their conduct to Wilson. In the light of this, however poor Hewitt's excuse may be, Wilson's excuse is poorer still: he simply hid behind the regulations, and one cannot avoid regarding him as the least attractive figure in the story.

Three staff-officers merit a brief mention. The Deputy Assistant Adjutant-General was Major John Waterfield of the 38th N.I.; aged forty-five, he had served through the Afghan War, commanded a local force in Bundelkhand (which had since been taken into the line as the 34th N.I.), graduated to staff duties in 1850, and held his present appointment since 1855. The Deputy Judge Advocate-General was Major J. F. Harriott, a cavalry officer aged forty-seven with no active service: he had been in the legal branch since 1844 and at Meerut since 1852. The Brigade-Major, Captain G. P. Whish, of the 60th N.I., was a son of the general who commanded the force sent to recapture Multan in 1848–9: he was forty-four and had been at Meerut since 1855. These three were near contemporaries, all in their forties.

The chief personal enigma at Meerut is presented by the officer commanding the 3rd Light Cavalry, Lt.-Col. (Brevet Colonel)

George Monro Carmichael-Smyth. It was he who, on the day of his return to the station after a short absence on leave, gave the order for a firing parade of the 3rd Light Cavalry skirmishers on the following morning, 24 April. That was the occasion of a refusal to accept cartridges, which led to the court-martial, the conviction and sentence of eighty-five out of ninety of the skirmishers, and the outbreak of 10 May. The question of why Carmichael-Smyth took this action has exercised historians and they have in general condemned him: but none of them gives an adequate account of his origins, attainments, or personality, and their views of him seem too simplified.

His grandfather was of the Carmichael family of the Earls of Hyndford and married an heiress of the name of Smyth; their son James added this name to Carmichael under his Smyth grandfather's will. This James Carmichael-Smyth, father of George, had a large family of eight sons and two daughters—George being the youngest of all. Six of the sons and the younger daughter came out to India from 1797 onwards, and the descendants of some of them and also of the elder daughter continued in the Indian services practically down to the end of the British Raj.[20] Colonel G. M. Carmichael-Smyth had one brother who served with distinction but returned home before he reached the country. He had three brothers in good positions while he was making his career in India, and possibly some nephews in India at the same time.[21] Membership of such a notable Anglo-Indian family must certainly have been not without influence on Carmichael-Smyth's character and modes of action. Junior, for instance, to the Bechers, they had not the same distinction: senior to the Lawrences, they lacked their gifts. They might, however, take rank with the Bombay 'Macnaghtens and Melvilles and Plowdens' of Octavius Sturges in the fifties, or 'the Plowdens, the Trevors, the Beadons and the Rivett-Carnacs' of Kipling in the eighties. To belong to this family in 1857 conferred a certain status in that old Anglo-India, gave certain pretensions, justified certain expectations.[22]

Another factor which cannot have been without influence on George Monro Carmichael-Smyth is that he was the Benjamin of this large family. Born in 1803, when his father was sixty and his brother, Thackeray's stepfather, already twenty-four, he was the last child of ageing parents. It is difficult to suppose that he did not undergo some spoiling in his nursery days or that his interests in India were not guarded and his progress watched over by his elder brothers above mentioned.

There are, also, certain features in Carmichael-Smyth's career which perhaps help to account for his conduct on the critical occasion at Meerut. It was a very ordinary regimental career, on the whole. He got a cavalry cadetship and so did not pass through Addiscombe. He came out to India in 1819 or 1820 and was posted to the 3rd Bengal Light Cavalry with which he remained throughout. He was, like Archdale Wilson, at Bhurtpore in 1826. His health then seems to have failed somewhat and he was on furlough on sick certificate from December 1827 to December 1831 and from March 1832 to September 1833, the greater part of six years. He got his captaincy in 1828 but his substantive majority only in 1852, though he had brevet field rank in 1846 and presumably earlier. He married first a Miss Jane Ross in 1838 (when he was thirty-five) and they had three sons, one of whom was later in the Police in the North-West Provinces. Newly married, he took part in the advance to Kabul in the First Afghan War, but his regiment had the good fortune to be sent back to India through the Khyber with Sir John Keane in 1839. The 3rd Light Cavalry, in the First Sikh War, missed Mudki and Ferozeshahr but were at Aliwal under Sir Harry Smith, where they took part in a charge with the 16th Lancers. At Sobraon they were used, with other cavalry, in a diversionary movement towards a ford upstream. They went up with the army to Lahore but were back at Jullundur later in 1846. They did not serve in the Second Sikh War. After the Mutiny, Carmichael-Smyth was posted to the newly-raised 1st, and then to the 5th European Bengal Light Cavalry. With many other Company officers he was retired on 31 December 1861. He was promoted Major-General, married a second time in 1879, and died on 29 April 1890 aged 87 (twenty-nine years after the death of Thackeray's stepfather) at 12 Royal Crescent, facing on Holland Park Road only a short distance east of Shepherd's Bush —a locality surely even then on the very edge of that part of the town inhabited by people of his sort and now much run down.[23]

In this ordinary career there are possibly two turning points. The first is the period of ill-health and furlough over the years 1828–33. The thirties, opening with Lord William Bentinck's Governor-Generalship, were the golden age of 'appointments'. It would have been natural for Carmichael-Smyth, through his connections, to have sought an appointment and just about at this stage of his life: one recalls how George Lawrence applied personally to Bentinck in Simla on behalf of his brother Henry. It can be supposed that this spell of sickness diverted or prevented Carmichael-Smyth from doing the obvious thing for a young man of his origins to get on in the Anglo-Indian world. He probably missed his chance of the interest, the rewards, and the distinction of an extra-regimental career, in which he saw such laurels won by so many who had started on a level (so he must have thought) with himself.

The second turning point was his service in the Afghan War, though not because of the campaign itself but because of the contacts which it brought with the Punjab in the last years of Sikh rule. Soon after his regiment's return from Kabul Carmichael-Smyth is found taking an interest in Sikh affairs. He claims that while stationed at Karnal in 1842, he received important information from a Sikh Sirdār, Ajit Singh, which he passed on to George Clerk. He seems also at this period to have entered into relations with a dubious personage in the Sikh service, Alexander Houghton Gardiner, about whom he seems to have corresponded with Henry Lawrence when the latter was at Khatmandu in 1844 or 1845. He might have met Lawrence when the latter was at Karnal in November 1843.[24]

Gardiner was a ship's deserter, probably Irish, who got service with Ranjit Singh but never rose above command of a battery or battalion. In the Sikh anarchy, he worked first with the Dogra brothers or Jammu family, and claimed to have been present at the murder of Kharak Singh. His rule however was to adhere to the *de facto* government, so that he served every faction in turn. He became notorious, while in the obedience of Jawāhir Singh, for carrying out with his own hands the mutilation of a Brahmin which nobody else would do. This was reported to Henry Lawrence on the occupation of Lahore in 1846 and he promptly deported Gardiner to Ludhiana in February of that year.[25]

Personal contacts, whatever they may have been earlier, between Carmichael-Smyth and Gardiner were doubtless renewed when the British forces moved to Lahore after Sobraon. It was however then only a few weeks until Henry Lawrence relegated Gardiner to Ludhiana. The 3rd Light Cavalry presently returned to Jullundur, from which Ludhiana is no distance away, and thus these contacts could continue. Out of them, it seems, there was born a volume published by Thackers at Calcutta in 1847 under the title of *A History of the Reigning Family at Lahore with Some Account of the Jummoo Rajahs, the Seik Soldiers and their Sirdars, edited by Major G. Carmichael-Smyth, 3rd Bengal Light Cavalry, with notes on Malcolm, Prinsep, Lawrence, Steinbach, McGregor and the Calcutta Review.*

The editor made the claim that the book was based to some extent on native manuscripts and information, but the extent may not have been great and one may wonder what facility he had in reading Persian or Urdu. The main source, as he also very fairly states, was Gardiner's notes. Carmichael-Smyth himself contributed an Introduction, written in a disagreeable and aggressive style, and containing nothing to admire. There follows the main text. What was the editor's contribution to this, one cannot say; it may be that Gardiner, an uneducated man, lacked ability to reduce his information to writing, though in later life he was a fluent storyteller. The book displays extreme hostility to the Jammu or Dogra family but otherwise, discounting Gardiner's general untrustworthiness, it is a source of some importance for the beastly story of the Sikh anarchy. Lastly, it contains an appendix of quotations from the works of earlier authors named on the title page with Gardiner's corrections of alleged inaccuracies set down in parallel.

It is understandable that the Company's military and civil officers, who had been watching the Punjab since 1839 and had just concluded the First Sikh War, should have shown interest in such a work, and there is a distinguished list of 197 subscribers from Napier and Gough and all the divisional commanders of the Bengal Army downwards. At the present time the most curious thing about the book is its attitude to Henry Lawrence, then at the zenith of his reputation and powers, from which he was presently to decline but only to sink in a final blaze of glory ten years later at Lucknow. Here is a volume openly based on the notes of a shady individual whom Lawrence had deported within the past twelve months from Lahore. It is stated in the Introduction that Lawrence had asked to see part of the work in manuscript, which had delayed publication, and one can understand that he wanted to know what Gardiner was going to put out. The scoundrel, as he was, is described in the Introduction as 'Captain Gardiner of the

Seik Artillery, who has for several years past supplied important information to the British Government without betraying his own, as all the intrigues which he brought to light were those of the Jummoo family and their co-adjutor the Pundit' (*sc.* Julla). To ram this home a footnote contains a quotation from a letter written to Carmichael-Smyth by Lawrence himself from Khatmandu, where Lawrence says 'if I were in Broadfoot's place, I should like to have Gardiner at my elbow'. It is no surprise to find in the appendix a liberal quantity of extracts from Lawrence's semi-historical fiction, *Adventures of an officer in the Punjab*, corrected by Gardiner. It is not unfair to say that this book is a hit at Lawrence and one may feel sure he was not shown the Introduction with the quotation from his Khatmandu letter.

As far as is known, this literary effort of Carmichael-Smyth's had no sequel for ten years—unless (who knows?) he emulated 'the gallant Captain Wetherby' as military correspondent of some *mofussil* (up-country) newspaper.[26] Shortly after the outbreak at Meerut, he penned an account of the events and his own experiences on the evening of 10 May. This is preserved by Chick and was probably composed in 1857.[27] It is a simply-written document, understandably a little reticent but in general straightforward, and a valuable source for so much of the evening's events as came under his personal observation. Then, apparently in 1858, he published at Meerut a broadsheet with his observations, extremely jejune, on the causes of the Mutiny: running to only two pages, it tabulates a number of alleged causes, with Carmichael-Smyth's opinions on each and some quotations from the press in support of these, but it contains one invaluable piece of information about his own actions on 23 April.[28] Finally, he printed and circulated privately a pamphlet, rebutting the charge of unpopularity made against him by Kaye. This must, it seems, have been printed in England between 1870 (when Kaye's second volume containing this charge appeared) and 1883 shortly before which date Carmichael-Smyth sent a copy to Rice Holmes.[29] No copy of this production has been traceable.

The *History of the Reigning Family at Lahore* does not give a very pleasant impression of him who claimed to be no more than its editor. To have associated with Gardiner is no credit—but after all that old pretender got along years later with Henry Durand and Richard Temple, who should not have been so deceived. The cuts at Henry Lawrence deserve censure. The impression left is that Carmichael-Smyth was pushing himself forward on a field for which his talents and experiences did not qualify him. That argues a strain of conceit—understandable from his background. His irruption into the field of Sikh affairs was perhaps lost time's revenge.

This would square with the oft-repeated allegation of his un-popularity in his regiment. That, however, is not to be accepted with too great facility. The allegation was first made publicly by Kaye in his second volume, published in 1870, and was coupled with dark hints of undue favouritism towards a certain Brijmohan (orderly to the Havildār-Major) of whom more anon.[30] Kaye, of course, did not footnote his text, except occasionally; he does not give his source for these allegations, neither the unpopularity nor the favouritism. They may have been verbal; if they were written, he destroyed them, for there is nothing whatever about these matters in his Mutiny Papers in the India Office. Rice Holmes in 1883 repeated the allegation of unpopularity and underlined it by stating that the pamphlet which, as mentioned above, Carmichael-Smyth had sent him did not alter his opinion.

In works of such magnitude and weight as Kaye's and Holmes', these allegations might escape legal action: for others to circulate them privately during Carmichael-Smyth's life might have been dangerous. Hence, one can understand that open allegations of his unpopularity by contemporary serving officers or others are not readily forthcoming. Mackenzie, an ensign of the regiment at the critical time, in memoirs published in India in 1891 (a year after Carmichael-Smyth's death) says nothing about his unpopularity. The six troop officers who, as will be told below, set down their knowledge on 27 April 1857 as to whether their Colonel had been warned on the evening of the 23rd that the cartridges would be refused, go out of their way to exonerate him from any express warning, without suppressing however the fact that the event must have been clear to themselves and him on the evening in question. The loyalty of Bengal officers to their fellows, their men, their corps, and the worst of their commanders was notorious, but however one reads them these important letters are strangely free from any suggestion that the Colonel of the 3rd L.C. was hateful to his subordinates or his men.[31] The same is true of Captain Craigie's 'objectionable note' of 24 April—also to be mentioned

in its place.[32] A private letter from Mrs Craigie exhibits some dis-
like, and refers to a certain Raman Singh as the Colonel's 'victim'.[33]
Neither at the Court of Inquiry nor at the court-martial over the
refusal of the cartridges on 24 April did the accused or any testifying witness allege anything against Carmichael-Smyth's manner or
temper on that occasion, as the men of the 19th N.I. at Berhampore had done in Colonel Mitchell's case.[34] It is just to say that
the available evidence of Carmichael-Smyth's unpopularity is not
very weighty or convincing.

It is also just, and pleasing, to set against this evidence one
chance record, neglected by previous writers, of what seems to be
an act of at least official benevolence on his part. During the
cholera epidemic in the Doab in the hot weather and rains of 1856,
Government distributed cholera pills, which seemed to have a good
effect—whether physical or psychological who shall say? In the
villages, as already mentioned, the distribution was made through
the chaukidārs (later, the chapātī-bearers); in the towns it was done
through the police *chaukis* (posts) and also through private individuals in the various quarters. In the report about the distributors
in Meerut, one reads 'Native Cavalry and Hoosainee Bazars and
vicinity—1. Col. Smyth, commanding 3rd L.C., 2. Mr. J. Jones,
3rd Clerk, Collector's Office.' No other officer of any native
regiment acted as a distributor. One could say it happened
because he was the senior officer of a native regiment in station;
but why then is he coupled with the obscure Jones? In the
Collectors' reports the distributors are quite warmly thanked for
their aid: it seems as if the task was voluntary and entailed some
trouble. Colonel Smyth, commanding the 3rd L.C., may be
thought to have done something for his neighbours on this
occasion.[35]

The figure which emerges from this darkened canvas is complex
and any judgement of him must take that into account. His good
record of varied active service proves his courage, which O'Callaghan should not have questioned—even obliquely. He was not
merely a stupid martinet as he is sometimes represented. He may
have had too good a conceit of himself but he produced something,
in his Sikh history, out of the common run for a regimental officer.
He may not have been too popular but a strong unpopularity is
not proved against him. The impression which one has about him
is that of a possibly disappointed and difficult character, a man

45

shadowed by promise not fulfilled and certainly deficient in judgement; a deficiency which often ruins all.

Some brief mention of the civil officials at Meerut will not be amiss, though they had little direct influence on the events of 10 May. The Commissioner of the Meerut Division was H. H. Greathed: he was marooned all the night of 10–11 May in his bungalow in the civil lines under the protection of his servants. He went with the Meerut column under Wilson to Delhi on 28 May, served as political officer with the Delhi Field Force all through the siege, and died of sickness during the final assault on the city. The Judge was George Blunt, a very senior man, who retired from the service with effect from 11 April 1857, so that it is uncertain whether he was in Meerut on 10 May. The Collector and Magistrate was R. H. W. Dunlop: he was on leave on 10 May in Kulu, or Spiti, and only got back to Meerut via Simla, Ambala, and the Ridge at Delhi about 12 June. The Deputy Collector and Magistrate was Alexander Johnston: he was killed on 27 May while assisting at an attack on a Gujar village. He was the senior civil official who was actually available on the evening of 10 May; he was replaced, pending Dunlop's return, by D. G. Turnbull, former Collector of Bulandshahr. The significant point which emerges from this enumeration is that the section of the *Meerut District Narrative* which relates to Meerut itself was not composed by any official actually present at Meerut on 10 May. The *Narrative* as a whole was compiled by Fleetwood Williams, the succeeding Commissioner, and the paragraphs dealing with the events of 10 May probably by Dunlop from information collected after his return in June, but in these circumstances it does not deserve quite the same credence as other similar official narratives.[36]

CHAPTER 5

MEERUT CANTONMENT IN 1857

A knowledge of the topography of Meerut Cantonment in 1857 is essential for any understanding of the events of 10 May or of the depositions and narratives relating to those events. The sources from which the topography in 1857 can, to a great extent, be recovered are descriptions by various writers and a few surviving maps.[1]

Descriptions actually contemporary with the Mutiny are those of Mrs Muter, Surgeon O'Callaghan, and an anonymous document printed in Chick. The American traveller Minturn gives a brief account of the place in the preceding year, 1856. It is also very worth while reading the much fuller account of Meerut and its ways of life presented by Thomas Bacon twenty years earlier.[2]

In England at any rate, there does not appear to survive any copy of a full map of Meerut prior to 1857 and there is only one partial sketch map dating from 1857, which is preserved among the *Kaye Papers* in the India Office: it shows the Dam-damma or Artillery School of Instruction, where the European population took refuge after the outbreak, and part of the northern face of the European lines. It was prepared by Lieutenant E. Jones of the Bengal Artillery to show the temporary defences of the Dam-damma, but it furnishes some interesting details.[3]

Next, and much the most important, is a map prepared in 1860 from actual survey by Lt.-Col. F. Alexander, the Executive Engineer at Meerut, on the scale of one mile to eight inches. It was prepared for the purpose of showing proposed alterations in the cantonment boundaries, and some proposed new construction in connection with the laying of the railway line which was to run up the western side of the station. There is no doubt that it shows the station in the main as it existed in 1857. The officers' bungalows in the area behind (east of) the main north–south range of the native lines seem rather scarce, and this may be due to lack of reconstruction after the conflagration of 10 May. The map shows only the cantonment, not the civil station nor the city: the area of those parts is almost blank. The street

47

names on this map can certainly be taken to be those of 1857; by the date of the next map, mentioned below, several of the main street names had been changed. The allocation of the large block of lines east of the church between European infantry and artillery may possibly not be exactly as in 1857.[4]

The last map which is of use for present purposes is a map of the Cantonment and Environs of Meerut surveyed by Major G. F. Anderson, Deputy Superintendent, in 1867–8; it was published in sixteen sheets on the scale of one mile to twelve inches in Calcutta in 1871, and in four sheets on the scale of one mile to six inches in 1873. Sheet 14 of the sixteen-sheet edition contains a long list of references to buildings all over the station and this list enables some buildings to be located which are referred to in the sources for the outbreak in 1857 and which seem to be in positions on the 1867 map conforming to the references to them in the 1857 sources. Otherwise, the 1867 map shows great changes from the 1860 map and the position which must have existed in 1857. Most notable of these is the complete disappearance of the main block of the native lines of 1857; what remains are what had in 1857 been merely two western projections at the north and south extremities of the lines. Between these now quite separated sets of lines, the racecourse occupies most of what had been in 1857 the native parade ground. This map does, however, cover more ground than the 1860 map and shows the civil station and a good part of the city of Meerut on its southern edge, and more of the Delhi road.[5]

The following description is, in consequence, mainly based on the 1860 map, and street names are given as they appear on that map (which also formed the basis of the sketch map at the end of this book).

The British station at Meerut dated from 1806 and was laid out to the north of the Indian city. The main natural feature of the area occupied by the British station was a ravine known as the Abū Nullah.[6] Such water as this carried seasonally flowed into the Kali Nadi of which the nullah can be regarded as a tributary or branch. In May, of course, it was dry, or practically so. It was deep and wide enough to call for bridges to carry the station roads across. It entered the station at the north-west corner, ran south for some way, then turned eastwards and flowed for over a mile but with many zigzags and with a wide northward bend between the Dragoon Bridge and the Begum's Bridge which are mentioned below. Somewhat east of the latter bridge the ravine turned south again and ran out eventually past the eastern side of the Indian city.

The longish west–east stretch of the Abū Nullah divided the station roughly into two halves. The so-called European lines of the British regiments and of the Bengal Artillery were on the northern edge of the northern half; the so-called native lines of the Indian cavalry and infantry were on the western edge of the southern half. It is important to realise that the two sets of lines were laid out at right-angles to each other and faced different ways, as well as being separated by the nullah and by a lot of ground. The European lines ran west–east and faced north: the main block of the native lines ran north–south and faced west.

Taking first the European lines, the cavalry lines (occupied by the Carabiniers) formed the western section, the infantry lines the central section, and the artillery lines the eastern section. The cavalry stables were on the edge of their parade ground. Behind them were barracks for the men consisting of large bungalows for about twenty men each. To the east came first the European infantry lines (occupied by the Q.R.R.) and then at the eastern extremity the artillery lines, again with barracks along their front. Near the centre of the whole range of lines was the church, which stood upon the verge of the infantry parade ground, just within the edge of the lines, and was the largest and finest in any North India station; farther out on the parade ground was the cemetery. Behind the church were the cavalry and infantry hospitals.[7] On the edge of the artillery parade ground was the large enclosed Artillery School of Instruction, commonly known as the Damdamma.[8] Behind the various ranges of barracks was an area occupied by the bungalows of the officers with their compounds surrounded by low walls: mainly, they were assigned to officers behind their own regimental barracks, but there was a good deal of intermixture.[9] This area was bounded on the south by a broad and tree shaded road, known as the Mall, the evening promenade of the European inhabitants. This ran right through from west to east. Between the Mall and the Abū Nullah was another area filled with bungalows and also with bazars. There was a bazar behind the cavalry lines known as the Dragoon Bazar, but the largest, known as the European Infantry Bazar, was behind the infantry lines: there was also an Artillery Bazar behind those lines. The crowded nature of this whole area, filled with buildings surrounded by walls, trees and ditches, was well-known to contemporaries.[10]

There was a road known as Terminus Road which ran south-westwards from the western end of the cavalry lines and crossed the nullah by a bridge.[11] The European cavalry and infantry lines were divided by a street known as Bridge Street, and this crossed the nullah by a bridge known as the Dragoon Bridge.[12] Two main north–south streets intersected the European infantry lines. Hill Street ran south-east from a point between Bridge Street and the church to meet the other of these two roads, Church Street, at a point not far north of the bridge by which Church Street then crossed the nullah. Church Street ran due north and south, and at the north ended at the churchyard wall. The bridge by which Church Street (after its junction with Hill Street) crossed the nullah was known as the Begum's Bridge, because it was constructed by the Begum Sumroo. A cross-road known as Chapel Street turned off from Church Street south-westwards, crossed Hill Street, then passed over the nullah by a bridge at the top of the northward bend which was not pukka, but only wood.[13] Further to the east, Baker Street, School Street, and Clement Street were large roads, running north and south. None of them was carried over the nullah by a bridge, for the nullah had, before intersecting with them, made its further southward turn.

Proceeding now to the southern half of the station across the nullah, Bridge Street was continued south from the Dragoon Bridge by Sudder Street. After a mile or more, Sudder Street stopped at a cross-road running west and east, and by turning east one could then reach the Delhi road, but Sudder Street did not itself run through any further. Chapel Street, which had crossed the nullah by the wooden bridge, then continued its south-western course and ran into Sudder Street not far south of the Dragoon Bridge. Just south of the Begum's Bridge, where Church Street had crossed the nullah, the road divided into three as follows. A road called Abū Lane branched off to the west, form-ing a chord across the northern bend of the nullah (between the nullah and the Sudder Bazar) and emerged at its western end into Sudder Street. The Delhi road went off in a south-westerly direc-tion and ran out past the western side of the Indian city; the Bulandshahr road, which was in fact the Grand Trunk Road, continued more or less south and ran out past the eastern side of the Indian city, which thus lay between the Delhi and Bulandshahr roads.

After making its southward turn, the nullah ran down to the east of the Bulandshahr road and roughly parallel to it. There were some bridges over the nullah on this stretch but one cannot be certain how many in 1857. The only one which matters and which certainly did then exist was on a road which came from the eastern face of the city, crossed the Bulandshahr road, and then went on over the nullah by the bridge now in question. This road then bore north-east and passed a large tank known as the Sūrajkund and eventually ran into a road which had originated at the eastern end of the Mall, ran more or less southwards and led eventually to Garhmukhteshwar, a well-known crossing place on the Ganges into Rohilkhand.[14]

The native lines composed the western face of this area south of the nullah. They consisted of a main block running north and south and facing west over the parade ground. From both the northern and southern extremities of this main block there were projections to the west, that is to say other blocks of lines running out westwards and facing in the one case south and in the other case north. Thus the native lines formed three sides of a rectangle round a large parade ground. Native lines consisted of rows of huts occupied by one or two men along the edge of the parade ground. In front of these, at least in infantry lines, were the bells of arms. To the rear of the lines of huts was the area allotted to officers' bungalows, messes and so forth. At Meerut, there was a large bungalow area to the rear (east) of the main block and a smaller number of bungalows to the rear (north) of the northern projection, but none to the rear of the southern projection. Sudder Street formed mainly the eastern limit of the bungalow area behind the main block: there was a road from Sudder Street behind or through the bungalows at the rear of the northern projection. The northern extremity of the main block was a quarter of a mile or more south of the Dragoon Bridge and from that point the lines and bungalows extended a full mile farther south; the western projections each extended for the better part of a mile.[15]

The western projection at the southern end formed the native cavalry lines: the native infantry lines consisted of the main north–south block and the western projection at the northern end. The

3rd Light Cavalry occupied the native cavalry lines, the 20th Native Infantry the main north–south block, and the 11th Native Infantry the western projection at the northern end.

There was a small Cavalry Bazar behind (south of) the native cavalry lines and one very large bazar, known as the Sudder Bazar, or Chief Bazar, serving the native lines as a whole. The Sudder Bazar lay in the angle between Sudder Street and Abū Lane, and extended nearly to the Delhi road on the east. It gave the name to Sudder Street which bordered it on its western edge. Its dimensions were a half to three quarters of a mile, both north–south and east–west, but its outline was naturally irregular. Its northern portion was nearer to the nullah and the Dragoon Bridge than was the northern end of the main native lines and it extended southwards about half-way down those lines. It was from the Sudder Bazar and parts of the city that the mobs or gangs emerged which committed many of the murders and most of the arson and looting on 10 May.

Farther east than the area just described lay the civil station. This mainly occupied the area between the Delhi road and the nullah after its renewed southern turn. It extended, however, also west of the Delhi road in rear of the native lines, and east of the nullah towards the Garhmukhteshwar road. It does not lend itself to exact description, consisting of the courts and offices of the civil administration and of the scattered bungalows of officials and subordinate staff.

Between the Delhi and the Bulandshahr roads, south of the civil station and east of the native cavalry lines, lay the city of Meerut. Whether it was still walled is not clear, but there were gates standing or ways of ingress which still preserved the names of gates. Round the northern edge of the city there was a route, by various interconnecting roads, from the Delhi road to the Bulandshahr road. It was then possible to go down the Bulandshahr road southwards to where it crossed the road mentioned earlier, which came from the eastern face of the city, crossed the nullah, and went past the Sūrajkund to the Garhmukhteshwar road.

It was by this route, some round and some through the city, that the 3rd L.C. troopers travelled on the evening of 10 May to rescue their eighty-five comrades from the jail. It is of great importance to realise that there were two jails at Meerut. The one now in question was known as the New Jail in distinction from the Old Jail; it was also called the Central Jail and the Civil Jail. It had actually been constructed, in spite of its name, as long ago as 1819. It lay upon the west side of the Garhmukhteshwar road only a little north of the point where this road was joined by the road from the city across the nullah and past the Sūrajkund. The New Jail formed a large rectangle of about 500 by 400 yards and was capable of taking over 4000 prisoners.[16]

The Old Jail is not marked on any of the available maps and the sources do not enable its exact position to be established. It is, however, clear enough that it lay somewhere between the city and the Sudder Bazar, probably not far from the north-western angle of the city. It must have been the original jail built when the station was laid out in 1806. It could take 1550 prisoners.[17] In addition to the prisoners in the two jails, there was on 10 May a small number of dacoits awaiting transportation who were confined in quarters in the compound of Major Williams' bungalow, he being (among his various duties) special officer for dacoity and thagī.[18] The prisoners from both jails were let out in the course of the outbreak, but they were released at quite different times and by quite different parties.

A few other buildings may be mentioned. The cutcherries (courts and offices) of the Judge and of the Collector and Magistrate were to the east of the nullah where it made its turn to the southward. The Collector and Magistrate's cutcherry was rather more to the south than the Judge's and thus rather nearer the New Jail. The situation of the treasury cannot be identified but it was probably part of, or close to, the Collector and Magistrate's cutcherry. On the morning of 11 May the bodies of the European and Eurasian dead were collected in 'the theatre'. Meerut, as Thomas Bacon already tells us, was much given to theatricals; the 1867 map marks both the Station Theatre and the Royal Theatre on the south side of the Mall between Bridge Street and Hill Street, and there were at one time four or five regimental theatres. The theatre now in question was probably the Station Theatre; by a mistake of the contractor it had been built the wrong way round—with its back to the Mall.[19] None of the sources in 1857 mention a club, nor can one be identified on the 1860 map; there is a club on the 1867 map, again on the south side of the Mall, quite near Bridge Street. Assembly Rooms also cannot be identified but probably existed; these to some extent supplied the place of the club in British stations in India—before the club became a general institution.[20] There was a second Protestant church which in 1857 was in charge of the Rev. A. Medland of the Church Missionary Society, but its situation is not ascertainable.[21] Chapel Street was named after and contained the Roman Catholic chapel for this was near the wooden bridge. This chapel served not only the local English, Eurasian and Indian Catholics but also the very large proportion of Irish in the Queen's regiments. There are references to the rum godowns: the old rum godowns were south of the European Infantry Bazar, the new in Clement Street east of the Artillery Mess. The sources also mention the shop of Elahi Buksh; this was on the corner of Abū Lane and Sudder Street.[22]

The bungalows occupied by individuals are even more difficult to locate. General Hewitt seems to have lived in the civil station, for when Colonel Carmichael-Smyth escaped on the evening of 10 May he went first to the bungalow of the Commissioner, H. H. Greathed, and then to Hewitt's.[23] Of Greathed's bungalow, we can only say that it was next door to that of Major G. W. Williams, and from the latter it was possible to see the road round the northern edge of the city which some of the 3rd L.C. sowars took on their way to the jail.[24] Carmichael-Smyth's bungalow was in the native lines, farther north than Captain Craigie's, for officers of the 20th N.I. hiding in Smyth's compound heard and joined the European troops returning north through the bungalow area, but Craigie's party did not. Captain Chambers' bungalow was opposite Craigie's and Lieutenant Mackenzie's a little up the road. Lieutenant Eckford, the Executive Engineer, and Surgeon Smith of the Veteran Establishment had bungalows next to each other in Sudder Street, near its northern end; and Whish, the Brigade-Major, was also housed in the native lines.[25] One would like to know where Archdale Wilson's bungalow was but it is uncertain. On his way to it Carmichael-Smyth was fired on near the rum godowns, and if this means the new rum godowns then the bungalow must have been in Clement Street, where what seem to be some rather large bungalows can be seen on the 1860 map. But, from the narrative of the Rev. T. C. Smyth, Wilson's bungalow appears to have been near that of a couple named Bicknell, with whom the Rev. T. C. Smyth lived; and one rather gathers that that was not so far from the church as Clement Street.[26] However, Wilson's bungalow was evidently in the European lines, rather towards the eastern end.

The cantonment and civil station thus described covered a very large space of ground and certain rough distances and dimensions should be kept in mind. The front of the European lines from west to east along the edge of the parade ground was some two and a quarter miles in length, about the distance from Kensington Palace to Piccadilly Circus. From the front of the European lines (their parade grounds) by Bridge Street or by Church Street to the bridges over the Abū Nullah was a mile, with the Mall half-way. From the Dragoon Bridge on to the nearest point of the native infantry lines was a good quarter of a mile farther, and on to the parade ground or down to the centre of the main north-south range as much again. The authorities at the nearest point of the European lines on the evening of 10 May were about as well able to make out what was going on in the native lines as persons at Marble Arch to make out what is going on round Victoria Station. From the front of the European lines to the northern edge of the city was again about two and a quarter miles; the diagonal from the artillery lines to the southern angle of the native lines a good two and a half miles; from the mid-point of the native cavalry lines to the New Jail was about three miles as the crow flies and more by the roads.

Two more matters may conveniently be dealt with here. The first is telegraphic communication. It is difficult to arrive at full certainty about the layout of the telegraph lines in the triangle Agra–Meerut–Delhi at this period. There was a telegraph line from Agra to Meerut: one would have thought that it would have followed the Grand Trunk Road, in which case it would have run up the road through Aligarh and Bulandshahr to Meerut (Agra itself was off the Grand Trunk Road, on a branch road from Aligarh); this seems to be confirmed by an allusion in a despatch from Hewitt.[27] There was also a line from Meerut to Delhi. Both the Meerut–Delhi and the Meerut–Agra lines were cut at the time of the outbreak, but at different times and in different circumstances. It is not clear whether the line went on northwards from Meerut to reach Karnal and Ambala after crossing the Jumna somewhere near the former place. A telegram survives which is marked as sent on 12 May from Meerut to Ambala and other

Punjab stations, but this may well have been carried by messenger from Meerut to Ambala and then distributed by wire from there.[28] From Delhi there was a line to Ambala and on the morning of 11 May the Delhi telegraph clerks were sending messages up this line to Ambala of the sort described as 'telegraphists' chatter'; and these were the first messages which conveyed to the Punjab the news of the outbreaks at Meerut and Delhi. They finally sent one official telegram by this line, on the orders of Brigadier Graves, at about 3 p.m. on the afternoon of the 11th: one of them returned from the Flagstaff Tower to the Telegraph Office (not far from the present Maidens Hotel) for that purpose.[29] In their narrative they do not record that they 'chattered' in this way with Agra over a direct line, nor that such a line was cut. If there was such a line from Delhi via Muttra on the west bank of the Jumna it must presumably have been cut in the early hours of the morning of 11 May, soon after the mutinous cavalry from Meerut entered Delhi. Such a Delhi–Agra line is marked on a map of 1857, which also shows the line north from Meerut to Ambala crossing the Jumna near Karnal: however, this same map does *not* show the direct line from Delhi to Karnal and Ambala, which beyond any doubt existed, while it shows a line from Agra to Meerut which does not pass through Aligarh, as it seems in reality to have done.[30] Thus, this map darkens more than it illuminates, and the existence of the Agra–Delhi and the Meerut–Ambala lines rests under the shadow of a doubt.

The second point to be mentioned here is the hour of the Sunday evening service at the great church in the European infantry lines. It is an indubitable fact recorded by several contemporary witnesses, that on Sunday 10 May 1857 the evening service at that church was, on account of the heat, fixed for a time half an hour later than the usual hour. To this fact much importance came to be attached by contemporaries, and by some later writers, because the idea got about that the mutineers in the native lines had intended their rising to take place while the European troops were in church at the evening service, with only side-arms, so that the rising could have got under way with impunity or even (so the tale is sometimes embellished) the European troops could have been surrounded and slaughtered in the church. It may be said at once that this story is mere legend, as will be proved when all the relevant times have been particularised. The first thing however is to ask at what hour did the evening service actually commence on the evening in question? Out of the numerous witnesses on this matter, only two, Mrs Muter, and the Rev. T. C. Smyth the senior of the two chaplains, state what this hour was and they agree upon it; the service was fixed that evening for 7 p.m.[31] From this it follows that the ordinary hour for the evening service was 6.30 p.m. and it can be inferred that the church parades would have fallen in on an ordinary Sunday evening at 6 p.m. while on that particular evening they would have fallen in at 6.30 p.m. That will hold even for the 60th Q.R.R., whose parade ground was nearest to the church, because time must be allowed for the parade to be fallen in, told off, and marched to church so as to be in good time before the general congregation began to gather in the building.

To this important piece of information may be added at this point these further details as to times. On Sunday 10 May 1857 the sun set at Meerut at twenty minutes to seven o'clock, and the moon rose within five minutes of nine o'clock that night, two days past the full and therefore brilliant as no English moon can be. Between about 7 and 9 p.m. on 10 May darkness reigned. The sun rose on 11 May at twelve minutes after five o'clock.[32]

CHAPTER 6

THE FIRING PARADE OF 24 APRIL
AND ITS SEQUEL

It was the hot weather, the season of reduced duties and of leave. Archdale Wilson was absent from the station on 24 April and did not return till near the end of April.[1] There were many other absentees.[2] There was no officer above the substantive rank of captain with the 20th N.I. on the critical day. It would be rash to see in this state of affairs a serious aggravation of conditions in Meerut, but possibly it was not entirely without influence. In Wilson's absence Colonel Jones of the Carabiniers, wholly without Indian experience, commanded the station; but he went on leave when Wilson returned and Colonel Custance then took command of that regiment.[3] There was no senior officer, except poor old Hewitt, with whom Carmichael-Smyth might have usefully conferred before issuing the orders which he did on 23 April.

Carmichael-Smyth himself went at the end of March to Hardwar, as president of a committee, to purchase remounts at the *mela* or fair. This broke up early because of cholera and he took short leave at Mussoorie. While there he heard of the first cases of incendiarism at Ambala, which followed the appearance there of the Enfield cartridges as the rifle-training progressed. He also met somebody who had fallen in with a party of sepoys proceeding on leave; this acquaintance told him that the havildār with the party had said, with reference to the Berhampore affair, the news of which had now got up-country, 'I have been 36 years in the service and am a havildār, but I still would join in a mutiny and what is more I can tell you the whole army will mutiny'. This produced a deep impression on Carmichael-Smyth.[4]

On the night of 13 April the first case of incendiarism occurred at Meerut, involving five huts, one being that of a sowar of the 3rd L.C. named Brijmohan, who was orderly to the Havildār-Major and, according to Kaye, of low caste and unduly favoured by Carmichael-Smyth. This case of arson is ignored by the standard histories, according to which Brijmohan's hut was burnt down on the night of 23 April preceding the fatal parade: for this there is

58

certainly evidence. Yet the burning on the 13th was recorded in the Meerut police records. One can only conclude that Brijmohan's hut was burnt down twice, and that something connected with him was an element in the prevailing tension so far as the 3rd L.C. was concerned.[5]

Carmichael-Smyth arrived back in Meerut on Thursday 23 April having no doubt, in the way of those times, travelled in a *palki* (palaquin) through the night; he must have arrived early in the morning. He would have sent for the acting Adjutant, Lieutenant Melville-Clarke, to come to his bungalow, and would then have been shown or told anything of moment which had occurred during his absence. One thing which he would have then been shown was the revised Platoon Exercise and the orders for its adoption. He then did three things during that day of 23 April.

His first action was to order a parade of the skirmishers of the regiment to be held on the morning of the following day, Friday 24 April, at which blank cartridges would be issued for firing and the men would be instructed in the revised drill with the cartridge end torn off by the hand and not by the teeth. This, it can be assumed, was the first in order of the three acts now in question, for it would have been decided upon as soon as he saw the revised Platoon Exercise.[6] Next, he wrote a letter to Colonel Curzon, the Military Secretary to the Commander-in-Chief, with the information that he had heard the whole army was going to mutiny, and reporting the words used by the halvidār about whom he had been told at Mussoorie: this was doubtless done in the course of the day passed indoors.[7] Finally, he sent for the Havildār-Major and his attendant sprite or orderly, Brijmohan, showed the latter the new drill and made him fire off two of the *old* cartridges in that way; upon which, according to Smyth, Brijmohan said that the men would be pleased at the change in the drill. This was probably between five and six o'clock in the evening, for it was the custom of the times for Europeans to stay indoors in the hot weather from about 9 a.m. at latest, till about 5 p.m. at the earliest.[8]

This train of conduct has elements of ambivalence. If Carmichael-Smyth believed that the whole Bengal Army was on the verge of mutiny, as he wrote to Curzon, he should have thought twice about ordering a parade for firing drill. If he thought that the revised loading drill would cure the men's uneasiness, it was pointless to bother the Military Secretary with a piece of alarming *gup* (gossip) garnered at Mussoorie. He seems to have wished to show at the same time by two barely consistent actions his alertness and his fortitude, to gain credit both for passing information on, and for applying orders received. It was not mere vanity or obtuseness on his part but rather a sense of crisis or differing possibilities, of recognition to be won as well as decision required; and the curious double movement of his mind chimes with his character as it had been shaped by his circumstances previously discussed.

The order for the parade was no doubt posted. Brijmohan went back to the lines and boasted that he had used the *new* cartridges and said that all the skirmishers would have to do so next day. Thereupon, two Muhammadan *naiks* (corporals), Pīr Ali and Kudrat Ali, told their comrades that these *new* cartridges were greased with beef and pork fat and would defile both Hindus and Muhammadans: the men then bound themselves by an oath (Hindus on Ganges water and Muhammadans on the Koran) not to use the cartridges until every regiment had consented to do so.[9] The evidence on these matters is not quite free from suspicion. Brijmohan had *not* used the *new* cartridges; but he may have lied out of mischief. The three testifying witnesses as to the oath are all Hindus and they fasten the blame on two Muhammadans who happened in fact to be the first two men to refuse the cartridges on parade next day. There is, however, ample confirmation of the state of feeling in the regiment that night.

Some time in the evening, Captain Craigie, who commanded the 4th Troop, sent a note to the acting Adjutant and commander of the 5th Troop, Lieutenant Melville-Clarke, which read as follows:

Go at once to Smyth and tell him that the men of my troop have requested in a body that the skirmishing tomorrow morning may be countermanded, as there is a commotion throughout the native troops about cartridges, and that the regiment will become *budnam* if they fire any cartridges. I understand that in all six troops a report of the same kind is being made. This is a most serious matter, and we may have the whole regiment in mutiny in half an hour if this is not attended to. Pray don't lose a moment but go to Smyth at once. 2. We have none of the objectionable cartridges, but the men say that if they fire any kind of cartridge at present they lay themselves open to the imputation from their comrades and from other regiments of having fired the objectionable ones.[10]

The Firing Parade of 24 April

This note is well-known because it went up to Simla with the file, and ultimately got into the Parliamentary Papers. Notwithstanding the regulation numbering of the second paragraph, its informal references to the commanding officer and its unsoldierlike disclosure of anxiety and urgency awoke the orderly-room prudery of Headquarters, and Meerut was called on to explain how this 'objectionable note' had been allowed to flutter up to those exalted heights—they excused themselves on the necessity of not missing a dāk.[11]

Less well-known, because preserved only in Smyth's *Account*, are certain other communications from the troop commanders, including Craigie. It seems that on the morrow of the Court of Inquiry, which followed on the parade, the story went about that Carmichael-Smyth had been warned that the men would not use their cartridges and had still persisted in holding the parade. On 27 April, Carmichael-Smyth ordered the acting Adjutant, Melville-Clarke, to write a circular letter to the troop commanders, asking whether any objection was made on the night of 23 April that the men would not use their cartridges and by whom it was made and what steps were taken.

Brevet Major Plowden (1st Troop) replied that a report was brought to him about 9 p.m. on the 23rd that the men would not use the cartridges and he ordered the man to inform the Havildār-Major for the Colonel's information. Lieutenant H. Gough (2nd Troop) said he received no report that the men would refuse the cartridges. Brevet Major Richardson (3rd Troop) said that his bearer told him that a man had brought a message that his men would refuse the cartridges and that Brijmohan's hut had been burnt down: this having been already reported by the Havildār-Major to the Colonel, Richardson took no action. Captain H. C. Craigie (4th Troop) said he received no report that the men would not use the cartridges but about 10 p.m. the Troop Colour Havildār brought a report that men of the troop had requested the native officers to solicit the Colonel to defer the parade until the agitation as to the cartridges had ceased. Feeling the importance of this, Craigie wrote to the Adjutant in strong terms (as we have seen above). Lieutenant Melville-Clarke himself (5th Troop) said he was told about 10 p.m. by one of his men that the men of the troop represented that, as no cartridges were being used in the station at present, they could not use them for fear of getting a bad character: Melville-Clarke told Smyth, who said there would be no alteration in orders. Captain G. A. Galway (6th Troop) said that on that night his Subadār sent word by his orderly that the men refused to go on parade the next morning and fire the cartridges, to which he replied that they would have to parade and do whatever was ordered.[12]

Carmichael-Smyth published all this in his own narrative and seems to have regarded the replies as helping his case. Certainly, Craigie very much watered down the content of his 'objectionable note'; Gough confined himself to a denial of having received a report of *that kind*, but whether he received some other message he did not disclose, though it is fair to say that in his reminiscences, published forty years later, he still revealed nothing of the sort on that evening. Plowden, Richardson and Galway all show that their men did send a message that they would not use the cartridges, while Melville-Clarke wraps the same thing up in the form of a representation that they could not use them, and confirms that he told Smyth. The Colonel was on the horns of a dilemma. He had given an order and could not withdraw in the face of explicitly threatened disobedience: he would then have been in the same position as Mitchell of the 19th N.I. at Berhampore, who was censured for coming to terms with men with arms in their hands. And rightly: for what use is an army that will not load and fire? It had not taken long for Carmichael-Smyth to be justified, if that was any satisfaction to him, in what he had written to Curzon, and condemned by events for having applied the orders which had arrived from Calcutta. Still, the revised Platoon Exercise was issued for use: someone had to grasp the nettle. Carmichael-Smyth did so—and was stung.

Craigie's apprehension of an immediate mutiny of the whole regiment was not justified by the event; but the parade of the skirmishers on the morning of Friday 24 April, issued in a serious breach of discipline on the part of eighty-five out of the ninety men present.[13] The men were to take three cartridges each and before Smyth came on the parade they refused to do so. Smyth then arrived and was told this by the Adjutant. He thereupon ordered Havildār-Major Baksh Ali to load and fire his carbine so as to show the new motions, and he did so. Smyth then ordered cartridges to be served out. The first was offered to Shaikh Pīr Ali Naik, who refused it, saying he would become badnām if he took it. Smyth said to him that the Havildār-Major had taken one but Pīr Ali said 'Oh! the Havildār-Major!' meaning, so Smyth thought, that the Havildār-Major in his position had to do so, and then adding that if all the men took one he (Pīr Ali) would do so. Smyth then ordered a cartridge to be tendered to Amīr Kudrat Ali Naik, who was Pīr Ali's rear file, but he also refused, saying that if all the regiment took one, he would. Only five non-commissioned officers accepted a cartridge, three Muhammadans and two Hindus: eighty-five non-commissioned officers and sowars refused to accept a cartridge, of whom forty-eight were Muhammadans and thirty-seven Hindus.[14]

When the cartridges had been tendered to all present Carmichael-Smyth ordered the five men who had accepted them to fall out and urged the others to accept the cartridges. None did so and there was a general murmur which Smyth thought was to the effect that if he ordered the whole regiment to accept the cartridges, perhaps they would do so. One may suspect that what the men really said was that if *all* the regiments accepted the cartridges, they would do so, for that would be in accord with what they appear to have sworn among themselves. Smyth then spoke to them again, pointing out that the cartridges were not greased, that they were the same as they had been using, and that five non-commissioned officers had not refused them.[15] This produced no effect. Thereupon Smyth had the parade dismissed as they were too large a party to send to the guard.[16] They were, however, taken off duty and confined to their lines.[17]

Smyth now reported the incident to the Brigade-Major, Whish, who laid the report before the station commander, Colonel H. R. Jones, of the Carabiniers.[18] Jones forwarded the report to Hewitt: he ordered a Native Court of Inquiry to assemble the next day and informed the Adjutant-General, Colonel Chester, at Simla. Chester brought the case to the notice of the Commander-in-Chief, General the Hon. George Anson, who commented demi-officially that it seemed a most outrageous case and summary dismissal would be no more than the culprits deserved.[19]

The Court of Inquiry assembled on Saturday 25 April. It consisted of seven native commissioned officers, four from the 20th N.I. and three from the 3rd L.C. with Captain Macdonald and Captain Earle of the 20th N.I. as Superintending Officer and Interpreter respectively, and with Major Harriott, the Deputy

Judge Advocate-General, present. Carmichael-Smyth gave his evidence, setting out what had occurred as narrated above. Evidence from the Quartermaster-Havildār of the 3rd L.C. and from a magazine *tindal* (foreman) was taken that the cartridges were the same in all respects as had always been in use, according to the tindal ever since he had been in the regiment, which was thirty-three years. The members of the Court examined them and agreed that they were the same as had been in use for thirty or forty years: no doubt they were blanks. One of the five men who had taken the cartridges gave evidence to the same effect and stated that they were unobjectionable and that he had taken them, but referred to the existence of a rumour that a new description of cartridge had been made up. The senior Hindu and the senior Muhammadan troopers from each troop were then called. The expressions used by them differ but the gist of their unanimous evidence was that rumour, doubt, and suspicion prevailed in regard to the cartridges and none of the sepoys in the station would touch them.[20]

The proceedings of the Court of Inquiry, with its conclusions that there was some rumour abroad but that the cartridges were unobjectionable, were forwarded to Simla. The Judge Advocate-General, Colonel Keith Young, recommended a court-martial: the Commander-in-Chief approved. He told the Adjutant-General on 29 April that no time must be lost in convening the court-martial and that Hewitt was to be told to carry out immediately its sentence, which the warrant would empower him to do.[21] Meanwhile, at the Artillery School of Instruction at Meerut, on 27 April, a squad of recruits told the drill-havildār they would not use the blank ammunition cartridges if ordered to do so: since they were only recruits they were dealt with by being paid up and dismissed forthwith.[22] Also in this interval, the news of the action of the 3rd L.C. skirmishers spread about. It met the 11th N.I., marching up from Allahabad to Meerut, some marches out of the latter station.[23] During this period after the Court of Inquiry, the eighty-five men were confined in an empty hospital under a guard of their own regiment.[24]

During the interval which elapsed between the firing parade or the Court of Inquiry and the court-martial, there were further cases of incendiarism in the cantonment. This was a repetition of a well-known pattern. Discontent among the sepoys was frequently expressed by the burning of officers' or non-commissioned officers' bungalows, regimental stores, or the like; usually by shooting burning arrows into the thatched roof. It is reported from Meerut on 7 May that fires were occurring almost nightly: an empty bungalow of the Quartermaster-Sergeant of the 3rd L.C., and an old N.I. hospital had been burnt, and on the 6th the Barrack Master's godown.[25]

The original proceedings of the court-martial do not seem to have survived, though Hewitt in reporting its outcome said that he would send them up to Simla. What is known of it is contained in a memorandum of 21 October 1857 by the Judge Advocate-General, Colonel Keith Young.[26] It sat on 6, 7 and 8 May, at the Mess of the Carabiniers. It consisted of six Muhammadan and nine Hindu native commissioned officers. Four of the Muhammadans and six of the Hindus were from the Meerut regiments: one Muhammadan from the 3rd L.C. and three from the 11th N.I., one Hindu each from the 3rd L.C. and the Artillery and two each from the 11th and the 20th N.I. The remaining five members were from the regiments at Delhi, one Muhammadan and one Hindu each from the 38th and 54th N.I. and one Hindu from the 74th N.I. The Subadār-Major of the 38th N.I. was the president. The names of the Superintending Officer and the Interpreter are not recorded.

Although it sat for three days the court-martial does not seem to have heard a great deal of evidence; but these courts were notoriously slow in their proceedings and the case was truly quite plain. Carmichael-Smyth gave a shortened account of what had occurred, making it clear that he had given a separate and individual order to each of the accused to take the cartridges and each had disobeyed and refused to do so. Kudrat Ali asked him if he had shown them the cartridges so that they might see whether they were old ones or new ones and Smyth replied that the *kotdafadārs* (native N.C.Os. in charge of the bells of arms) had the cartridges in their hands and the men could have examined them but refused to touch them. The court asked Smyth why he told the men they would have to fire instead of merely ordering them to do so. Smyth said the parade was in the order book the day before, with orders for each man to receive three cartridges. He himself attended the parade because he wanted to show the men the new way of loading. When he came on the parade, he was told by the Adjutant that the men had not taken their cartridges and that was why he ordered the Havildār-Major to fire and then spoke to the men.

Matadeen, the first-named of the accused, proffered their defence. It was less a defence than an excuse. He said that Brijmohan Singh (*sic*) had told his comrades that he had fired off two of the *new greased* cartridges. About 7.30 p.m. on the 23rd, they were discussing this and the parade fixed for the next day with the Colonel and Adjutant present and the *new* cartridges to be used, and were speculating whether any Hindu or Muhammadan would refuse the cartridges. A number of them said to each other that if they used the cartridges they would lose their caste and be unable to return to their homes. They then decided to report the position to their troop officers so as to save their caste, and this was done through the native officers. When they came on parade the next morning they did not know what had been done or said the night before by the troop officers. The Adjutant came on parade and then the Colonel. The latter said he had invented something and urged them to fire the cartridges, because this would please the Commander-in-Chief, and earn praise for them and for him (the Colonel), and the affair would be published in the papers. He then called the Havildār-Major and ordered him to load and fire. The Havildār-Major was about to bite off the cartridge when the Colonel ordered him to tear it. The Colonel then called for the cartridges. These were brought by the kotdafadārs wrapped up in cloth. The Colonel asked if they would take the cartridges and they said they would not; they had great doubts about them and hence the Colonel had to try and persuade them—a thing he had never done before. He then dismissed them and they asked to make a statement and said that if the other regiments would fire one cartridge, they would fire ten. The Colonel said there were no other cartridges for other men and they said that there were pistols. The Colonel then finally dismissed them.[27]

On the whole this can only be called a lame and evasive explanation. It rather confirms, without explicitly admitting, the fact of the sworn agreement not to take the cartridges, which, if it had been investigated and proved at that stage, would have aggravated and extended the offence. It was not true to say that they did not know what the troop officers had done: some, as Galway, had returned a sharp and immediate answer; while Craigie's action was almost certainly known and its failure obvious. The suggestion that the cartridges, when brought, were wrapped up is intended to fit in with Kudrat Ali's question to the Colonel as to whether they had been allowed to examine the cartridges. But how could troops, ordered to take ammunition, be allowed to pick it over first?

Yet this statement cannot be entirely dismissed. It confirms, as was repeated independently months later in the depositions before Williams, that Brijmohan said he had fired the *new* cartridges. It must, I think, be accepted that this was what he said and that this started an acute suspicion among the men as to what they were to be made to do upon this parade. One may hold this, although, even had they been quite certain that the old cartridges were to be used, the men would probably have refused them, because, as the affair of the 19th N.I. proves, the trouble was now about *paper*, not external greasing. If the English had invented the supposed trick with the new, why should they not have already polluted the old? So the reasoning ran. Still, on any given occasion, if there was some direct reference to the use of the *new* cartridge, feelings and suspicions became still more inflamed. The words attributed to the Colonel are very curious. Why this reference to publication in the papers? It seems an unlikely idea to arise in the men's minds and not in the least calculated to soothe them. But if the Colonel was fond of publicising his ideas, if he did himself *write for or to the papers*, some such remark might have slipped out. One cannot help a suspicion that the Colonel's words, as given by Matadeen, are not pure invention.

By the votes of fourteen out of fifteen members of the court, the whole of the accused were convicted and were sentenced to imprisonment with hard labour for ten years; but the court asked for favourable consideration on the ground of good character and of their having been misled by rumours. Hewitt, in reviewing the decision, rejected these grounds of mitigation and held that they rather aggravated the offence. He therefore confirmed the sentence as to the majority of the prisoners, but on the ground of their being very young and misled by older men, he remitted one half of the sentence on eleven men who had been less than five years in the service.[28]

On the following morning, Saturday 9 May, the whole of the troops at Meerut, European and native, were paraded on the European infantry parade ground. They were formed into three sides of a square. The native infantry and cavalry regiments were without ball. The European troops were armed. By this, it is meant, it seems, that the European infantry and cavalry had ball and the Bengal Artillery ammunition for the guns. The 60th had no more than the ten rounds per man issued in January; from the events of the following evening, it is clear that additional ammunition was not issued until then. Still, ten rounds per man was presumably enough for the purpose on this occasion. It seems likely that the Artillery had grape. It is said that all the European troops, 60th, Carabiniers, and Artillery were ordered to load.[29]

After the court-martial, the condemned men had been confined under a guard of two companies of the 60th and twenty-five Carabiniers.[30] They were now marched to the parade ground: this was a distance of over two miles, for their place of confinement was presumably still in or near their own lines. They were marched into the square, the sentence was read out, they were stripped of their uniform, and were then publicly ironed. The irons were not painful or heavy, but were shackles such as were used in Indian jails: men could move long distances in them if they got away, without having them removed.[31] The shackling of eighty-five men, however, was a long process. It occupied over two hours. While it was going on the condemned men made much outcry, taunting their comrades or appealing for rescue. Finally, they were marched off the parade ground under guard of a company of the 60th, down to the New Jail, again a distance of two full miles. As they left the parade ground their outcry continued; they abused their officers, and particularly Carmichael-Smyth, at whom some of them flung their boots. At the jail they were handed over to the civil authorities, who of course had a force of warders and jail guards, but now asked for a military guard also: this was supplied in the shape of twenty-four sepoys of the 20th N.I., the Rifles returning to their own quarters and duties.[32] The long and painful scene of the parade imposed a great nervous strain on the native troops. In the afternoon of the 9th, the troop officers of the 3rd L.C. visited the condemned men at the jail for the purpose of paying them up and found them in the greatest dejection, which aroused the keen sympathy of at least one of the officers.[33]

Hewitt reported to the Commander-in-Chief the same day the outcome of the court-martial, the publication of the finding and sentence (without mentioning his reduction of it in the case of eleven men), and the fact that the condemned men had been ironed in front of the brigade: the remainder of the native troops were, he said, 'behaving steady and soldierlike'. General Anson approved of the sentence but expressed his regret at the 'unusual procedure' of public ironing. It is the general view of historians that Hewitt, aged and in failing health, was enfeebled in will power and power of command; his superiors at the time came to the same conclusion. How comes it that an officer in that condition resorted to an 'unusual procedure' and an exercise of such stern severity as the ironing on parade?

The question has not been asked or considered previously but there is only one possible answer. This procedure was suggested by someone else: it is in the highest degree unlikely that Hewitt originated the idea. There can be only conjecture as to who proposed it. Archdale Wilson is not a likely candidate, for he also was an officer somewhat given to hesitation. It is probable that one of the staff officers was responsible. Nothing much is known of them. Hewitt's confirmation of the sentence, recorded by Colonel Keith Young, does not read as if it was Hewitt's own production. It is extremely clear, precise, and vigorous and reads as if it was the work of an officer trained in legal process: it seems probable that it was composed by Harriott, the Deputy Judge Advocate-General.[34] He therefore is one possibility as the person who suggested the public ironing. There were also Whish, the Brigade-Major, and Waterfield, the Deputy Assistant Adjutant-General: there is nothing to suggest that either of them was responsible. On the other hand, one odd little fact may point to Harriott. On the evening of 10 May Harriott brought the first information of the outbreak to Carmichael-Smyth at the latter's bungalow, and, when shots were then heard, Smyth at once advised Harriott to be off in Smyth's buggy.[35] Harriott, of course, was not a regimental officer, and his presence was useless; but there is something a little odd about the promptitude with which Smyth sent him off. Smyth probably knew or suspected that in any disturbance the men would be out for his (Smyth's) blood: did he believe that they would be out for Harriott's too? And was that because Harriott was known to have recommended the ironing parade? This is the only scrap of evidence which points to him, or anyone, in this connection, and the whole matter remains pure conjecture.

CHAPTER 7

THE OUTBREAK
A: THE NATIVE INFANTRY LINES

On the evening of 9 May a native officer of the 2nd Troop of the 3rd L.C. came to the bungalow of Lieutenant Gough, the temporary troop commander, under pretence of making up the accounts. After a time he informed Gough that a mutiny of the native troops at Meerut would take place on the following day; the native infantry was going to rise, the cavalry would do the same and release their comrades from the jail. Gough went at once to his Colonel and reported this, but Carmichael-Smyth treated the report with contempt and reproved Gough for listening to such idle words. That same evening Gough met the Brigadier and told him the story, but Archdale Wilson also was incredulous. Two of the deponents before Major Williams, the *sheristadār* (court registrar) and one of the *tahsildārs* (sub-divisional revenue official) at Meerut, stated that it was rumoured on the 9th that the sepoys would mutiny. On the evening of the 9th the Commissioner (Mr Greathed) and his wife were dining with Colonel Custance of the Carabiniers: she told him of a report, which she had probably heard through her servants, that placards had been seen in the city calling on all true Mussulmans to rise and slaughter the English.[1]

There is next day, 10 May, some evidence that at about 2 p.m. a prostitute in the Sudder Bazar was told by a sepoy that the native troops would mutiny that day. The evidence is not very satisfactory. The prostitute was named Sophie, and she had a mother named Mehree. She is supposed to have told her mother, who in turn told another woman named Zeenut: the latter told a woman named Gulab Jan, living in the bungalow of Surgeon Smith, presumably in the servants' quarters in the compound. Gulab Jan declared that she told Smith, who treated the story as bazar gup. Smith perished, so his evidence is lost. Gulab Jan and Zeenut deposed to these alleged facts. Sophie deposed and denied that she heard of the outbreak in advance; one might not be impressed by that. Sophie, however, also said that at the time her mother Mehree, the link between her and Zeenut, was away at Ludhiana:

70

enquiries were made by the Kotwal and confirmed that Mehree was away at the time. There was, perhaps, more motive for Sophie to lie and for friends of hers to lie about her mother's absence, than there was for Gulab Jan to lie about hearing and repeating the report. Still, the evidence is not wholly convincing.[2]

On Sundays the Delhi telegraph office closed at 9 a.m. and re-opened at 4 p.m. Before it closed in the morning on 10 May the line to Meerut was open. When it re-opened in the afternoon, communication had been severed. The line was carried across the Jumna by a cable between two cable houses on the opposite banks. The assistant in charge sent his two signallers over to the cable-house on the eastern bank, but from there they were able to call back. The line had been cut beyond that point: it is said that it was cut near Meerut but the evidence as to where it was cut is wanting.[3]

Mrs Rotton, the wife of the Rev. J. E. W. Rotton, one of the chaplains, was begged by her ayah not to go to the evening service because of danger and disturbances. This however was only a quarter of an hour before the time of the service and the disturbances had then long commenced, so this has not much significance.[4] A Eurasian Risāldār of the 3rd L.C. was told, on the afternoon of 10 May by two men of the regiment that the whole of the regiment intended next morning to give in to Colonel Carmichael-Smyth an application to General Hewitt for the release and re-employment of the eighty-five condemned men.[5]

These are all the facts recorded as to any signs of discontent or plans for an outbreak between the time of the ironing parade on the morning of 9 May and the actual commencement of the events of the evening of 10 May. What was the hour of that commencement?

To answer this question an elementary point must first be noted. The evidence is mainly to be found in the *Meerut Depositions* and the various deponents who mention the time of an event are speaking of *different stages* in the sequence of happenings. They mention in fact different hours from five till after six o'clock but it can easily be seen that they are describing successive stages. The detail will appear as we proceed, but for our immediate purpose it will help if the scheme of events is summarily set out as follows:

(a) Cry or rumour in the Sudder Bazar that the European troops were coming, the bazar and its mobs being then still quiet.

(b) Flight of sepoys from Sudder Bazar to lines.
(c) Uproar in the native infantry lines, the officers coming down and trying to keep their men (especially the 20th N.I.) under control.
(d) Uproar spreading to cavalry lines.
(e) Party of cavalry set out via the city to rescue their comrades from the New Jail.
(f) Loss of control over the native infantry.
(g) Mobs break out in the Sudder Bazar and among the bungalows.

The whole sequence of these events is reflected in the *Meerut Depositions* and occupied a full hour or more, from soon after five until getting on for half past six o'clock. The stage (c) occupied quite a considerable time before the stage (f) was reached: the stage (d) was subsequent to the beginning of the stage (c), and the stage (e) followed the stage (d) by a certain, though quite short interval.

It is the hour of the stage (a), the raising of a cry or rumour in the Sudder Bazar that the European troops were coming, which fixes the commencement of the outbreak. A havildār of the 11th N.I. and two havildārs of the 20th N.I. state that this hour was about 5 p.m. Two servants of Captain Macdonald of the 20th N.I. state that Captain Chambers of the 11th N.I. came to their master's bungalow to warn him of the disturbance about 5 p.m. One of the Meerut tahsildārs states that his guard were at about 5 p.m. talking of a mutiny having commenced. Other testimony indicates that the firing on the infantry parade ground, which marked stage (f), was heard between 5.30 and 6 p.m. and a number of artillery men were attacked by mobs in the Sudder Bazar—stage (g)—at about 6 p.m. It is clear that stage (a) (the first outcry in the Sudder Bazar) occurred just after 5 p.m.[6]

At this hour then—just after 5 p.m.—a cry was raised, or a whisper was spread, in the Sudder Bazar that the European troops were coming to deprive the native regiments of their arms and ammunition. There is evidence to this effect from a sowar of the 3rd L.C., two havildārs of the 20th N.I. and two havildārs of the 11th N.I. The bazar itself was at that stage quiet and rioting in the bazar did not break out at that moment.[7] The depositions rather give the impression that the cry or rumour originated among men of the 20th N.I. and that is expressly stated by one of the 11th N.I. witnesses: men of the 3rd L.C. do not seem to have been initially concerned.[8] Sepoys of the 20th and 11th N.I. began to run back to their lines, where the rumour spread through the general body of each of the two infantry regiments.

In General Hewitt's first report of 11 May he wrote: 'I am led to think the outbreak was not premeditated, but the result of a rumour that a party was parading to seize their arms, which was strengthened by the fact of the 60th Rifles parading for evening church service.'[9] This idea was, in Major Williams' opinion, supported by the evidence collected by him, and he accepted a statement by one witness which he thought showed that the rumour was started, or circulated, by a cook boy of the 60th Rifles.[10] Williams' elaboration of Hewitt's first idea was accepted by Rice Holmes and has been recently re-stated by Mr S. N. Sen, but it will not stand examination.

The later addition, in the form of the cook boy, may first be dealt with.[11] The sole evidence for his existence and action is contained in the deposition of a havildār of the 20th N.I. reading as follows: 'I stopt a musician [by which he means a bandsman of his regiment] named Dareean and asked him what was the matter? He said he had just heard from a cook boy of the Rifles that the artillery and rifles were coming to take away the arms and ammunition of the native regiments.' Now this is hearsay. The deponent neither saw nor heard the cook boy; he was merely told by Dareean that the latter had heard something from a cook boy. Dareean himself did not give evidence. It is uncertain whether Dareean had really himself seen and heard the supposed cook boy, or whether he stated as an experience of his own what some other person had told him or what was being passed round the bazar. Even if a cook boy existed it is not proved that he came from the European lines with news which he thought true, or with a mischievous report which he knew was false; he may merely have been in the bazar and have said something—whether foolishly or maliciously—to give substance to a rumour already in progress. Absolutely nothing at all is proved by the sole piece of evidence relating to the supposed cook boy and his alleged action ought not to be used as the foundation or support of any theory concerning the events of that evening.

Next, as to the possible connection with the church parade, this is a wholly groundless suggestion. The rumour was flying round the bazar by about 5 p.m. The hour fixed for the parade was 6.30 p.m. and the first men to appear on the Rifles' parade ground did so a little before six. The times do not fit. The rumour preceded the parade by an hour, roundly speaking. Then, the parade was in white, and not in green service uniform. On the arrival of news of the outbreak, the first thing which the riflemen did was to rush to their barracks and put on their green jackets. Nobody who saw a few knots of men gathering in white could have taken that for a duty parade of the kind in question. Hewitt's suggestion on this point was hastily made without proper consideration of the times involved or the character of the parade, and cannot be accepted for a moment.

There were good reasons at that juncture for taking this line as to the cause of the outbreak. It is obvious that the Divisional General, the Brigadier, and the staff must have desired to dissociate the outbreak from their own previous proceedings and to make out that it arose in a sudden and unforeseeable manner, against which they could not have guarded. Of course, they did not wish to admit that it was a direct consequence of the ironing parade or that they ought to have taken precautions or exercised vigilance which they had not done. More than this, Gough had received a warning and he had told the Brigadier, and the Brigadier had done nothing. For Archdale Wilson at least, it was of the highest importance to make out that the outbreak was unpremeditated. In this report of Hewitt's the way is open for a denial, if necessary, that the outbreak was in fact the mutiny of which Wilson had been warned on the previous day: it was nothing of the sort, *that* warning had been a myth, *this* outbreak was unpremeditated—the work of a hot-weather evening panic. Otherwise where would Wilson have stood? Not, we may be sure, in command of the Delhi Field Force four months later.

The origin of this outcry or rumour is therefore a question which will call for further consideration in the proper place. Suffice it to grant that it arose in the Sudder Bazar about 5 p.m. and was carried back to the native lines. What then *immediately* happened is not easy to determine because we receive no real information of what took place in the lines until the European officers received the alarm and reached the scene. This was after a certain, though not very lengthy, interval.

The fullest account which we possess of what passed when the officers came down to the lines relates to the 20th N.I.[12] At about 5.30 p.m. several officers of this regiment were sitting in the bungalow of the officer commanding the regiment. The source does not name him but, as far as I can judge, he was (Brevet) Major Taylor, no doubt in temporary command (sometimes referred to by his substantive rank of Captain). Lieutenant Pattle appeared and informed them that a disturbance had commenced in the lines, whereupon they all went down thither. At that stage there was no uproar and so they did not arm themselves. At the same time an officer of the 11th N.I., Lieutenant Chambers, came to Captain Macdonald of the 20th N.I. at the latter's bungalow and gave him some information, upon which Macdonald put on his sword and rode off to the lines, telling his wife to go over to Mrs Chambers.[13] The officers of the 20th N.I. walked through the lines, trying as they went to reassure the sepoys: these were therefore evidently gathered outside their huts in a state of agitation. When they had passed through the lines they came to the regimental magazine, and here they found a number of bazar *badmashes* (scoundrels) blocking the road which came from the bazar. One witness states that these people had followed the sepoys who had rushed back to the lines with the outcry from the Sudder Bazar, and he puts the number of this bazar crowd only at about seventy.[14] Taylor thereupon ordered the grenadier company to disperse this crowd, and the first definite act of disobedience occurred. The sepoys of the grenadier company did not move in response to his order.

Thereupon, the Christian drummers and musicians armed themselves with sticks and carried out Taylor's order. Another quarter of an hour passed, during which the officers continued their efforts to reassure the sepoys. This must bring us to a time between 5.45 and 6 p.m. It was then observed that some of the sepoys were beginning to steal away with loaded muskets; these must presumably have been men on guard duty and therefore armed, for the bells of arms had not yet been broken open. Some of the officers chased these men and tried to make them return. At this moment, it would be about 6 p.m., a sowar of the 3rd L.C. galloped into the lines, calling out to the sepoys. His words as recorded are peculiar; he said that the Europeans were coming and that if the sepoys intended to do anything, they should do it at once. This sowar came from the direction of the Brigade-Major's bungalow or office and was perhaps one of his orderlies.[15] Thereupon, the situation got entirely out of hand. The sepoys rushed forward, the bazar people joined in, and now the bells of arms were broken open.

Something of the same kind had been going on with the 11th N.I. but we have no such precise narrative. Surgeon O'Callaghan was in his bungalow between 5 and 6 p.m. dressing to go for a ride with Colonel Finnis (the officer commanding the 11th N.I.) when he saw the servants going down to the front of the compound and looking out towards the lines. He himself, still dressing, went down and had a look and then returned, put on his uniform, and went down again.[16] He did not himself go down to the parade ground and so what he says as to what took place there is not direct evidence, though deserving fair credit. The rumour about the European troops spread from the 20th N.I. and the bazar people to the 11th N.I. and a Pay Havildār sent a naik to inform Colonel Finnis, which must mean that the sepoys were gathering as those of the 20th had done.[17] In fact, the sepoys seem at an early stage to have tried to get into the bells of arms, but another Pay Havildār locked these up and ran to inform one of the captains.[18] The officers came down to the parade ground and tried to calm the men: the officers had then got the keys of the bells of arms.[19] The 20th N.I. had now broken open their bells of arms and got the weapons and ammunition and they now began to fire at, or in the direction of, the 11th N.I.[20] O'Callaghan recognised the sound of firing with ball cartridges. Finnis thereupon rode over towards the 20th.[21] Their fire continued and Finnis' horse was hit, whereupon he turned back on foot.[22] At this moment, he authorised one of his officers, Captain Dennys, to ride to the Brigade-Major's to ask for help.[23] Then Finnis himself was shot.[24] Thereupon the 11th also rushed their bells of arms and got their weapons, and the officers withdrew.[25] O'Callaghan was urged first by a European N.C.O. and then by a native officer to fly. He got his horse and made his way across the broken ground in rear of the 11th N.I. lines to the Dragoon lines, as did most of the other officers: he started at a footpace but on the urging of the native officer put his horse to the gallop.

It is a highly probable supposition that the officer sent off by Finnis reached the Brigade-Major, Whish, and that the latter acted upon his request: but it is possible, no doubt, that Whish had already taken some action himself on account of the uproar in the lines of the 20th. Whish may then have sent to warn Hewitt and urge him to make his way to the European lines; Hewitt did so, but he was escorted by Lieutenant Warde of the 11th N.I., so it seems possible that Finnis had sent him a message direct. No stigma attaches to Hewitt for acting in this way; it was clearly his proper course to place himself at the head of the European portion of his command which would now have the task of over-coming the outbreak of the native regiments. Another officer of the 11th N.I., Lieutenant Möller, sent a sergeant of the Carabiniers, whom he encountered near the Dragoon Bridge, with a message to the Carabiniers.[26] O'Callaghan found Colonel Custance of the Carabiniers already on the parade ground and the regiment assembling. This seems rather earlier than one might expect and argues for such a message having been sent up. Whish himself then rode off to Wilson in the Artillery lines: Whish must have started for Wilson's not much before 6 p.m.

It seems then almost certain that the sowar who galloped into the lines of the 20th N.I. did in fact come from the Brigade-Major's and had learnt of Finnis' request or of the Brigade-Major's actual message to the European troops: either would quickly be known to the orderlies, sentries, servants, and the people in neighbouring compounds. One must therefore draw a distinction between his message and the outcry started by the sepoys in the bazar. That outcry started much earlier, around 5 p.m.: the sowar makes his appearance at a time getting on for 6 p.m. The bazar outcry has no connection with any real event or movement in the European lines: the sowar brought genuine information that the European troops had been sent for.

When the 20th N.I. got finally out of control and Finnis was killed, the officers of the 20th had to disperse and suffered casual-ties in the process. It is not surprising that, in the confusion which now reigned, the accounts of their movements should be rather difficult to disentangle.

Immediately after Finnis was shot, Captain Macdonald of the 20th N.I. was shot, and at the same time a Mr Tregear, who was Inspector of Education and was spending the day in the lines—as whose guest is not recorded. This occurred near the regimental magazine. A Pay Havildār got Macdonald into the Sergeant-Major's bungalow, where it seems he died.[27] This outbreak round the magazine and the shooting of Finnis and Macdonald were mainly the work of the right wing of the regiment.[28] The lines of the two wings were divided by what was known as the centre street, and in these final moments the officers were in that street still trying to keep control of the left wing. They failed, the bullets were flying, and the sepoys urged them to leave. Slowly and sadly, they walked away.[29]

One officer, Lieutenant Humphrey, had his horse shot under him and was himself fired at on the ground but escaped and hid all night in an outhouse of the hospital. Ensign Lewis was wounded and chased but managed to get on a passing carriage and escaped. Six officers went off on foot together, Major Taylor, Lieutenants Henderson, Shuldham, Pattle and Tytler, and Assistant Surgeon Adley. After numerous escapes from the mobs, they took refuge in an outhouse, in fact a servants' latrine, in the compound of Colonel Carmichael-Smyth's bungalow. Taylor, Henderson and Pattle took the risk of going off separately from there and were all killed: the other three remained there for five hours, that is to say, till about 11 p.m., when they heard the European troops marching by and joined them.

Taylor and Henderson seem to have gone back to the lines when they left this refuge. Henderson was shot at and wounded by a sepoy: a havildār got him into the hospital, gave him water, and hid him in a back room, where presumably he died.[30] Taylor, after a sepoy had threatened him with a musket, was cut at by a butcher from the bazar and presumably wounded. A Pay Havildār hid him in a hut (what he calls 'the baboo's house') but it was a stifling refuge and Taylor with the havildār's help got to his own bungalow, whither the havildār also took another unnamed officer—perhaps Pattle.[31] Another officer, Captain Earle, somehow hid in the lines till about half an hour after sunset, that is till about 7 p.m. He then made his way to Taylor's bungalow where he found the latter still alive. Taylor made him take his (Taylor's) buggy in order to go to the Brigade-Major's. However, he does not seem to have found that possible, but by dint of hard driving got through to the European lines. Attacked at several points along his route, notably near Surgeon Smith's bungalow and Elahi Buksh's shop, he evidently therefore went up Sudder Street and over the Dragoon Bridge, finally joining the European troops on the Mall. Taylor must later have set out himself but was murdered on the road: his body was found near Elahi Buksh's shop.[32]

Earle (in Taylor's buggy) was one of the stragglers in an exodus, mainly over the Dragoon Bridge, which took place from the bungalow area behind the native lines while the disturbance in the native regiments developed over this space of an hour to an hour and a half. There were no doubt a number of Europeans, men or women, who were preparing or (like Mrs Craigie and Miss Mackenzie) had even started for the evening church service. For these to get their carriages moving and start for safety was easy: others who perhaps had no such plan were soon warned of what was afoot. A stream of vehicles was soon to be seen hastening up Sudder Street, and one of these it was, no doubt, on to which Ensign Lewis of the 20th N.I. clambered. This was the shortest and most certain route of escape. Those who struck out towards the Delhi road and the Begum's Bridge presently ran into the mobs and some of them had to turn back or were killed. Those who attempted to get away on foot, sometimes in disguise, suffered the same fate and so did some who were caught in their bungalows. By about 7 p.m. the area was emptied of most of the Europeans and those who remained were defending themselves against the mobs or were lying hidden or dead in their compounds or about their houses.

By this hour the entire 20th N.I. had dissolved in mutiny: there is no record of any part of that regiment remaining loyal. On the other hand, there were in the 11th N.I. about 125 men who remained loyal. They were kept for some time in the native lines and then submitted to being disarmed and were told to go to their homes. Unarmed, they said, their chances of arrival were small. They were then offered and willingly accepted service in the police. Their arms were later restored and 90 of them remained on duty till the end of the Mutiny, the remainder taking leave and making for their homes.[33]

CHAPTER 8

THE OUTBREAK
B: THE NATIVE CAVALRY LINES

The 3rd Light Cavalry was the regiment directly involved in the firing parade and its consequences and one would have expected that, when the outbreak came, it would have begun among them: indeed the outbreak is often vaguely ascribed to them, with the implication that the native infantry joined in. It comes as somewhat of a surprise to find that the evidence points to the disturbance in the cavalry lines having followed, not preceded, that in the infantry lines. This seems to be indicated, somewhat obscurely, by two out of the three deponents from the cavalry regiment.[1] More significant, perhaps, is the fact that none of the infantry deponents alleges that the infantry broke out following upon some disturbance in the cavalry lines, and if the facts had not been notoriously against it this would surely have been suggested: as it is, all infantry witnesses make their outbreak follow upon the bazar outcry and do not mention the cavalry at all.[2] Once the cavalry had risen, they took to their horses, and the consequence is that their actions then ranged farther and moved faster than those of the infantry. This increases the difficulty of co-ordinating in point of time what was occurring in the native infantry and cavalry lines respectively.

There is no clear statement about the initial stages of the outbreak of the cavalry. It seems to have started about 5.30 p.m., even a little after, the time when the officers of the 20th N.I. were getting down to the lines. It no doubt began with gatherings in the lines and on the parade ground, coalescing into a general pandemonium. The regiment got its horses from the stables, and also its arms, which (not being firearms) were apparently not consigned to locked bells of arms like the weapons of the infantry. In this state the officers found their men careering about the parade ground, some in uniform, some in undress, most of them in wild excitement.[3]

Colonel Carmichael-Smyth was entertaining to dinner his regimental Surgeon, Surgeon-Major Christie, and his regimental Veterinary Surgeon, Philips. He says it was about 6 p.m. and they had done dinner when Major J. F. Harriott, the Deputy Judge Advocate-General, came over with the news that the bazar people were collecting and that Macdonald had told him there was a row in the 20th N.I. lines: since Harriott must have met MacDonald on his way down to the lines, the time seems to be rather before than after 6 p.m. Shots were then heard which Carmichael-Smyth says he 'knew was not in order because it was Sunday': why they might have been more in order at that hour on a weekday is not clear. Smyth thereupon put Harriott into his (Smyth's) buggy and sent him off: a possible reason for his prompt dispatch has been mentioned at the end of chapter 6 above. Christie and Philips went off in another buggy; their fate will be mentioned below.[4]

Major Fairlie, the officer of the day, and Lieutenant Melville-Clarke, the acting Adjutant then appeared and Carmichael-Smyth told them to go down to the lines and tell the men to stand to their horses. Carmichael-Smyth was Field Officer of the week and now ordered his horse to be saddled but before it was ready Jemadār Maun Singh, the Havildār-Major, and the ill-omened Brijmohan appeared and reported that the regiment was in a disturbed state. Gough says that a party of men had set out to murder the Colonel but he received a warning and made his escape: it seems likely that Maun Singh, the Havildār-Major and Brijmohan brought this warning, though Carmichael-Smyth understandably does not mention this. At the same time as they arrived, the six officers of the 20th N.I. entered the compound pursued by sepoys, who must have desisted from the chase on seeing a party of Europeans in the compound, for otherwise the six could not have found the refuge which they did. Carmichael-Smyth thereupon went off with two orderlies, his own and the one attached to the Field Officer. They were assaulted on the way but got through. Smyth went to the Commissioner's, Mr Greathed's: they tried to shut the gate against him but he forced his way up to the bungalow, was told the Greatheds were out, and warned the servants. In fact, the Greatheds were hidden on the roof by the servants. Smyth then went to Hewitt's bungalow but found he had left. He then went on to the Brigadier's, being fired on near the rum godowns and from the Brigadier's compound; he ultimately joined the Brigadier on the Artillery parade ground.[5]

Carmichael-Smyth was never censured for his conduct on this evening, nor was any enquiry into it ordered: that should be sufficient answer to the criticisms which were levelled at him by some of his contemporaries, extending on the part of O'Callaghan to a thinly-veiled accusation of cowardice, which with the Colonel's record of active service in mind one cannot for one moment entertain.[6] It can be taken as certain that his own appearance on the parade ground would only have inflamed the situation and it is highly likely that Fairlie and Melville-Clarke urged him not to come down. It was quite proper for him to turn to his other duties as Field Officer of the week, to place himself at the disposal of his superiors, and to seek in the course of his flight to warn the General and the Commissioner. The six officers of the 20th N.I. had escaped from instant danger and it was probably better for them that Carmichael-Smyth should clear off, and the mutineers be thus diverted from searching the bungalow. The circumstances were all against, and did not call for, any reckless heroism on Carmichael-Smyth's part: for his faults, whatever they were, he was punished by being forced into conduct which lost him some reputation, but he cannot justly be blamed.

When the officers, or some of them, reached the parade ground, they seem to have attempted to bring the men to their senses by sounding the assembly.[7] This was probably Fairlie's and Melville-Clarke's order, in pursuance of the Colonel's command. By then, however, something had happened which was only realised a little later on. A considerable party of the men had left the parade ground and gone off to the New Jail to release the condemned sowars. Their number is estimated at 50.[8] Some went round the north of the city taking thus the road to the Sūrajkund.[9] Some few went through the city, entering by the Kamboh Gate, probably in the north-west angle, and apparently going out by the Shahrah Gate, presumably leading to the Sūrajkund: as they passed, they called on the people to join them in a war for religion.[10] The head jailer had given orders at 5 p.m. for the prisoners to be counted and this had been done and he had made his inspection: it was then that he saw a cloud of dust announcing the approach of the sowars. They must have gone at full gallop and the distance is upwards of three miles; one must suppose them arriving around 6 p.m. and leaving the parade ground about 5.45 p.m., which would be before any officer had got down to the parade ground. The extra guard of the 20th N.I. fraternised with the sowars, who rode into the jail and took possession of it. The head jailer rushed off to the Magistrate. The rescue party got their comrades out and smiths were fetched to knock off their fetters. It seems as if eventually the rescued men accompanied their rescuers back to the regiment. None of the other prisoners in the New Jail were released by the sowars at this time: the contrary has been repeatedly stated, at the time and in books written since, but the evidence of the head jailer is available, and it is categorical and indisputable on this point.[11]

Mackenzie and Gough have both left us a narrative of the events passing before their own eyes, written down in 1891 and 1897 respectively. Neither of them was, it seems, among the first to reach the parade ground. Gough says his servants brought him the alarm about 5 p.m. and told him then that the native infantry lines were on fire: but that, from other evidence, cannot be earlier than 5.45 p.m., or indeed more like 6 p.m., so that his recollection of the hour is loose. Immediately afterwards, the native officer who had warned him the previous day of the impending mutiny, galloped up with two orderlies in great excitement with the news that the native infantry had mutinied and were killing their officers, and that the cavalry were arming; further confirmation that the cavalry outbreak began after the infantry outbreak had gone some way.[12] Firing could now be heard from the infantry lines and Gough mounted and rode first of all down there. He found pandemonium and the sepoys fired at him. He then went off, with the native officer and orderlies, to the lines of his own Troop.[13] There he found all in confusion, men galloping about, the lines on fire, a mob at the magazine. He says he was the one Englishman there but that cannot be so, for most of the officers were by then somewhere on the parade ground. He could not bring the men to obedience and after a time shouts to kill him were raised. He then saw the Regimental Quartermaster-Sergeant, whose name he gives as Cunninghame, galloping up, pursued by sowars.[14] The appearance of these latter, in open mutiny, brought over the sowars whom Gough had been trying to hold. He and Cunninghame were urged to clear off and they did. They forced their way through some part of the bazar, where there were crowds of armed men. Gough then made for the Commissioner's: Mr and Mrs Greathed were friends of his, he had met them at church in the morning and wished to warn them. On reaching the house he was told by the servants that they had left; in fact, the servants were concealing them on the roof. The Greatheds overheard his colloquy with the servants, who thus persuaded him to go away, thinking this was the safer course for their master and mistress. Gough then went on to the Artillery lines, still escorted by the faithful native officer and two sowars; these then left him, to return to their comrades, with whom they declared that their duty lay.[15]

Mackenzie received the alarm from his bearer 'at the hour when better folk were on their way to church': he then heard the sound of firearms.[16] This indicates a time about 5.45–6 p.m. That seems early to start for a service at 7 p.m. Mackenzie himself mentions the change of the hour of the service but also emphasises that the change of time was not known to the sepoys. If that was so, there can hardly have been general notification of it in the native lines, for if there had been the sepoys would have known. Officers or their families then might not all have known of it and might have started out for the normal 6.30 p.m. service at about 5.45 p.m.: the adventures of Mrs Craigie and Mackenzie's sister indicate that they did in fact start at about that hour. Mackenzie himself says he was informed at the time that the hour of the service had been changed but his words seem to indicate that he heard of this just after the outbreak and not necessarily that he or his sister had heard of it before she and Mrs Craigie started out.[17]

It is at this point that Mackenzie gives his own story of meeting the Regimental Quartermaster-Sergeant, which cannot be reconciled with Gough's. Mackenzie says that on leaving his gate he met the Quartermaster-Sergeant, whom he does not name, flieing on foot from his house in the lines. He told Mackenzie that the troopers were coming 'to cut us up'. He refused Mackenzie's suggestion that they should stick together, went into the bungalow garden and over the wall to the next compound, being attacked as he did so by a small mob, including some of Mackenzie's servants: the latter's chaukidār wounded him in the lip with a spear, but he got away. In the next bungalow the Sergeant warned two officers, who proceeded to arm and mount; their names are not given. They gave the Sergeant a third horse bare-backed. They then found both entrances blocked, but a sweeper showed them a gap in the wall behind some outhouses by which they all three got away and reached the 60th Rifles' lines.[18]

After warding off a blow from a sepoy, Mackenzie saw a number of sowars galloping up and to his utter surprise they attacked him with their swords. He was rescued from this melée by the appearance of Craigie at his gate a little down the road, and the sowars made off. Stifling their anxiety for their womenfolk, the two officers galloped down to the parade ground where they found most of the other officers. The men were careering about in wild excitement but to Craigie it appeared that some of them seemed to hesitate at joining in the uproar. He was, as Mackenzie stresses, a good linguist with much influence among the men and he managed to gather forty or fifty around him in a group apart. They then somehow (presumably from the shouts and the taunts) learnt of the party which had gone on the jail rescue.[19]

Craigie set off with his party of sowars, Melville-Clarke, the acting Adjutant, and Mackenzie, to try and stop the rescue. They went round the north of the city. At one point they met a *palki-gārī* (palanquin carriage with horses) containing a European woman with a sowar alongside running his sword into what was already a corpse: Craigie and Clarke despatched him.[20] Mackenzie was swept from his saddle by a severed telegraph wire, no doubt when they had turned south on the Grand Trunk or Bulandshahr Road east of the city.[21] The troop rode over him but he escaped injury, caught his horse and overtook them. They had started at a smart trot but were now at a gallop and out they went past the Sūrajkund and round to the jail.

They were, of course, too late. It was already dusk on this outward journey and it seems that it must have been 6.15 p.m. when they left the parade ground and the rescue party had half an hour's start. According to Mrs Craigie, they met the escaped prisoners, to whom the rescuers had given arms and mounts, before they reached the jail. Mackenzie says they found the imprisoned men released from the building and the smiths at work on their fetters. The guard of the 20th N.I. fired on them and they had to ride off back to the cantonment. This, when they turned, appeared fairly in a blaze, the bungalows fired on all hands. They returned at breakneck speed and Craigie sent four volunteers to see to the ladies and then, so it seems, also gave Mackenzie permission to go and see what had happened to them. Mackenzie called for more volunteers and went off with a dozen men. Craigie and the rest returned to the parade ground. It was by this time dark: the hour must have been about 7 p.m.[22] Craigie and the rest of the officers, taking the colours, made for the European lines, presumably over the Dragoon Bridge to the Carabiniers' lines.[23] Smyth and Gough had gone separately: Fairlie got a bullet in the cantle of his saddle: Galway somehow was left behind, for he was hiding in a tope on the parade ground in the line of fire when some rounds were discharged from the guns at the northern end of the parade ground towards moonrise.[24]

Mrs Craigie and Miss Mackenzie had set out for church, it would seem, a little before six. Their road took them by the regimental Mess of the 3rd L.C.; they saw the servants leaning over the compound walls looking towards the infantry lines and were warned by them to turn back, which they did. These movements, and the location of the Mess, are not easy to understand; for after turning back they fell in with a mob on the edge of the bazar, who were chasing a Carabinier. They courageously succeeded in getting the man into the carriage, and with him reached home. They got down the guns in the bungalow but did not know how to load them. The four men sent by Craigie then appeared and afterwards Mackenzie and his party; and Mackenzie proceeded to load the guns. Mackenzie felt some uneasiness about the men whom he had brought. He therefore took the ladies out and called on the sowars to defend them which, with an outburst of emotion that cast them to their knees, they swore to do. After a time, Craigie himself returned from the European lines: this would have been about 8 p.m. He approved a plan Mackenzie had formed and the whole party took refuge in the small cell of a Hindu temple in the compound. The servants brought news that the body of Mrs Chambers, with her unborn child, was lying in her compound opposite. The loyalty of the sowars was uncertain. They heard, strangely enough, nothing of the European troops, not even of a mounted party, which Mackenzie mentions as having been sent to clear the cantonments and rescue any survivors, but as having lost its way.[25] A mob beset the compound gate but was dispersed by one of the servants firing into it. Towards midnight they harnessed up the carriage, put the ladies and the Carabinier in it, and a postilion on one of the horses, and drove off with the two officers mounted one on either side. They charged through a knot of troopers, and got down a road on to the parade ground. They made their way across this until they reached what Mackenzie calls a 'short length of straight road leading to the stables of the Carabiniers'. Those stables stood on the edge of the European cavalry parade ground but it is true to say that the comparatively short and straight stretch of Terminus Road led to the western end of the Carabiniers' stables: the party came by this road to a bridge where a picquet had been posted with a gun and there was in fact a bridge carrying Terminus Road across the Abū Nullah, Thus they reached safety.

It appears that the remainder of Craigie's sowars accompanied the officers when they withdrew to the Carabiniers' lines. Other sowars also rejoined and about 80 or 90 altogether remained loyal.[26]

CHAPTER 9

THE OUTBREAK
C: THE BAZAR MOBS

When the first outcry was raised by sepoys in the Sudder Bazar, and these began to rush back to their lines, the bazar within itself was and still remained quiet, but the sepoys making for the lines gathered in their trail a crowd of the lower and more disorderly castes.[1] This was the crowd which blocked the end of the road to the bazar at the rear of the 20th N.I. lines and which could not be dispersed though forced to yield a few yards by the Christian drummers.[2] When the 20th N.I. passed out of control, somewhere about 5.45 p.m., this mob seems to have scattered instantly, with the disorderly sepoys, through the bungalow area to the east of the native lines and to have begun to plunder the bungalows, to set them on fire and to murder Europeans and Eurasians. Of such a mob frenzy quickly takes hold and, if plunder is their first and dominant appetite, arson and murder also break out at once. Sepoys or sowars led or incited these mobs in some episodes but in the main the mobs were formed of the badmashes from the bazars and these were often the murderers and incendiaries.[3]

They were certainly the criminals in the notorious murders of Mrs Chambers, Mrs Macdonald, and Veterinary-Surgeon Dawson (attached to the Artillery) and his wife. Mrs Chambers was the wife of Captain Chambers, Adjutant of the 11th N.I. Their bungalow was opposite Craigie's, and thus distant from their own lines. At some stage Lieutenant Möller (Le Champion Möller) of the 11th N.I., who had made his way to the Carabiniers' parade ground, returned to the native lines in an effort to fetch Mrs Chambers away: he got near enough to her bungalow to see her in the veranda but was then forced back by half a dozen 3rd L.C. sowars. It must be very doubtful whether he would have succeeded in conveying her to safety. He could not have disguised or concealed her. She was pregnant, and she was eventually murdered and mutilated with the unborn child. The culprit was apparently known to be a Muhammadan butcher and three days later Möller went to the bazar and arrested him and he was hanged. Presumably Möller traced the butcher by imperious enquiries in the bazar: he does not record that he witnessed the murder but one wonders whether he could identify the man because he had seen him with a mob round the bungalow, though Möller does not say this.[4]

Mrs Macdonald had been told by her husband to go over to Mrs Chambers, so that evidently the Macdonalds' bungalow was also quite close to those of Craigie and Chambers: she did not however do so. Before she had got ready, news was brought to her that her husband had been shot; she would have gone to him, but at the same time the mob had appeared and fired the bungalow. The ayah and the *dhobi* (washerman) hid Mrs Macdonald and her children in a *bheestie's* (water-carrier's) hut. The chaukidār was getting ready to flee and it was decided to accompany him and his family. Mrs Macdonald and the children were dressed in native clothes and the three servants set out with them. They followed a lane past the elephant sheds, which were probably just at the rear of the bungalow area, and got out on to a road, where they were stopped by a crowd which proceeded to examine the women. The chaukidār tried to protect Mrs Macdonald by saying she was his sister-in-law but, when her face was seen, she was cut down: her body was much mutilated. The servants got away with the children, whom they hid for the night in a Christian pensioner's house and brought into the Dam-damma next morning.[5] Dawson and his wife were in bed with smallpox: he came out on the veranda and fired at the mob and was himself shot. To avoid contagion with Mrs Dawson, the mob threw torches at her till her garments caught fire and she was burned to death.[6]

Another victim was Mrs Courtney, whose husband was the proprietor of the hotel. When the firing was heard, her coachman, according to his own account, was ordered by his mistress to get the carriage and take her, with her two children, towards the city: probably she meant to get away by the Delhi road or even across to the Grand Trunk Road. Near the gate of the city (which gate is not known) they ran into a crowd. Mrs Courtney ordered the driver to take her to the Deputy Collector's and he struck off towards the Sudder Bazar, that is to say northwards. The mob followed, but they met some of the 3rd L.C. who interfered to protect her, a notable fact. They got to the Deputy Collector's gate but it was closed against them by a Muhammadan jemadār. The coachman was knocked off the box and Mrs Courtney and the children were killed by a mob.[7] This story seems inconsistent with the statement, attributed by an unknown writer to Mrs Craigie, that Mrs Courtney was the woman who was being attacked (though already dead) by a sowar, when her husband and Melville-Clarke, *en route* with their party to the jail, killed the man.[8] The coachman's reference to men of the 3rd L.C. cannot be to Craigie and his party. Bodies were seen near the Deputy Collector's house but are described as those of a woman and two men.[9] Two Deputy Collectors made depositions but neither refer to this incident.[10] One of them, Wazir Ali Khan, said that at dusk he shut up his compound and spent the night in fear and trembling: it seems as if it may have been his gate which was shut by his jemadār, without the Deputy Collector knowing of Mrs Courtney's arrival. It seems that the coachman's story is true, and Mrs Craigie's alleged statement an error, and that this was another murder by the mob, after sowars had helped the victim to escape from her first attackers.

It seems probable that, when the native infantry passed beyond control, the news travelled back in a flash from the watching crowd of ruffians to the Sudder Bazar itself, and that was when violence within the bazar itself broke out. There is evidence that the native infantry guard at the Kotwali, the head police station, somewhere in the middle of the bazar, received some message from a sepoy about 5.30 p.m., and withdrew not much later.[11] Some European witnesses fix the time when they were attacked as nearer six o'clock than five.[12] These indications fit in with the moment when the native infantry got out of hand. That meant, for the bazar mob, that a substantial part of the reserve forces of order had broken down, while the remainder, the European troops, would have their work cut out: the mobs nearest at hand turned to pillage and arson.

There seems to be no doubt that the cantonment police failed in this crisis on the whole to stand to their duty. The prime object of Major Williams' enquiry, which brought forth the *Meerut Depositions*, was to elucidate the behaviour of the police: that, in passing, is a defect of these important documents wherein the evidence as to the origin and course of the outbreak generally is really a by-product. Scattered *passim* through those pages are statements that men in police uniform were seen among the mobs taking part in their acts of violence. Williams in his introductory *Memorandum* speaks of 'culpable negligence and wilful disregard of their first duty as policemen'.[13] He blames for the loss of police control the officiating Kotwal, who was himself a Gujar (set a thief to catch a thief), by name Dhunna Singh. The relevant depositions do not seem entirely to justify this. They seem rather to show that Dhunna Singh, who was only officiating in his post, made some attempt to keep his men together under control: they prove two arrests of plunderers, of whom the second was a Gujar, and the latter was released as a condition of the mob abandoning the plunder of the house of a Bengali merchant in which they were engaged.[14] That does not seem altogether culpable amid the wild doings of that night. Major Williams, if slightly unfair to the Kotwal, was entitled to claim that the police did not entirely fail.

There were a number of European soldiers in the bazar, the greater number being Artillerymen, from whom alone we possess depositions. They were well into the bazar: some were near the Kotwali. Apparently not far from there was a shop known to the men as 'the pop shop' which sold ginger beer, bottled lemonade and the like.[15] This presumably was a favourite goal for those airless, dusty hot-weather evening walks which yet were a relief from the close barrack-rooms and the dull atmosphere of the lines. Some were alone, most in twos or threes. Some of them, loitering along, were suddenly warned by a galloping sowar of the 3rd L.C., shouting to them to clear out for the sepoys were making a bobbery.[16] They were set on with sticks, swords, and stones, and took to their heels; dodging and fighting, some got away but several were killed. Some escaped over the bridge near the Roman Catholic chapel, which is probably the plank or wooden bridge in Chapel Street.[17] Lieutenant Furnell of the Mounted Police brought one party to safety by that bridge but they were not the same as any of the deponents.[18] There were also Carabiniers and Riflemen in the bazar but none of these made a deposition. One Carabinier was chased out and rescued on the edge of the bazar by Mrs Craigie and Miss Mackenzie.[19] Several Riflemen were killed. At the capture of Delhi, four months later, some Artillerymen thought they recognised the 'pop shop man', and the man they so identified was put to death.[20]

It seems that in the area round the north-western edge of the bazar, along Sudder Street or between the bazar and the Abū Nullah, there were bungalows allotted to officers holding appointments under civil departments and to retired officers and pensioners.

At least, we can identify undoubtedly in this area a group of bungalows thus occupied. One was occupied by Lieutenant J. Eckford, who was Executive-Engineer. He heard the uproar from the lines about 6 p.m. and then the sound of shots, and saw the crowds gathering round the bazar, and Europeans hurrying northwards on horses or in buggies. He had with him an old pensioner named Chapman, employed no doubt in his office work, and who lived not far away. Chapman saw four Riflemen killed near the bungalow. About 7 p.m. Eckford was told that a mob had killed his next door neighbour, Surgeon Smith, whose bungalow was on fire: they then came on to him, but he drove them off on this occasion with a shot from his double-barrelled gun. About twenty minutes later, a larger mob appeared. Eckford and Chapman had now been joined by an escaping Rifleman. This mob was largely composed of sepoys. They battered their way in. Eckford was attacked by a sowar of the 3rd L.C. whom he wounded with a pistol shot, but received himself a severe sword cut in the head: the Rifleman got him into the next room. Eckford gave his double-barrelled gun to the Rifleman, who attempted to escape but was killed in scaling the wall. Chapman got away to the gardener's house. Eckford collapsed on the portico where a tree shaded him from view: he lay unconscious for two hours, then staggered out, found his way to where his wife and sister and child were hiding in the servants' quarters and they all managed to get away by a dry nullah to the Carabiniers' lines. Chapman remained in hiding till morning and then got away. He passed the house occupied by two pensioners, Kinly and Markoe, and saw their corpses. Mrs Markoe and a Mrs Cahill, who lived in the Markoes' compound, had escaped from the mobs which had attacked their house soon after sunset, at the same time therefore as Eckford's and Smith's. Chapman, going on, found his own house and his wife safe, owing to the timely arrival of the Carabiniers.[21] Another victim of the mob in this area was the junior among the officers of the 3rd L.C., Cornet Macnabb, whose body, much disfigured by sword cuts, was found in the ditch near Surgeon Smith's bungalow. He had shared Mackenzie's bungalow.[22] He had gone with Gough to church in the morning and afterwards had gone to spend the day with a friend in the Artillery lines where, on hearing of the outbreak, he had borrowed a horse and tried to get back to his own regiment: according to Gough, the body was only identifiable because of his unusual height and the wrong braid on his uniform coat about which Gough had chaffed him on the way to church.[23]

Returning to the more southerly area, between the Sudder Bazar and the city, about 7 p.m. occurred the release of all the prisoners in the Old Jail, to the number of 720: this was effected by a body of sepoys three or four hundred in number.[24] This was the first release of convicts and it seems to be through some confusion with this event that the idea arose of the sowars having released the convicts from the New Jail when they rescued their comrades. On such occasions the convicts, of course, made off as fast as they could for their villages, like those from Agra, the muffled clank of whose fetters, as they hurried up the Muttra road in the fog and darkness with the cantonment ablaze behind, puzzled Mark Thornhill.[25] The sepoys who released these at Meerut urged them to do something for the Army, which had released them, before they dispersed to their homes. It is therefore clear that the object of the release was to re-kindle the outbreak and increase the confusion in that quarter, but it is not clear whether the convicts in fact responded to this invitation. Mobs however were ranging about far into the night. Joseph Henry Jones, no doubt a Eurasian, living in a bungalow near the Old Jail, set out soon after 5 p.m. on horseback for church, but turned back from the Begum's Bridge because of the disturbances. He saw the Old Jail release, his womenfolk were saved by Bibi Lane, no doubt the Indian wife of a European or Eurasian, and Jones himself escaped with difficulty in company with a relative, John Arot.[26] A European pensioner named Hughes was killed in the same area, but his wife was saved by their Muhammadan landlord.[27]

Adventures which belong rather to the periphery of the area of riots were those of the Commissioner, Mr Greathed, and of Lieutenant Furnell. Greathed had been out of the station and had only returned one day previously. The servants made him and his wife take refuge on the roof and then denied their presence to the mobs who came to search for them, and even to those, such as Carmichael-Smyth and Gough, who would have tried to get them away. An Afghan pensioner, nephew of Jan Fishan Khan, also tried to warn or protect them and was wounded by the mob.[28] The servants stuck to their own plan and later in the night got them down to the garden where they remained in hiding until the morning when they were able to reach safety.[29]

Lieutenant Furnell of the Mounted Police has left us the longest and most detailed account of personal adventures on the evening of 10 May which we possess. At the time that he made the deposition, he marked the route of his wanderings on a map, which one would very much like to see: but he did not penetrate deeply into the mob-ridden area, and in one particular he gives what may well be the wrong time for an incident. His bungalow seems to have been in the southern portion of the European lines between the Mall and the Abū Nullah, and there he was waiting for the *dāk gārī* (mail coach) to take him to Delhi (this was a lucky escape for him) when he heard of the uproar. He mounted and rode over the wooden bridge (in Chapel Street), met two Artillerymen in flight, and escorted them to their lines. There he was begged by a crowd of women and children to fetch help, as all European Artillerymen had been called on duty and only the native golandāz were left. At this point, which must be about 6.30 p.m., he describes the bringing in of a wounded woman with a child, who could have been Mrs Law, but the true time of her escape was between 10 and 11 p.m., in which case his memory is at fault. Furnell set out to find European troops. In the road leading to the Brigadier's house he found the body of Veterinary Surgeon Philips: he was attacked by some police, fired on from the Brigadier's compound and had to charge through a mob, which dispersed on the cry that the Carabiniers were coming. Hereabouts bungalows had been burnt. Going on, Furnell warned a pensioner named Larke and gained the Carabiniers' lines. A captain of the Carabiniers offered to accompany him with thirty men; they set out but near the Horse Artillery lines the Carabiniers were recalled. Furnell collected five volunteers, went down to the women's barracks, and got them away to the hospital. He then remembered that he had left his watch, his money, and some treasury drafts on his table, so he set off again to his own bungalow and retrieved them. He was then chased by two mounted men, probably sowars of the 3rd L.C., over the Begum's Bridge (southwards) and along Abū Lane, where he saw several bodies, to Elahi Buksh's, where he encountered another mob. He struck off then into the broken ground to the west of Sudder Street, got down into the nullah, and so to the Dragoon Bazar and lines.[30] Furnell's story gives us a glimpse of arson and mob violence in the area north of the Abū Nullah but not as far up as the Mall, for he mentions that the

destruction stopped short of this: the time was probably after
7 p.m.

The last stage of the mob violence was reached after 10 p.m.,
when from the surrounding country bands of villagers came in,
particularly Gujars. It is said that they numbered thousands,
which sounds somewhat exaggerated. These bands set fire to the
unoccupied Sappers' and Miners' lines which were at the rear and
slightly south-east of the Artillery lines: the rioters were probably
coming in from that quarter and happened upon these lines before
they reached the bazars and the city. The only persons living in
these lines were a Conductor (that is to say a pay-clerk or other
administrative rank), named Sergeant Law, with his wife and
children. He and one girl were killed: his wife was wounded but
escaped with the other children, the eldest girl so badly wounded
that she died in the morning, a boy also injured but who recovered.
The party was found by an Artillery Sergeant and brought into
the Artillery lines. The same assailants made attacks on other
houses in that quarter but were beaten off, and they actually got
into the Artillery lines and did some plundering but were driven
off by a picquet. This seems to have been about midnight and after
this the European lines were unmolested.[31]

Finally, at 2 a.m. these villagers and Gujar mobs released the
prisoners from the New Jail—839 in number—who had remained
locked up after the rescue of the sowars, though it seems that the
jail guards decamped after the rescue, fearing rightly that punishment would fall on them.[32]

One is bound, in treating of the history of the Mutiny, to concentrate attention on the adventures of the Europeans. All the
same, it is true that from the beginning of the mob disturbances at
about 6 p.m. far into the night there were riotous attacks on
Indians in the bazar areas. These were directed at shopkeepers
and were mainly for purposes of plunder, though a Bengali mentions that the mob broke the bottles of wine which he had in stock
and that may have been an act of Muhammadan fanaticism. In
these incidents, sepoys as well as the mobs took part, at least in the
earlier hours before the sepoys left the station. The sufferers
alleged that the officiating Kotwal, who was himself a Gujar,
afforded little help or protection, and gave free rein to his caste-
fellows in their plundering. However, it has already been seen
that probably he could do no more than he did, for there is no

doubt that the great majority of his police abandoned their duty and joined the mobs.[33]

To close this account of the mob violence, one incident may be examined for which either the mobs, or possibly the sowars who went on the jail rescue, may be responsible, the cutting of the telegraph line to Agra. Though nobody in Meerut seems to have noticed the fact, the line to Delhi was cut before 4 p.m., as has already been mentioned. The Agra line was not cut at that time. There can be small doubt that it came into Meerut up the Grand Trunk (or Bulandshahr) Road, between the eastern edge of the city and the Abū Nullah. It must have been somewhere here that Mackenzie was swept out of his saddle by a severed wire. That would have been a little after 6.30 p.m., so by then the line was cut. Before this, however, two telegrams had been sent off to Agra with news of the outbreak: the first was complete, the second was interrupted by the cutting of the wire. Both telegrams refer to an outbreak by the 3rd L.C., and not to the native infantry. Therefore, they can hardly have been sent before 6 p.m. One can also infer that the Telegraph Office was nearer the native cavalry lines than the native infantry lines: it was probably by the Grand Trunk Road near the north-eastern corner of the city.[34] The conclusion is that the line to Agra was cut not much before 6.30 p.m.

The first telegram was the famous message from the sister of the Postmaster at Meerut to her family at Agra: it is said to have been received at 9 p.m. which is inexplicably late, but this must mean received by the addressee and delivery must have been in some way delayed at Agra. It read: 'The cavalry have risen, setting fire to their own houses and several officers' houses besides having killed and wounded all European soldiers and officers they could find near their lines: if aunt intends starting tomorrow please detain her from doing so as the van has been prevented from leaving this station.'[35]

The despatch of the second, broken telegram is recorded in the *Meerut District Narrative*, its receipt and text in the *Agra Division Narrative*. It seems to have been official and addressed to government but it consisted only of the following words: 'The 3rd Cavalry have broken out in mutiny, and are killing all Europeans they meet. We are——.'[36]

Thus, it was the fuller message to the aunt in Agra which Mr Colvin, on the morning of the 11th, relayed to Lord Canning.

CHAPTER 10

THE OUTBREAK
D: THE EUROPEAN TROOP MOVEMENTS
AND THE EUROPEAN LINES

To begin with the two officers in command, General Hewitt escaped from his bungalow somewhere in the civil lines and was escorted by Lieutenant Warde of the 11th N.I. Whether Warde had been sent to look for him by Finnis (before the latter was killed) or encountered him *en route*, we do not know. Hewitt was apparently in some disarray and it is not clear where he first went. For a considerable time he was not with Archdale Wilson: he must however have joined the latter with the European troops, before these moved off sometime between 7 and 7.30 p.m., and he must have accompanied them in their march to the native parade ground and during their operations there; otherwise Wilson could not have used the presence of the divisional commander as relieving him of responsibility under the regulations.[1] Wilson himself received the news of the outbreak from Whish, the Brigade-Major, to whom Finnis had sent another officer of the 11th N.I., Captain Dennys. When Whish galloped into the Brigadier's compound, Wilson at once sent messages to the Artillery and the Carabiniers to join him on the Rifles' parade ground. Wilson himself rode off at once, being fired on, it is said, by his own guard. One may surmise that his promptitude and decision, not markedly characteristic of the man, owed something to what Gough had told him the evening before; Wilson knew at once what had happened.[2]

The Carabiniers were probably the first of the European troops to be alerted: the front of their lines was a mile or so north of the rear of the 11th N.I. lines, but the intervening ground was broken and gardens, walls, bazars, and buildings obscured the view. However, they were nearer to the native lines than the other European troops. When the officers of the 11th N.I. dispersed and left their lines, one of them, Lieutenant Möller (Le Champion Möller), found at the Dragoon Bridge a sergeant of the Carabiniers and sent him with a warning to the bungalow of Lt.-Col. W. N.

Custance, commanding the Carabiniers: Möller himself followed and reached the bungalow shortly afterwards. He says that from the bungalow he saw the regiment turning out, so the bungalow was close to the parade ground. Another of the 11th N.I. officers, Surgeon O'Callaghan, left on horseback, walking his mount across the broken ground. On the urgings of a native officer he put his horse to the gallop and went first to Custance's bungalow, found the latter had already left, and so went on to the parade ground. He found the regiment turning out and went up to Custance and reported what he knew: Custance returned brief thanks and O'Callaghan drew aside, slightly rebuffed.[3]

The Carabiniers armed, saddled and mounted with all speed. The N.C.Os. then proceeded to call the roll of the several Troops. This took quite a time. This proceeding is criticised by O'Callaghan. Kaye recorded the roll call in his account of these events and thereupon Custance wrote to him and denied, apparently, that it had taken place. Kaye somewhat hastily accepted the denial, declaring that he could not easily trace the source of his information; this shows that he was over-anxious to avoid any controversy, for a glance at Chick's pages would have put him on the track of O'Callaghan's account, from which of course he had taken this point. However, Kaye then met and had a letter from Le Champion Möller, who declared that he had heard the roll call in the Troop nearest him: Kaye passed this on to Custance, who replied that Möller must have heard the roll called in one of the dismounted Troops. Kaye then published his letter to Custance and the letter he had received from Le Champion Möller, saying he must leave the matter to the judgment of the public. I do not think there is any doubt that O'Callaghan (supported in this case by Le Champion Möller) is correct and that the roll was called. Nor does one see why the statement should have been traversed. The regiment was half dismounted; on a Sunday evening many of the men were absent from the lines. It seems essential that the roll should have been called in order that Custance might know what effective force he had at his disposal and Le Champion Möller quite rightly says that no good sergeant would omit to do so, as he cannot report his men present otherwise. Custance's denial was undoubtedly made in perfect good faith. The truth may be that he was preoccupied with his officers and with watching the mounting conflagration in the native lines and did not observe the roll call: this may be confirmed by the departure of the captain and thirty men who went off with Lieutenant Furnell, as mentioned in the preceding chapter, evidently without the knowledge or permission of Custance, since they were recalled as soon as their absence was noticed.[4]

Le Champion Möller presently left the Carabiniers to go in search of Mrs Chambers, as mentioned in the preceding chapter. O'Callaghan remained and accompanied the Carabiniers throughout their subsequent movements until the European troops started back from the native parade ground when he lost them and came back with the Artillery. O'Callaghan has left two accounts of the Carabiniers' movements: they are the accounts of an eyewitness shortly after the events, they are coherent and are in agreement and supplement each other, though in a few places they may be a little obscure or not quite explicit. In these circumstances, however, they are the fundamental authority for what happened to the Carabiniers.[5]

While the roll was being called it was still daylight but the sun was setting; this means it was just after half past six. Darkness had fallen while the Carabiniers were still standing on their parade ground and even then there was a delay, occasioned, as O'Callaghan heard, by waiting for a staff-officer who apparently arrived soon after dark. They then prepared to move 'under the guidance' (as O'Callaghan puts it) of Major Waterfield, the Deputy Assistant Adjutant-General.

Le Champion Möller says that the Carabiniers were ordered off 'in broad daylight'. If he means that they actually moved off in daylight his testimony must be rejected in favour of O'Callaghan's: Le Champion Möller did not remain with the Carabiniers, while O'Callaghan did; and their movements as next described by the latter would be entirely inexplicable unless they were moving in the darkness which set in by about 7 p.m. and lasted till after 9 p.m., when the moon had risen.[6]

They did not then take the road to the left, leading straight down to the native lines, but turned off to the right—for what purpose or object O'Callaghan could never hear. This reference to 'the road to the left' seems to refer to Terminus Road which led to a bridge across the nullah and then to the north-west corner of the native parade ground: the Carabiniers could have got off down Terminus Road by passing through their own stables and barracks. They moved off, however, at a trot to the east along 'a narrow road or causeway leading apparently into the dark and silent country' (O'Callaghan's phrase). After proceeding in this way for some time, they dropped to a walk, halted, and turned about, retracing their steps: they were thus turned about after two or three miles. They ultimately verged off to the left (which means, I think, that they turned down Bridge Street), debouched on the left rear of the native lines, skirted behind and to the north of these lines, turned them at their western extremity and wheeled left on to the 11th N.I. parade ground. From this it is plain that O'Callaghan means by the 'left rear of the native lines' the rear of the eastern end of the lines of his own regiment, the 11th N.I., and it follows that the Carabiniers ultimately came down to Bridge Street and crossed the Dragoon Bridge.

When Wilson left his bungalow he must have gone first to the Artillery parade ground, for that is where Carmichael-Smyth, as Field Officer of the week, found him.[7] O'Callaghan, who is not here an eyewitness, says the Artillerymen worked with a will to get out the guns and that the guard of the 11th N.I. at the Dam-damma had to be disarmed by force: called on to lay down their arms, they refused to do so or to quit their post till formally relieved, an honourable performance on their part, which resulted in their being fired on and several of them wounded. The Rev. T. C. Smyth says that on his way home from the church, after the dispersal of the congregation, he was saluted by this guard shortly before the disarming party arrived. He says that he drove home about half past seven or a quarter to eight and that after his arrival at his bungalow, which was close to Wilson's, he heard a shot and this was the shot which killed Philips. The Rev. A. Medland also says that he heard Philips' death-cry after he had reached home. These times are puzzling. Christie and Philips left Carmichael-Smyth's, one may be pretty sure, before 6.30 p.m. and they should have been at the end of their drive by 7 p.m. at the latest. It is hard to believe that the disarming of the Dam-damma guard took place as late as 7.30 p.m., by which hour the Artillery should already have moved off. On the other hand Mr Smyth certainly would not have left the church till 7 p.m. or a few minutes before. The evidence is confusing but points to the Artillery having been still on their parade ground at 7 p.m. and somewhat after.[8]

The Rifles may have anticipated Wilson's order. While officers and men were gathering on the parade ground for evening church parade, that is to say not much after 6 p.m., a Rifleman too breathless to speak arrived at one end of the parade ground and Captain H. F. Williams at the other end brought the news to the acting Adjutant, Lieutenant Ashburnham.[9]

Thereupon the men in their white drill uniforms seemed to melt away without orders to their barracks, reappearing armed in their green service dress, but in fact they acted upon the orders of Williams, being joined by a considerable number of those who were not on the church parade, so that very quickly something like 800 men were armed and ready for orders.[10] Captain Muter, the senior officer on parade, despatched the first fifty under Lieutenant Austin to take over the treasury which had, of course, a native guard. The treasury is said to have been a mile and a half away and must have been near, or actually part of, the Collector and Magistrate's cutcherry in the part of the civil station which lay north and east of the Abū Nullah where that watercourse took its southerly turn east of the Begum's Bridge. The guard obeyed an order to ground arms and the treasury was secured, a useful though not a vital gain.[11] The Rifles then had to be issued with additional ammunition beyond the ten rounds issued to each man on the change of weapons in January. This entailed a considerable delay; the native guard at the regimental magazine took to flight but the ammunition then had to be got out and distributed. It can be concluded that the regiment did not move off before dark: the Artillery had by then joined with the Brigadier who may have come on earlier. Hewitt must also have been there. The Carabiniers were, of course, not at the rendezvous.[12]

The column of artillery and infantry probably went down Church Street and along the Mall. Captain Earle, who was among the last to leave the lines of the 20th N.I. and who went over the Dragoon Bridge, met them: that would have been in Bridge Street or in the Mall nearby and the time was probably about 7.45 p.m.[13] The column then wheeled to the right, taking the route afterwards followed by the Carabiniers along the rear of the 11th N.I. lines and so reached the north-west corner of the native parade ground, as the Brigadier did not wish to entangle his force in the narrow crowded streets.[14] The Carabiniers arrived at the same position between 8.30 and 9 p.m.[15] The other column had moved at an infantry pace and may perhaps have got into position about 8.15

p.m. Darkness was still complete: moonrise was not till 9 p.m. and it would be a little later than that before the moon lit up the ground, and the heavy smoke veiled any light from the flames of the burning buildings.[16]

The European troops now found themselves drawn up more or less in echelon, the Rifles to the left in advance, the Artillery to the right and slightly in rear of the Rifles, while the Carabiniers were still farther to the rear, as one might say in reserve.[17] No substantial body of mutinous troops were visible: even the din of the mobs had grown subdued.[18] Muter's company of the Rifles was to the front in skirmishing order and he went to Wilson and asked if they were to load with bullets and shoot straight, to which Wilson replied 'Yes: for execution, you see the position.'[19] Thereupon some volleys or rounds were fired into the area of the burning bungalows where Muter seems to have thought that the forms of sowars galloping about could be distinguished though this is rather improbable at that hour.[20] It was then thought that the mutineers were occupying a *tope* (group of trees) further over to the southwards out on the parade ground. The guns were ordered to the front and discharged three rounds into this tope. If there were any mutineers there, this sent them off: perhaps there was a party which had remained to observe the movements of the European troops. Lieutenant Galway of the 3rd L.C. who was hiding in this or another tope was endangered by the fire of the guns. It seems as if, when the Artillery was in action, the moon had still not risen or was barely up, in which case the discharge must have been rather at random.[21] After this the European troops were formed up and moved off eastwards across the parade ground. They seem to have then entered the lines by one of the roads leading inwards, probably about in the centre of the main block; they cannot have passed through or near the southern section of the lines, for their movements were inaudible to Craigie and his party in their hiding place in his compound.[22] The force then turned up Sudder Street and withdrew to the European lines by way of the Dragoon Bridge.[23] In its passage it gathered up a number of Europeans or Eurasians who had succeeded in remaining hidden. Among these were the surviving officers of the 20th N.I. from Carmichael-Smyth's compound and the pensioner Chapman and his family; the Eckfords were not picked up, so perhaps they had already left.[24] Numbers of other people are said to have emerged, and some in such terror and haste as to be in danger of being crushed under the wheels of the guns.[25] It seems, however, that some of the survivors were rescued not by the passage of the main force but by a party of the Carabiniers sent out to search for them; this party presumably swept a number of the side roads and thus picked up additional refugees.[26] Finally the force regained the Mall and bivouacked along it near the Carabiniers' lines, that is to say rather towards the western end; the bridges were covered by guns and picquets were thrown out right into the Artillery lines.[27]

There is not a great deal to be said about incidents or disturbances in the European lines. The action of bazar mobs in that area was limited and has already been noticed in the preceding chapter, where also the sad story of the Law family has been given. However, according to Mrs Muter, when she came away from the church, she found the broad road that leads to the bazar crowded with men and saw two Artillerymen being pursued by a throng, but herself passed unnoticed. She is probably referring to Church Street but this riotous outbreak did not spread, no doubt because shortly afterwards the approaching European troops were seen or heard.[28] Veterinary Surgeon Philips was shot and his companion, Surgeon-Major Christie, wounded and disfigured in the road near the Brigadier's house: according to the Rev. T. C. Smyth this was after his own return home, which seems inexplicably late. Mr Smyth says this was the work of five sowars and also states that at about 10 p.m. a bungalow opposite to his was fired by five troopers—the repetition of the number five is a little odd.[29] Contrary to many rumours and reports after the outbreak, there was certainly no attempt by the 3rd L.C. as a whole to invade the European lines. The incident of Philips and Christie and the pursuit of Furnell mentioned in the preceding chapter are the only clear cases of any sowars appearing in that area. Guards of the 11th N.I. behaved in a manner deserving praise: the one at the Damdamma stood its ground with honour and disaster to itself, the one at the Treasury surrendered peaceably, and another at the Deputy Paymaster's kept its treasure for several days. A guard from the 20th N.I. stood firm at the Joint Magistrate's. The guard at the Brigadier's fired on him and on others, while two guards are said to have listened quietly to a request (made by the Judge and the Magistrate to the General and Brigadier) to send guards to the treasury where Muter had anticipated them and to the Jail, but immediately afterwards to have fired on passers-by and made off. It is not recorded whether these were from the 11th or 20th N.I.[30]

On the morning of 11 May a force was sent out to reconnoitre to the south-west of the station. Gough says it was a small force of cavalry and artillery, the *Meerut District Narrative* that it was a strong force of all arms, and one may suspect that Gough is more correct.[31] It went out early at daybreak, that is to say about 5 a.m., and, in accordance with the practice of the time, was brought back by 8 a.m. to escape the sun.[32] This force went down on the right side, that is to say to the westward, of the Delhi road, no doubt reconnoitring villages, topes, or any other cover near the line of its advance: it did not, of course, come upon any of the mutineers, who at that hour were approaching the bridge of boats at Delhi. The force cannot have gone, in the time, more than four or five miles. The Brigadier had come down to the native infantry lines and was making arrangements to collect the bodies of those slain in the outbreak; and here Carmichael-Smyth, who had been with the reconnoitring force, rejoined him.[33] The bodies were collected and brought into the theatre, where that evening a dramatic tragedy was to have been performed.[34]

There is no exact and complete list of the casualties at Meerut: nor is that an exceptional thing. Published reports seldom give the names of private soldiers or even non-commissioned officers, and many of the slain were European or Eurasians in quite humble positions whose identities were unrecorded or unrecognised. General Hewitt gave the loss of life as 'about forty' and the Rev. T. C. Smyth states that he and his colleague, Mr Rotton, had buried thirty-one, but there were others.[35] Eight commissioned officers were killed—Colonel Finnis, Captains Taylor, Macdonald and Henderson, Lieutenant Pattle, Cornet Macnabb, and Veterinary Surgeons Philips and Dawson. Then there was the retired Surgeon Smith, and the Inspector of Education, Tregear. Next we have three officers' wives—Mrs Macdonald, Mrs Chambers and Mrs Dawson, and then Mrs Courtney and two children, making together six more. In subordinate positions or among pensioners were Sergeant Law and two children, Markoe and Hughes, another five in number.[36] Five Riflemen appear to have been killed at or near Eckford's bungalow.[37] Three Artillerymen are named as having been killed in the bazar (Conolly, Cairns and Benson).[38] These are the victims whose names and the circumstances of whose deaths are clearly known. They add up to twenty-nine, which is very close to the Rev. T. C. Smyth's figure.

The *Depositions*, however, provide evidence of numerous other deaths, which may in some instances overlap with these known cases, but certainly add a considerable number to the tally. There was a group of bodies near the Old Jail variously estimated at from eight to fifteen: it may have included Mrs Macdonald's but, allowing for that, it probably accounts for an additional ten.[39] A sergeant of the 60th mentions four bodies somewhere north of the native lines: they might have been the Riflemen killed near Eckford's but he does not say they were men of his regiment.[40] Another deponent, probably a Eurasian, mentions the body of a woman separately, and the bodies of two women and a man together, somewhere in the southern area near the city.[41] Two other deponents mention the bodies of two men and a woman.[42] There were probably additional European soldiers killed in or around the bazar, and non-military victims who are not mentioned in the *Depositions* at all. With these cases mentioned in the *Depositions*, and allowing for those which are not, one can hardly add less than twenty to the twenty-nine identified cases. That makes forty-nine. There seems good reason to place the total at around fifty rather than at about forty, as Hewitt did.

CHAPTER II

THE HANDLING OF THE
EUROPEAN TROOPS

The Government of India, on 28 June 1857, removed General Hewitt from the command of the Meerut Division. That is at least some justification for the opinion that the handling of the European troops on the evening of 10 May was not creditable. However, Wilson was left to fight another day; and the decision to remove Hewitt was taken by Sir Patrick Grant in Calcutta, when he certainly did not have full information about all the circumstances on the evening of 10 May. So his decision is not conclusive. It cannot have been uninfluenced by the outcry against the Meerut commanding officers which rose immediately and grew louder as the disasters of May and June 1857 accumulated, disasters for which these officers at Meerut were held indirectly responsible in addition to their alleged defaults on that evening itself. Every historian has added his voice to the chorus of blame, but in detail often injudiciously and in general perhaps excessively. At any rate, the fair and right way is to scrutinise with care the steps which were taken that evening and the charges based upon them.

The first and most sweeping charge is that of delay in bringing the European troops into action. This is given some colour by taking the time limits as about 5 p.m., the first outcry in the bazar; and 8.30 p.m., the arrival of the Carabiniers on the native parade ground. Those limits are, of course, too wide. One has to take the hour at which the news reached the European troops or their commanders, which was about 6 p.m. on the parade ground and 6.15 p.m. or after at the Brigadier's bungalow; then one has to take the arrival of the Artillery and the Rifles on the 11th N.I. parade ground, and that was not much after 8 p.m. So the interval is at once reduced to about two hours or slightly more. Major Harriott, the D.J.A.-G., when he was the prosecuting officer at the trial of the ex-King of Delhi, stated in his speech that the native regiments had reckoned upon a delay of about an hour and a half. The difference is not very great.

True, such a lapse of time seems excessive for an emergency;

but this emergency, like many others, was a surprise. The European troops were not cantoned at Meerut to guard the population against their fellow soldiers of the Bengal Army. The ironing parade had been a strain but it would be difficult to insist that it ought to have been followed by a disarming as at Mian Mir (Lahore). Lesser precautions would have brought on an outbreak which might have been avoided. The mutineers chose their hour so that two hours of moonless dark would fall just as the European troops were getting ready to move, and a Sunday evening was chosen as the one when there would be the least readiness in the European lines, as Gough rightly points out. Wilson and Carmichael-Smyth, and perhaps others, had heard Gough's report: events proved them wrong in brushing it aside but they were not disentitled to do so, as matters stood on the evening of the 9th. Hewitt could not be on the spot when the first orders had to be given. Wilson personally lost not a moment when the news of the outbreak was brought to him. What delayed the Artillery and the Rifles was the disarming of native guards and the issue of ammunition to the Rifles. The system of native guards was part of the established military order devised without a thought for such a catastrophe as this, and there is nothing to prove that the limited quantity of ball cartridge actually issued to the Rifles in the peace of January was anything unusual. It seems, considering the apparent time of the Artillery's move, that this part of the force cannot have moved off the European parade ground till getting on for 7.30 p.m. and, if so, they did not do too badly to come out at the western end of the 11th N.I. lines not much after 8 p.m., though it was thought, by Gough and others, that their actual pace of marching was rather slow.

What actually happened to the Carabiniers that evening, and why, are the most vexed and vexing questions in the whole episode. The doubts which have been raised about the roll having been called before they moved off were considered and dismissed in the preceding chapter. It seems that the roll was called, and it is difficult to understand why Colonel Custance disputed the fact, for it was the proper thing to call the roll and there was nothing culpable in any delay so caused. The real trouble begins when the Carabiniers left their parade ground.

It is not explicitly stated by O'Callaghan, but it is to be inferred from his narrative, and it has been generally held that the Carabiniers went astray. If so, it was evidently when they took 'the narrow road or causeway leading apparently into the dark and silent country'. No attempt has been made by previous writers to identify this road: O'Callaghan himself does not do so, but that might be either because he had only been ten days in the station and could not recognise the road, or because at the time he wrote he preferred not to be explicit. It is nevertheless possible to submit a conjecture on the point.

When Bridge Street emerged from the northern front of the European lines, the road presently inclined to the north-west across the Carabiniers' parade ground and became the Sardhana road, leading to the former domain of the Begum Somroo. When Hill Street (the next road eastwards) emerged in the same way, it went on straight northwards and became the Roorkee road; some way out it passed the cemetery on its right (east). There was a short road, running due east and west outside the front of the lines and named Cross Street, which linked the Sardhana and Roorkee roads (or, if it is preferred, Bridge Street and Hill Street). Where Cross Street ran into Hill Street or the Roorkee road, there was a junction of five roads. Hill Street came up from the south; Cross Street came in from the west; the Roorkee road went out to the north. A continuation of Cross Street went on to the east until it ran into the western wall of the hospital compound at about its mid-point where it then became necessary for anyone to turn either left (north) or right (south) along the side of the compound. The fifth road at the junction was a road known as Cemetery Road. It went off to the north-east, just beyond the Roorkee road and between that road and the continuation of Cross Street. Cemetery Road ran in this way to the south-west corner of the churchyard and then turned north alongside the churchyard wall to the north-west corner of the churchyard. At that point it threw off a branch to the west, and both this branch and the continuation of Cemetery Road itself northwards led to the cemetery which lay north of the church. From the stretch of Cemetery Road beyond the north-west corner of the churchyard, it was possible to turn off again eastwards right on to the Rifles' parade ground. In fact, the shortest road route from the Carabiniers' parade ground to the Rifles' parade ground was precisely by Cross Street and Cemetery Road and a body of troops following this route was moving, as O'Callaghan says, eastwards. The topography here described is shown on the inset to the sketch map attached at the end.

However, in complete darkness the road junction must have been confusing and it seems that the Carabiniers went up the Roorkee road instead of finding their way into Cemetery Road just beyond the Roorkee road. One cannot say whether the Roorkee road was a 'narrow causeway' but it certainly led 'into the dark and silent country'. There was, of course, a change of direction, but in the dark O'Callaghan may not have observed this; his moving eastwards is right as to the direction on leaving the parade ground and right also about Cross Street. Thus, the conjecture here proposed accords with the data supplied by O'Callaghan and with the topography at the time: if it remains a conjecture, there is certainly no alternative explanation. There is no other road within the possible area of the Carabiniers' movements which fits O'Callaghan's description, except the Roorkee road. No map shows any road or track of this description running west–east across the parade ground parallel with the front of the lines, and the existence of such a road or track must be ruled out.

Any movement eastwards by the Carabiniers would *prima facie* be merely the carrying out of Wilson's order to join him on the Rifles' parade ground, and the route by Cross Street and Cemetery Road was in fact the shortest which the Carabiniers could take for that purpose. Whether, therefore, one confines judgment to the established fact that the Carabiniers did move eastwards, or whether one accepts the above conjecture as to their actual route, the simple explanation of their movements is that they were obeying Wilson's orders and making for the Rifles' parade ground. Then, when it was realised that they had taken the wrong road, it would also have been apparent that they must be too late for the rendezvous and so they were turned round and taken to the real objective of the European troops, the native parade ground, which would have been known to Major Waterfield, who was with them.

There is however certain evidence which confuses (one is tempted to say, bedevils) the issue, for it indicates the possibility that the Carabiniers received an order to go to the jail and that this was their objective at the time when they went out of their way. This evidence, however, is of such a kind that it needs to be very carefully weighed.

It will be remembered that General Custance, as he then was, wrote to Sir John Kaye in 1870 contradicting Kaye's statement that the Carabiniers' movements had been delayed by a roll call. Kaye wrote in reply saying that he was perfectly convinced (his conviction was shaken afterwards by Le Champion) by the documentary evidence which Custance had afforded him that the statement that there was a roll call was based upon erroneous information, and he also said in parenthesis that he would have been satisfied with Custance's own denial. Later on in the letter he added the following remarks:

I may add to this that from a careful perusal and collation of the several documents which you have sent me, containing the evidence of officers and non-commissioned officers of your regiment, it appears that the Carabiniers, when preceding towards the lines of the native battalions, were counter-marched, by order conveyed to you by a staff-officer and marched towards the gaol, which lies, at a considerable distance, in a different direction. It seems that on reaching the gaol, it was found that the prisoners had already escaped, so the Carabiniers were marched back again towards the native lines. On their return, darkness having set in, they lost their way, although under the guidance of the staff-officer who had directed you to the gaol.[1]

Le Champion (Möller), in his letter to Kaye in the same correspondence, wrote that 'the Carabiniers were in broad daylight ordered not to the mutineers' parade ground close by, but to the prison some miles off'. A footnote in the *Meerut District Narrative* refers to the Dragoons having been sent on an errand to the gaol.[2]

The documents which Custance sent to Kaye are, so far as can be ascertained, no longer extant. What Kaye says that they proved conflicts in almost every particular with O'Callaghan's account of the Carabiniers' movements. Kaye says the Carabiniers were proceeding to the native lines when they were countermarched: O'Callaghan says they were proceeding away from the native lines when they were turned about. Kaye says an order was brought to them by a staff-officer while they were moving: O'Callaghan says the staff-officer arrived before they left the parade ground. Kaye says that they countermarched towards the gaol: O'Callaghan says that after they were turned about they made their way to the native lines and parade ground. Kaye says they reached the gaol and found the prisoners released: O'Callaghan says nothing whatever of such a dénouement. Kaye says that they went astray after being turned about: O'Callaghan implies that they did so before. If the documents really contained what Kaye said they did, then

O'Callaghan's narrative must practically be discarded: such a conclusion is inadmissible.

It may be stressed that O'Callaghan's description of what happened just before the Carabiniers turned about—'we moderated our pace to a walk; then the bugles sounded a "halt", and lastly "threes about", and we commenced retracing our steps'—is quite incompatible with the idea that the regiment was arriving at the jail to deal with mutinous soldiery or escaping prisoners; they would have come at a trot—perhaps ending in a gallop. Such details of their actual movements cannot be fabricated or inexact, and they exclude the idea that the Carabiniers had arrived at or near the jail when they turned about.

O'Callaghan says that at the beginning of their movement the Carabiniers turned off to the right, 'for what purpose or with what object, I could never hear'. O'Callaghan was strongly critical of the handling of the European troops that evening: he personally accompanied the Carabiniers; he had ample opportunity, and ample time, to learn the purpose or object of their movements before he wrote his earlier account (preserved in Chick) or his later account (in his pamphlet). It is incredible that he should not have learnt either that the Carabiniers really were ordered to go to the jail or that there was some general belief or rumour that they had been so ordered, and incredible that he should in that event have omitted to mention the matter.

O'Callaghan makes the rather curious remark that after darkness had fallen on the Carabiniers' parade ground, 'still there was a delay, occasioned, as I heard, by waiting for a staff-officer'. This would imply that three orders or messages reached the Carabiniers; first Wilson's original order to join him on the Rifles' parade ground, secondly another to stand fast and wait for a staff-officer— for otherwise how could the Carabiniers have been waiting in this way?—and thirdly, the order (whatever it may have been) which the staff-officer brought. Wilson in his official explanation of his actions that evening mentions no order sent by him except his original order to join him on the Rifles' parade ground. In regard to what happened to the Carabiniers, he is not quite open, for he states that 'on the road to the lines I was joined by the Carabiniers'.

Wilson thus does not record in his official explanation that he ever did order the Carabiniers to the jail. It is not easy however to believe that he suppressed the mention of such an order, if it had been given; for it must in that case have been known for certain to a number of officers, some of them quite high-ranking enough to make sure that the true facts were reported. Nor is there necessarily any reason why Wilson, writing his explanation in October 1857, should have suppressed the fact that he gave such an order (if he did so). Looking back now, one would say that such an order was unwise; but at the time it may not have been. The fog of war was thick that evening. Wilson might have received a message that the 3rd L.C. were attacking the jail and he might have ordered the Carabiniers to go and drive them off and control the prisoners: he need not have suppressed any mention of such an order if in such circumstances it had been given. The actual events at the jail could not have been known in the European lines until the arrival of Craigie with most of the 3rd L.C. officers; that was not much earlier than 7.30 p.m., which was well after the Carabiniers had moved and after any order for them to go to the jail had been given. Gough seems to have arrived earlier but he certainly did not know what had in fact happened at the jail and he does not say that he had been aware of the attempt to rescue the imprisoned sowars or of Craigie's efforts to prevent this. However, it can be supposed that before Craigie arrived with the true story a report was brought, by Gough or by someone else, of a cavalry attack on the jail, whereupon Wilson might have diverted the Carabiniers thither: there is no other conceivable reason for such an order being given, and if it was given in such circumstances Wilson had no need to conceal the fact.

If the Carabiniers were ordered to go to the jail, the best and shortest way was for them to go down to the Mall and then eastwards along it to the far end and then straight on down the Garhmukhteshwar road, on which the jail was situated. It would have been possible to reach the jail by making their way eastwards along the parade ground and then southwards through the Artillery lines, by School Street, and so to the end of the Mall and the Garhmukhteshwar road. It was a longer way round and in darkness certainly more difficult. It is hard to understand why it should have been taken. If on the other hand the Carabiniers were simply trying to get to the Rifles' parade ground for the rendezvous originally ordered, then the route by Cross Street and Cemetery Road was the shortest and best.

The footnote to the *Meerut District Narrative* was most probably added by Fleetwood Williams in 1858 when he was compiling the *Narrative* by combining the District Officers' reports. Le Champion was not with the Carabiniers and his statement to Kaye was made in 1871, though he says he had referred to his 'Memoranda'. Neither of these sources is of much value to strengthen the evidence. It is worth noting that when Malleson edited the combined edition of Kaye–Malleson in 1880 he transferred from the Appendix to a footnote to the text some extracts from Le Champion's letter about the roll call and the sending of the Carabiniers to the jail which he designated, too hastily, as 'unimpeachable testimony' but he left Kaye's actual text unaltered.[3] Three years later Rice Holmes in his 5th edition accepted the story without any attempt at analysing the evidence and made the over-confident statement that the Carabiniers had been sent to the jail.[4]

At the present day, it can only be said that the evidence is not sufficient to establish that the Carabiniers were ordered to go to the jail. This conclusion does not infringe the good faith of General Custance or of the officers or non-commissioned officers who made the statements sent to Kaye in 1870. There is no direct statement by General Custance that he received an order to go to the jail: Kaye makes it clear that Custance denied the roll call but he particularly does not say that Custance himself made any statement about the order to go to the jail, only that this (and certain impossible facts) emerged from Kaye's own perusal and collation of the documents.

Kaye's statements about the documents are such that one cannot now say what the documents did contain. It may very well be that what they really contained were statements of belief, or opinion, or later reports that the Carabiniers had been on their way to the jail when they went astray. Such an idea might have prevailed among the officers and men of the Carabiniers when afterwards discussing their regiment's rather mysterious movements that evening. From them, the story could have been spread about and the *District Narrative* footnote and Le Champion's statement could both rest upon this kind of belief or rumour just as well as on actual fact.

After the Carabiniers reached the native parade ground, it is said that one of their officers, Captain Rosser, offered to pursue the retreating mutineers.[5] There are variations in the reports of this incident: it is said that Rosser wanted to take two squadrons and three or four guns, or one squadron and two guns. On enquiry by Sir John Kaye in 1868, it was denied both by General Custance and by Sir Archdale Wilson that the offer was made to either of them or was brought to their notice and this we may believe. It is doubtful whether the Carabiniers, who were lying back 'in reserve' as O'Callaghan puts it, were anywhere near Wilson, and it is entirely likely that even Custance did not hear what Rosser said: nor was there any reason for him to act upon it if he had. On this subject, Wilson adds that he did not believe that any of the force knew that evening that the mutineers had made for Delhi.[6] That is for practical purposes true. Hewitt had been told by Le Champion (Möller) that the latter had heard some plundering sepoys shouting to each other 'to Delhi!'[7] This however was hardly conclusive information of the movements of the whole mass of mutineers. The expectation would be that they would disperse to their homes in Rohilkhand, Oudh, and the Doab and seek concealment among their families in various directions: and it is a fact that this is what most of them thought of doing at first. Except for Le Champion's story, there was nothing to contradict this assumption.

The alternative possibility was that the mutinous regiments, or a large contingent of them, would be hanging round the station through the night with the idea of making incursions from one quarter or another, in search of plunder or to effect further destruction. This was a possibility to which it was right that the officers in command at Meerut should be very much alive. It was what actually did determine their withdrawal from the native parade ground and their disposition of the available force in bivouac on the Mall. They had lost contact with the mutinous regiments: more accurately, contact had never been gained. In the circumstances, they cannot be blamed for holding their forces on their own ground instead of launching them quite blindly into the night.

Their failure to pursue the mutineers is the second main charge which is constantly laid against Hewitt and Wilson. The preceding paragraphs have shown that this charge is basically unsustainable, because it was not known whither the mutinous regiments had gone. Apart from that, a pursuit was hardly feasible and if undertaken would not, in all probability, have produced the effects expected. At the time Sir Patrick Grant, who succeeded Anson as

Commander-in-Chief, took the view that if a wing of the 60th with a squadron of the Carabiniers and some guns had been sent in pursuit the insurrection would have been nipped in the bud, but this was the opinion of an officer who was nowhere near the scene of events and had not the material before him to form a sound judgment.[8] Lord Roberts, writing years later with all the weight of his own military experience, concluded that nothing would have been gained by pursuit and the mutineers would not have been overtaken before they reached Delhi.[9] That is the right judgment. It cannot be supposed that the European troops, as they stood on the native parade ground, were ready equipped for a forty mile night march. Cavalry sent in pursuit would have been liable to be ambushed by the native infantry or the latter would have escaped by dispersing. Even the native infantry did not, in bulk, reach Delhi till the early hours of the afternoon next day: the European infantry would not have got there before the magazine blew up. It is fanciful to suppose that the sight of a few of the Carabiniers on the east bank of the Jumna next morning would have made any difference.[10] If they had managed to get into the city, they would probably have been destroyed, and if they had got to the cantonment their arrival would have more probably precipitated the outbreak there, just as the rumour of the approach of European troops had done at Berhampore and at Meerut itself. There is no real ground for claiming that the appearance of European troops was calculated to restrain an incipient mutiny: the evidence suggests the contrary. There are no sound arguments to support the view that the commanders at Meerut were culpable in failing to launch a wild pursuit into the night; they did better to hold their force together for the protection of the station.

The point on which the handling of the troops at Meerut can really be criticised seems to be in regard to the original order issued by Wilson for the Carabiniers as well as the Artillery to concentrate on the Rifles' parade ground. It is true that this order brought the wings to the centre and the horse to the foot. However, it drew back the Carabiniers and they were the nearest to the scene of disorder. Moreover, the order in a sense immobilised the Carabiniers. Under orders to close eastwards, they could not probe southwards. It would have turned out much better if Wilson's first message to the Carabiniers had been that he was going to move with the other European troops on the Dragoon

Bridge and the Carabiniers were either to stand fast till he sent for them to join him or were to move down Bridge Street and await him near the junction of the Mall. Wilson of course knew the ground and he had been told by Whish, who had learnt from Dennys, where the trouble had broken out. Wilson consequently knew that he must move on the native lines over the Dragoon Bridge and not by the Begum's Bridge, which would have put him the wrong side of the Sudder Bazar. If he had sent an order to the Carabiniers in the sense suggested, he could have told them also to push a troop or half a troop at once down to or across the Dragoon Bridge, so as to secure his essential crossing-point. Even without Wilson actually adding such a direction, Custance might have taken that action independently, once he knew that the Dragoon Bridge was the first objective. Apart from the tactical advantage of securing the bridge, such a party of Carabiniers between the Dragoon Bridge and Elahi Buksh's shop would have frightened back the mobs and would have saved Surgeon Smith, the Eckford, Markoe, Cahill and Chapman families, and very likely Taylor and MacNabb: Craigie could have got from it an escort to go back and bring his party away at once. Thus, the initial mistake was committed by Wilson in failing to order a concentration on the flank nearest to the scene of danger and nearest to the bridge which he was bound to use in moving on the native lines. Needless to say, but for this initial error, the Carabiniers would not have gone off into 'the dark and silent country', though that was not a direct consequence of Wilson's actual order.

In saying the Carabiniers moved 'under the guidance of Major Waterfield' and then tacitly indicating that they took the wrong road, O'Callaghan implies that Waterfield was in some way responsible. That is not tenable on the facts as recorded by O'Callaghan himself. He makes the Carabiniers move off along his 'narrow road or causeway' on which they continued until they turned back: there was no track, road or causeway running west-east across the infantry parade ground: the only possible conclusion is that the divagation occurred before they even reached the infantry parade ground. In that case, the mishap occurred on a road or roads adjacent to the Carabiniers' own lines and which must have been familiar to their own officers and N.C.Os. after two months in station. It follows that they went astray at a point where they cannot have been dependent on Waterfield's guidance.

If he was supposed to guide them at all it can only have been through the infantry or artillery lines at the far (eastern) end of the infantry parade ground, on the very doubtful supposition that they were ordered to go that way to the jail: he cannot have been responsible as a guide at the point where they did go wrong. The divagation certainly did not occur, as Kaye seems to have thought, on the road back from the jail: O'Callaghan's narrative makes it certain that they diverged before, and not after, they turned back, and also that they never reached the jail. All that can now be said is that in the darkness the leading files took the wrong road; such an event is not unprecedented, and no individual, certainly not Waterfield, can now be saddled with the blame.

It is the case that the conduct of Hewitt and Wilson at Meerut is sometimes unfavourably compared with that of Colonel Gillespie on the occasion of the mutiny at Vellore in 1806. This comparison is entirely unfair. That outbreak of the native troops occurred within the fort at Vellore and a body of Europeans succeeded in retaining possession of part of the walls and of the interior. An officer got away to Gillespie at Arcot with an exact account of the position. Gillespie moved in haste with cavalry to Vellore and then was unable to force his way into the fort; he had to wait for guns and even then it was the assistance of the Europeans holding out within the fort which enabled him to recapture it. Thus at Vellore, Gillespie had exact information of the position, he had to deal with mutineers shut up in a known position, and there was a force acting on his side within the fort itself. None of these conditions existed at Meerut: Hewitt and Wilson were in an entirely different and much more difficult position.[11]

If one is to compare Vellore and Meerut at all, the most interesting point is in relation to the time factor. It will be appreciated that, if troops are to get ready to move from one point to another, the time needed to get them ready is the same whether they are to move fifteen miles or three miles. Now Arcot is sixteen miles from Vellore, and Gillespie received the news at 6 a.m. and reached Vellore at 10 a.m.; he certainly moved with cavalry at speed, once he had started, and the actual ride probably took at most two and a half hours. If that is so, then even in the early morning it took an hour and a half to turn out the cavalry with which Gillespie set off. That is not really much less time than it took to turn out the troops at Meerut on a Sunday evening. Gillespie had a simple problem and his action was crowned with success, and that is why it was thought so speedy and brilliant. On analysis, it turns out that in the only point where comparison is relevant there is little to choose between what was achieved at Arcot and at Meerut.

A final word may be said about disarming on the Mian Mir model which was referred to in passing above. Could such a step have been taken at Meerut? At Mian Mir intelligence of widespread disaffection was brought, as at Meerut, by only one native officer on the evening of 12 May. There was a ball that evening which was not postponed but at which the officers of the European regiments were privately warned. There was a general parade next morning and at the end of the parade the Indian regiments found themselves face to face with the British regiments and the Artillery fully armed. Ordered to lodge their arms, the Indian regiments obeyed. Now in the first place the officers at Mian Mir knew what had happened at Meerut and they were backed by the authority of Montgomery, acting in the absence of John Lawrence; at Meerut the officers had no such precedent and no such support (in spite of the Berhampore episode). I doubt if they could have felt justified in carrying out a summary disarming on the morning of 10 May on the strength of what one native officer had told to a cavalry subaltern (Gough). If they had felt so justified it might have been technically possible, though secrecy would have been difficult. Psychologically, it was impossible for either Hewitt or Wilson without higher authority.

CHAPTER 12

TO DELHI

The Delhi road, running south-westwards from the Begum's Bridge and passing just west of Meerut city, forks a little farther on: one branch turns off sharply to the west to Baghput on the Jumna, the other is the direct road to Delhi on its south-westerly course. The distance to Baghput is about thirty miles: here the Jumna could be crossed by a bridge of boats and on the western bank the traveller could take a road southwards which brought him first to the cantonment of Delhi upon the Ridge and then to the Kashmir Gate in the northern wall of the city, a distance of about twenty miles from the river crossing, making fifty miles altogether from Meerut. By the direct road, the distance from Meerut to Delhi is about thirty-eight miles: the main stages were Begumabad at twelve to thirteen miles; Mooradnagar at eighteen to nineteen miles; and Ghaziuddinnagar (now Ghaziabad) at about twenty-nine miles. Just beyond the last place, the road crossed the Hindan River by a bridge and so came to the eastern end of the Delhi bridge of boats across the Jumna, below the north-eastern corner of the Red Fort (or more accurately of the separate fort of Selimgarh). Across the bridge of boats was the Calcutta Gate in the eastern face of the city wall.

The bulk of the sowars and sepoys who left Meerut at nightfall on 10 May took the direct road to Delhi. There is a certain amount of evidence of their progress along it. Begumabad, Mooradnagar and Ghaziuddinnagar are all mentioned, as are also some smaller places—Mulleeana, Rethanee, Bhorboral, Mouza Bessokur, Sekree (these are the spellings in the sources). These small places cannot always be found on recent or comparatively recent maps but can be traced on older maps, notably on a map of the Meerut District prepared in 1831 by Captain W. Brown.[1]

In the fork between the main Delhi road and the road to Baghput, quite close to both roads, lay the village of Mulleeana. The chaukidār of that village, so it appears, deposed that the sowars and sepoys passed there in small bands of twenty or thirty, some in uniform and some in undress, and that they were throwing away their arms and equipment. The time when this was observed was not stated. Undoubtedly, the bulk of the native troops left the station during the dark hours between sunset and moonrise, from 7 p.m. to 9 p.m. The villagers would at first have kept in their villages, closing their entries: they might later have come out to join in the plunder. How much they could really observe of the flight of the regiments is far from certain.[2]

Few certainly were those who took the Baghput road, men undoubtedly whose homes were in the region between Meerut and the Jumna or across that river. The bulk of the three regiments went on past the fork down the main road to Delhi. They gathered into some kind of assembly near a village called Rethanee, about three miles from Meerut.[3] Here they decided on their course of flight, or rather of action. Munshi Mohanlal, an intelligent and reliable witness, afterwards overheard a sowar of the 3rd L.C. in Delhi explaining to a sepoy that before the outbreak at Meerut they had no idea of coming to Delhi and at this assembly there was at first a disagreement as to the direction of movement. It was urged, so it seems, that to move off towards Rohilkhand (eastwards across the Ganges) or towards Agra (southwards down the Doab) without guns would be dangerous. Those were, no doubt, the regions where (together with Oudh, beyond Rohilkhand) most of the men had their homes and to which they would first incline to disperse, but this argument apparently swayed their opinion. According to the sowar, after a long and deliberate consideration, the decision was given to move on Delhi, because possession of the city could easily be obtained and, with possession of the Magazine and the person of the King, would give a great advantage which could be exploited by holding the city for months against the English. By whom these arguments—dangers of dispersal homewards without artillery, easy success of a *coup de main* at Delhi, possibilities of its exploitation—were advanced, we do not know.

However, while Mohanlal's informant may have spoken quite truly as to the ideas of a large section of the mutineers and their change of mind at Rethanee, there must obviously have been at least a group which argued at Rethanee in favour of the Delhi plan. It is also the case that Lieutenant Möller states that on his way towards Mrs Chambers' bungalow he passed sepoys plundering his own regimental magazine (presumably, therefore, 11th N.I. sepoys) who were calling out to each other 'Quick, brother, quick!

Delhi, Delhi!' Since it was this outcry which caused Möller to try and get permission, first from Hewitt and then from Wilson, to ride to Delhi with a warning, his record of the sepoys' words seems to be indubitably what he thought at the time that he heard. If he is right, then the idea of a flight to Delhi was abroad well before the bulk of the sepoys had left the cantonment. The conclusion would be that a section or a group had begun to put this idea about at that early stage, and swung practically the whole of the mutineers round to it at the meeting at Rethanee, imposing a positive course of action aimed at developing and extending the rebellious movement in preference to the merely negative course of flight and dispersal to their homes or to remoter parts.[4]

When they moved off from Rethanee, the mutineers tended to break up into small parties again to a certain extent but there seems to have been what one may call a main body which kept together. At Bessokur, which is a mile or two short of Begumabad, a body of two or three hundred sowars passed through about 10 p.m. At Sekree, halfway between Begumabad and Mooradnagar, that is to say about four or five miles beyond Bessokur, the sowars passed at midnight, the sepoys about five hours later.[5] Travellers from Delhi, who crossed the Hindan between about midnight and one o'clock, then fell in with parties of sowars: they left the road and went by the fields to Mooradnagar and then by by-paths to Mooree, which is a little north-west of Begumabad, but their coachman stuck to the road and fell in with further parties, he says, right as far as Bhorboral, which is on the Meerut side of Bessokur.[6]

One deposition contains a reference, which is pure hearsay, to some cavalry horses having been brought in to Hauper from Goolaothee. These places are not on the Meerut–Delhi road, but on the Meerut–Bulandshahr, or Grand Trunk Road. Hauper is twenty miles from Meerut, Goolaothee south of it twenty-eight miles from Meerut. It seems to have been assumed that this was a case of a party which went down that road from Meerut, but that is not really probable. A more likely explanation is that this is a trace of some party which decided to break off eastwards at Mooradnagar or beyond and make for the Ganges, leaving Hauper on their left: approaching the Grand Trunk Road, they decided to let their military mounts go and cover the rest of their journey inconspicuously. There may have been other parties who acted in a similar way.[7]

None of the times must be taken as by the clock and the evidence was collected several months after the events, and so no very clear picture can be formed. Some features emerge. The cavalry naturally outdistanced the infantry, which of course moved more slowly and probably with more frequent rests. The infantry may have remained more compact than the cavalry, but even in the case of the latter there was at least one substantial body of several hundreds holding together. Other cavalry parties ranged ahead or lagged behind this large body; some were at the Hindan when the large body was a dozen miles farther back at Sekree. Some parties broke away but the mass of the three regiments held on to Delhi, straight down the main road and not, as sometimes stated, along by-roads. They committed some acts of violence or plunder on their way.[8]

Hewitt's despatch of 11 May states that, the electric wire having been destroyed, it was impossible to communicate the state of things except by express, which was done to Delhi and Umballa. The messenger to Umballa apparently reached his goal, for there is extant a telegram dispatched from Umballa to other Punjab stations on the 12th over the signature of Waterfield, which was most probably carried by this messenger. It does not seem that the messenger to Delhi got through. No account of events there on the 11th by any officer mentions his arrival, which must have become known if it occurred. The evidence is that the first intimation of the events at Meerut received at the cantonment on the Ridge by Brigadier Graves, the officer commanding at Delhi, was in the form of a message calling for military help sent up from the city between 9 and 10 a.m.[9]

It is also recorded that one message at least was sent by the civil authorities in Meerut to those in Delhi, carried by a police sowar.[10] It was no doubt sent to the Commissioner and Agent to the Lieutenant-Governor of the N.W.P. at Delhi, Simon Fraser, whose residence was at Ludlow Castle north of the city about a mile from the Kashmir Gate. The story seems to appear first in a few lines in a native newswriter which was put in evidence at the trial of the ex-King of Delhi and mentioned that sometime during that night Fraser did receive a message from Meerut. The existence of a rumour to this effect is also mentioned by Mainodin, with the added details that on the sowar's arrival Fraser had not yet gone to bed but was asleep in his chair, that his jemadār woke him, and that he put the note in his pocket and went to bed. That version has since appealed to the imagination of many.[11]

Probability, however, is against the arrival of any messenger from Meerut and against the receipt by Fraser of any message of this kind.

Almost conclusive evidence against it is provided by the evidence of Mrs Peile that Fraser was at 'Marshall the merchant's' when he heard of the arrival of the mutineers. Now Marshall's premises were near the present Maidens Hotel, farther from the city than the Residency at Ludlow Castle. Supposing Fraser received a message, put it in his pocket and went to bed, he would have found it on his dressing table the next morning, put there by his bearer. He would then certainly have driven straight down to the city, not *away* from it to Marshall's. There is no reason to doubt Mrs Peile's evidence: she was at the Flagstaff Tower on the 11th and Marshall was there also.[12]

The first of the Meerut mutineers to reach Delhi were a party of the 3rd L.C., probably about thirty in number, who reached the eastern end of the bridge of boats about 7 a.m. There was a toll post there and they murdered the toll collector, who perhaps tried to interfere with them. They then crossed the bridge. From what subsequently happened, it must be inferred that a single sowar from this party then entered through the Calcutta Gate and rode round to the Lahore Gate of the Fort. The remainder turned down to the left below Selimgarh on to the tract of ground along the river bank or channel below the eastern wall of the Fort. This tract was known as the *Zer Jharokha* '(the ground) below the balcony' or 'under the lattice', because in the Fort wall above was a jharokha, a balcony with stone lattice-work, where for some two centuries the Mogul emperors had been wont to show themselves to their subjects on special occasions or even at times daily.[13]

The single sowar who appeared at the Lahore Gate of the Fort talked with the guard of the 38th N.I. there, telling them of the Meerut events and the coming of the mutineers. His presence was reported to the commander of the King's bodyguard, Captain Douglas, whose lodgings were above the long vaulted entrance passage within the Gate. Douglas came down and spoke with the man, who repeated his tale and said he had come for a drink and a pipe with the guard. Douglas tried to have him seized but he made off. Meanwhile, one of the sepoys of the 38th N.I. carried the news inside to the doorkeepers of the *Diwan-i-Khas* (Private Audience Hall) on the eastern face. The King's apartments were close by, and also those of his physician, Ahsanullah. The doorkeepers told the physician and almost immediately he was summoned by the King.[14]

The King exclaimed to Ahsanullah 'Look! the cavalry are coming by the road of the Zer Jharokha'. Ahsanullah, looking out, saw about fifteen or twenty sowars approaching. His first thought was to have the postern door, near the foot of the so-called Saman Burj, closed, as it gave access to this part of the palace.[15] This had scarcely been done when five or six sowars came up close to the door and raised the time-honoured cry for justice, *Dohai*! *Dohai, Pādishah*! Another court official, Ghulam Abbas, had also been summoned and now arrived. It seemed to him that thirty or forty sowars had collected. He was sent by the King to fetch Douglas, who must just have returned within the Gate after his colloquy with the single sowar. He came over with Ghulam Abbas and parleyed with the sowars from a platform between the Diwan-i-Khas and the King's private apartments.[16]

Douglas is reported to have told the sowars to go to the Kotla of Firuz Shah, the old palace of that emperor lying on the Jumna bank just south of the present city.[17] This apparently they started to do, proceeding south along the river bank below the eastern wall of the city. In this wall, slightly south of the Fort, was the Rajghat Gate. They found it open (or it was opened to them) and by it they entered the city.

Meanwhile either a messenger or a rumour had caught up with Fraser at Marshall's. The mutineers' argument with the toll keeper and his murder together with the crossing of the bridge and the deviation on to the Zer Jharokha must be reckoned as allowing time for a messenger riding post haste to reach Fraser or for this astounding rumour to spread. He drove down at once in his own buggy from Marshall's to the Lahore Gate of the Fort. He arrived there at the time when Douglas had gone inside after his colloquy with the single sowar, it may well be while the parley was in progress with the mutineers on the Zer Jharokha. He got down from his buggy and walked in under the gateway, apparently in search of Douglas, for he told a chaprāsī, Bakhtawar Singh, to give Douglas a message to join him at the Calcutta Gate. Douglas came back to the Gate of the Fort, which had by then been shut with his buggy inside: he was given the message, went outside and borrowed a buggy from a native officer of the King's bodyguard, Dildar Khan, and drove down to the Calcutta Gate. He there found Fraser, with the Judge, Le Bas, and the Collector and Magistrate, Hutchinson, and several other Englishmen.[18]

Le Bas's previous movements are not known. Hutchinson had been sitting as Magistrate at his court at the cutcherry which was behind St James's Church. The *Darogah* (police officer) from the bridge of boats came to him with the news that there had been an outbreak at Meerut and the mutineers were approaching Delhi. Hutchinson told him to go and close the Gate and then drove off in the direction of Fraser's house, that is to say towards the Kashmir Gate *en route* for Ludlow Castle. He shortly returned to the court: it seems possible that he met Fraser on his way to the Fort. On his return, Hutchinson told Mainodin, who was in court on a case, to go and warn the Kotwal at the Kotwali in the Chandni Chauk. Mainodin on his way met the watchman from the Rajghat Gate who told him of the mutineers' entry: he went back and warned Hutchinson, who asked where Le Bas was, then went himself to the Kotwali and afterwards to the Calcutta Gate.[19]

In the interval between Hutchinson's departure for the Kashmir Gate and his return, the Joint Magistrate, Sir Theophilus Metcalfe, arrived.[20] From a window in the cutcherry he saw a party of mutineers crossing the bridge of boats. Perhaps in agreement with Hutchinson, he went to arrange for guns to be fetched from the Magazine to be trained on the bridge. He went first to the bungalow occupied by the Assistant Commissary of Ordnance at the Magazine, Lieutenant George Forrest of the Veteran Establishment, which was probably near the Magazine.[21] They went down to the Magazine together but as there were neither Artillerymen nor gun-cattle the plan could not be carried out. With Willoughby, the officer commanding the Magazine, they went through to a small bastion on the river face of the Magazine and from there they watched the arrival of a fresh and much larger body of mutineers. Metcalfe and Willoughby then went down to see if the Calcutta Gate was closed (Hutchinson had given the order for this) and Willoughby shortly returned, while Metcalfe remained for a time with the group of Englishmen round Fraser.

Forrest and his companions observed from the Magazine bastion the crossing of the bridge by this second, larger party of mutineers. Forrest recorded what he saw twice, once in a written report made out only three weeks later, and subsequently in verbal evidence at the trial of the ex-King of Delhi early in 1858. He says the time was about 9 a.m.: this is not in his earlier written report but in his evidence at the trial. In the written report, he says that he saw the mutineers marching in open column, headed by the cavalry, that the Calcutta Gate was already occupied by a body of cavalry, and that the mutineers were admitted directly to the palace; these last two details are certainly inaccurate. Some eight months later, he said in his verbal evidence that he saw some cavalry in front (nearly a regiment), followed by the 11th and 20th regiments of Native Infantry, marching up in military formation, he would say with fixed bayonets and sloped arms: it is certain that the bulk of the infantry arrived in the early afternoon, about five or six hours after the cavalry, as would be expected, so that here again Forrest is inaccurate. He was no longer young and broke down during his escape with Vibart's party. His evidence therefore cannot be accepted quite literally. What he must really have seen was the large party of cavalry which was referred to as the main body in the description of the mutineers' flight together with some infantry which must have kept up by running at the stirrups or getting up behind and which perhaps included groups from both the 11th and the 20th N.I. The distinction from the original party of sowars, in time of arrival and in composition, is clear but is sometimes overlooked.[22]

This second body of mutineers was also observed by Mrs Aldwell, the Eurasian wife (after the Delhi massacre, the widow) of a Government pensioner. Her testimony is independent of Forrest's but agrees with it. The Aldwells lived in Daryaganj, the quarter which formed the south-eastern corner of the city above the Jumna, largely inhabited by pensioners or subordinate employees of Government, European or Eurasian: their house was close by the Khairati Gate, situated south of the Rajghat Gate, and giving access from the Jumna bank. Mrs Aldwell was told by one of her syces, between 8 and 9 a.m., of the arrival of mutineers from Meerut, but that they had not even crossed the bridge: the arrival of the earlier party at 7 a.m. was apparently still unknown in Daryaganj. She and her neighbours saw this body cross the bridge about 9 a.m. which agrees with Forrest's evidence. She says that a good part were cavalry, and some infantry, again agreeing with

Forrest. This second body also turned down the river bank, for the Calcutta Gate was closed, and passed close under the parapets of the Aldwell house, some of them firing at the spectators. Thus they did not enter by either the Rajghat or the Khairati Gates. Mrs Aldwell thought they were going to the jail to free the prisoners: the jail was near the kotla of Firuz Shah, to which Douglas had directed the earlier party. It can be then surmised that this body eventually managed to get into the city by the Delhi Gate, which was in the south wall very near the south-eastern angle, and close to which they would pass, whether bound for the jail or for the kotla of Firuz Shah.[23]

The group of Europeans remained near the Calcutta Gate. Fraser's escort of Jhajjar sowars was with them. These are not mentioned in the story of his arrival at the Fort and would have hardly accompanied him to Marshall's: but for the sake of his dignity and on account of the fate of his predecessor and homonym, William Fraser, he would have been accompanied by several of them as orderlies, and he may have sent one of these back to fetch the whole escort down to the Calcutta Gate.[24] A crowd had also gathered round when the news of the closing of the Gate spread. Metcalfe presently went off to Daryaganj and there he fell in with mutineers and after many hairbreadth escapes he got away to Paharganj, where Mainodin sheltered him until he could escape to Jhajjar.[25] Thus Metcalfe seems to have encountered some of the large body of mutineers who had got into the city and were starting to plunder and massacre in Daryaganj.[26] Presently, half a dozen sowars came galloping round the Fort walls to the Calcutta Gate: these again seem to have been from the recently arrived large body. They fired their pistols at the Englishmen. Fraser seized a musket from a policeman and shot one of the sowars. His escort deserted him. He and Hutchinson got into a buggy and made for the Fort, attacked by more sowars on the way. Douglas threw himself into the palace ditch and injured his ankle: he was dragged inside by his servants, and there Fraser, Hutchinson and Douglas, with others, were all later murdered.[27]

A full and detailed account of the further events at Delhi on 11 May requires a separate study and is excluded from these pages. The aim of the preceding paragraphs has been to trace the movements of the Meerut mutineers at the end of their journey to Delhi. As the day proceeds, they are lost to sight in the general turmoil, merged with the mutinous regiments at Delhi, the fanatics, and the mobs. Only two definite pieces of information need be mentioned to complete their story. Somewhat later in the morning, perhaps towards 11 a.m., a party of the 3rd L.C. sowars debouched from the road leading from the Magazine and the Fort into the open space lying outside the Kashmir Gate Main Guard. They were on the south side, facing the Main Guard on the north: on the east was St James's Church with William Fraser's monument in front of it and opposite on the west was Skinner's house. Within the Main Guard were now the usual guard, supplied that day by the 38th N.I., and eight companies of the 54th N.I. which had come down in answer to a message sent up to Brigadier Graves, probably by Fraser from the Calcutta Gate when the arrival of the large body of mutineers was perceived. Colonel Ripley, commanding the 54th N.I., brought this force, or part of it, out of the Main Guard into the open space and gave the order to open fire on the sowars. The 54th thereupon fired high, the 38th did not fire at all: the sowars discharged their pistols, severely wounding Ripley and killing four of his officers: the sowars then reined round and disappeared back into the city. One of the officers killed was Ensign William Waterfield of the 54th N.I., a nephew of Major Waterfield at Meerut.[28]

Finally, the main part of the Meerut infantry arrived in the early afternoon: it is said that it did not arrive as a compact force but that it came in by straggling parties.[29] As the day wore on, the mutinous soldiery, whether from Meerut or Delhi, invaded the Fort, and the King and his family found their courtyards, their gardens, and even their dwellings turned into encampments and barracks, for an excited, undisciplined, and weary mob. Thus had the Meerut mutineers attained the goal they chose at Rethanee. They were at Delhi. Yet it was still a long way to Delhi—*hanoz Dillī dūr hai*: many of those who take that road never arrive, and those who get there cannot be sure of returning whence they came.

CHAPTER 13

CONCLUSIONS

The essential question to be asked about the Meerut outbreak is whether it was planned in advance or whether it arose through chance circumstances on the fateful evening. Put thus, however, the question conceals ambiguities. There are really three questions. Was the outbreak an episode brought on by some chance happening on the evening of 10 May? Or was it planned in Meerut itself during the preceding days or weeks? Or was it part of a plan matured much longer and with much wider scope? The second of these three questions must be considered first, because it is in relation to this question that the evidence is clearest and the answer to it enables the first of the three questions to be disposed of also.

Was, then, the Meerut outbreak planned in Meerut itself during the days or weeks preceding 10 May?

Some good authorities have held that there was no previous preparation or plan at all even among the regiments at Meerut, or at least not among the bulk of the sepoys: this last qualification, however, is pointless because, even if the bulk were not aware of any plan, they could yet have been moved according to the plans of a small group or groups. Rice Holmes was of this opinion, which seemed to him to be borne out by the evidence in the *Meerut Depositions*, though that is by no means the case when the *Depositions* are collated and closely analysed. More recently, Mr S. N. Sen has stated this view of the Meerut episode in still more absolute terms. Both Rice Holmes and Mr Sen accept the story of the cook boy, which is quite unsubstantiated, and the connection of the church parade with the panic in the native lines, which is disproved by the facts. Neither of them refers at all to two facts which make it absolutely certain that the outbreak was indeed premeditated and planned in advance among the Meerut troops.

These two facts are the report brought to Gough on the evening of 9 May and the cutting of the telegraph line to Delhi between 9 a.m. and 4 p.m. on the 10th. The report brought to Gough is particularly remarkable in forecasting that the infantry would rise and the cavalry would follow them: considering that it was the cavalry who were aggrieved by the court-martial sentences, one would have expected the opposite, but in fact what Gough was told is exactly what actually happened. One cannot fall back on coincidence when one finds not one fact of this kind but two facts, followed by an actual outbreak which the report foretold and to which the wire-cutting is obviously relevant. One can only conclude that the report was a true report of something for which the plans had been laid by 9 May and the wire-cutting on the 10th was a part of the plan.

It must, then, also follow (and this disposes of the first of the three questions) that the panic in the bazar was not mere chance. It would be too much if there was a plan for a rising on the evening of the 10th and at just the time required a chance incident started a panic which got the already planned movement under way. It must be concluded that the panic in the bazar was deliberately provoked and was the first stage of the plan. The pattern at Berhampore was being repeated. The firing parade had brought to a head the suspicions about the cartridges. Now, the panic cry was started at the chosen moment by some group of organisers. As at Berhampore, these leaders lurk in the shadows but the outcry in the bazar and the rush to the lines are their work, operating on the idle groups of sepoys gathered in the bazar.

This conclusion is confirmed by the quite elaborate and skilful nature of the plan as revealed in action and sequence of events. The outcry was raised at about 5 p.m., just an hour and a half before sunset. As Major Harriott said in his address at the trial of the ex-King of Delhi, the mutineers reckoned that they would have about an hour and a half before the European troops could be collected and brought down to the scene: in the event, the period was somewhat longer. However, on that calculation and with an uproar starting about 5 p.m., the European troops would have arrived just about as darkness fell. The darkness would last for two hours until the moon rose. This timing thus allowed the maximum time for disturbances to develop in the native lines before darkness and the European troops simultaneously arrived, whereupon the native troops would be able in the darkness to get away. Further, by the outcry starting in the Sudder Bazar and not in the lines themselves, the bazar mob was put on the alert and induced to join in: the Sudder Bazar lay on, or close to, the route which the European troops must take and riots in that bazar were a distraction and to some extent a danger to their movements. Thus, by bringing the bazar mobs into the affair in this way, the native troops could hope to divert part of the European forces and increase their own chances of mischief and of escape. The plan in fact was to gain the maximum advantage by careful timing and by diversionary outbreaks in the bazar while the whole bulk of the native troops were worked up into a state of pandemonium and were then withdrawn under cover of darkness before the Europeans could strike effectively: the scheme was perhaps completed by the release of the prisoners from the Old Jail as darkness fell, so as to introduce at that moment fresh forces of disorder.

It cannot possibly be supposed that such a skilfully devised plan was worked out, even by a small group of leaders, between the dismissal of the ironing parade on the morning of 9 May and the communication to Gough that evening or the cutting of the Delhi telegraph wire sometime in the middle of the day on the 10th. This is evidently a plan which took longer to mature than that. It must be regarded as having been evolved during the period of slightly over a fortnight between the firing parade and 9 May. It was so evolved in anticipation of the court-martial verdict, which could be foreseen with certainty.

What could not be similarly foreseen were the sentence, the manner of its execution, and the arrangements for the confinement of the condemned men. It follows from this that the rescue of the sowars cannot have been one of the original elements of the plan. The outbreak does not centre round that at all, as is sometimes supposed. It was planned on quite different lines, without regard to a rescue of this kind. The rescue was a secondary movement, a last minute addition to the plan, made by men of the 3rd L.C., which in any case was not the leading regiment according to the plan as laid out. It was the 20th N.I. which took, or was given, the leading part.

To identify the organisers or leaders is impossible, though their existence is a necessary inference from the facts. They, or all of them, are not likely to be found among the condemned men who were in some sort of confinement from the firing parade onwards, which would have constricted their freedom of action. The two naiks, Pīr Ali and Kudrat Ali, who were said to have organised the oath and were the first to refuse the cartridges, are therefore not to be regarded as ringleaders but more probably as the immediate tools of the real organisers. The decision to make for Delhi again shows the organising group at work for it was contrary to the natural impulse, and probably to the first intentions, of the bulk of the sepoys: the idea seems to have got abroad while the sacking of the native lines was still going on but the decision was only generally accepted at the assembly at Rethanee, where it seems that the mass was swayed by the few.

The evidence from Meerut itself does not show conclusively what collusion there may have been between the Meerut and Delhi regiments or between the regiments and the Delhi Court. The decision to make for Delhi argues in favour of some collusion: it was so full of possible risks that it could hardly have been taken merely in reliance on the general cohesion of the Army and without some persuasion that the Delhi regiments were pledged to join. The cutting of the Delhi telegraph wire also indicates a previous intention to make Delhi the objective of the rising and a need to prevent premature news reaching the authorities there. The proximity of the two stations and the opportunities for consultation with Delhi native officers at the Meerut court-martial make collusion easy to suppose. Nevertheless, conclusions cannot be drawn as to the relations between the Meerut and Delhi regiments and still less as to the relations between the regiments and the Delhi Court, without a fuller study of the Delhi outbreak and the whole evidence bearing on this: such a study cannot be included in the present volume.

The answer to the last question as to whether the Meerut outbreak was part of a plan longer matured and wider in scope is not to be found in the evidence of what happened at Meerut itself. For that question, what is significant is the position of the Meerut episode in a series of events. The various incidents at Barrackpore, the Berhampore outbreak which went so far and then stopped short, the case of Mangal Pande which went off like a damp squib, have the appearance of a succession of attempts to start an insurrectionary movement in the Presidency Division as near as possible to the seat of Government. These efforts failed. It would be natural then to shift the scene and try what could be done up-country, where regiments were thicker on the ground, the men nearer their homes, and the seat of power farther away. Such designs might evolve out of nothing more than the correspondence between regiments which undoubtedly went on: or they might represent the original and the revised plan of organisers who remain invisible. The chapātī distributions and Waterfield's spinning wheels episode, outside the cadre of the military movements, must be reckoned similar attempts to prepare disturbances over a wider field in conjunction with the military risings which it was hoped to initiate in the Presidency Division. The dates and succession of episodes fit in with the supposition of a sustained effort to produce an outbreak in February or March which failed and was followed by a sudden, and perhaps somewhat unexpected, success in quite a different quarter in May.

There are stories that the outbreak at Meerut was a premature explosion which anticipated a general plot throughout the Army for a concerted rising on a given date. This is usually said to have been three weeks later, Sunday 31 May. The origin of that version seems to be the opinion of Mr J. (later Sir John) Cracroft Wilson, the experienced Judge of Moradabad, of which he had convinced himself by 'carefully collating oral information with the facts as they occurred', but his information and evidence remain unrecorded. The plan, according to him, was for the sepoys to rise and exterminate their officers and other Europeans and European troops during the morning church service. It is curious how this preoccupation with an attack on the Christians in church recurs: it was never realised except at Shahjahanpur on 31 May, which may be Wilson's 'facts as they occurred'. An alternative and more absurd version fixes the date as Sunday 24 May, the birthday of Queen Victoria: on that day the troops were to turn out to fire *feux de joie*, the sepoys were to possess themselves (how, it is not made clear) of balled cartridges and were to turn their weapons on their European officers and European troops. Carmichael-Smyth claimed—after the event—that his action at Meerut had brought on this premature explosion and ruined the far more dangerous plan. The facts of the Meerut episode by no means support such an idea. If the Meerut troops had really acted in a panic on the spur of the moment on the evening of 10 May, the theory might hold water. It would be very improbable that they would deliberately plan, as they did, during a full fortnight in advance, an *émeute* which would anticipate a vaster scheme concerted for three weeks later, to which they were privy. That is more particularly so, when once it has been realised that the outbreak did not revolve round the rescue of the sowars which was an addition and not the centre of the affair at all.

Some other questions have been discussed fully enough in the text. Carmichael-Smyth's part was not the blunder of a stupid martinet. It falls under a superior category of historical events. It was one of those cases where a man has the opportunity to perform a certain action and does so because it is natural to him, it is in his character: but the action is performed in circumstances which exaggerate its effects beyond all expectation. It is a real case of historical contingency: it makes or mars a fortune or at least a reputation, while changing the course of events. The handling of the European troops was not by any means open to the sweeping condemnation which it generally receives, but deserves criticism on one tactical point which turned out to be vital and for which the responsibility must rest on Archdale Wilson.

Another question about the Mutiny which historians are fond of asking is whether the movement was a military mutiny or a general rebellion. This question again is *mal posée*. How general must a rebellion be in order to be a general rebellion? To talk, on the other hand, of a military mutiny is to bring in a concept of military law—disobedience to lawful orders, violence offered to superior officers, acts of a kind which in the case of an individual or of a unit can be classified under that category for adjudication and punishment by a suitable tribunal. A general rising of an entire army of its nature passes beyond the bounds of mutiny: and when the personnel of the army is linked as that of the Bengal Army was to the population of a certain territory, the rising of the army is in itself a rising of the people of that territory, with the possibly incomplete support of the civil population, less well-armed or organised. Where the Meerut episode can perhaps be made to throw a little light on this problem of the nature of the Mutiny is in the historical analogies which can be found for some aspects of it.

There is an interesting analogy between the behaviour of the mutinous regiments both at Berhampore and Meerut (the identity of the pattern has already been noted) and the behaviour of revolutionary crowds which has been studied in relation to the French Revolution by G. Lefebvre, whose analysis has recently been restated and publicised in England by G. Rudé. It results from this analysis that the process of the formation of a revolutionary crowd begins with an assembly of people, of which the time and place may be governed by chance. The composition of the assembly, however, is by no means miscellaneous but generally presents a certain unity of economic status, occupation, and locality. It is obvious that the sepoy regiments each formed a unity of that kind with a higher degree of cohesion than the specimens of revolutionary crowds studied by Lefebvre, a cohesion resting not only on the regiment in itself with its military discipline, but also on the strata of population and the localities from which it was recruited. Next, the assembly of people with its inchoate tendency towards some kind of violent demonstration is frequently converted to actual violence and to unity as a crowd engaged in such action through the injection of an element of panic: precisely the same is true of the sepoy regiments at Berhampore and Meerut, propelled from a state of suspicion and discontent into a state of violence and mutiny by a panic cry that other troops were approaching in order to disarm them. Further, in these cases of revolutionary crowds, it is often found that the panic is fed and the transition to violence forwarded by some group or groups of leaders or organisers who remain in the background and who can only occasionally or imperfectly be identified: enough stress has already been laid on this factor in relation to the outbreaks at Berhampore and Meerut. Thus, these episodes, far from being, as they seemed to contemporaries, examples of unprecedented malice and unaccountable wickedness, can be classified as belonging to a historical genus which becomes manifest when relations between constituted authorities and those subject to them become strained to an extreme degree.

On a wider plane, an analogy may also hold between the general situation out of which sprang the actions of the revolutionary crowds in eighteenth-century France and the state of the Upper Provinces of the Bengal Presidency in 1857. In France, there was a widespread condition of discontent shared by several groups—lesser bourgeoisie, artisans and journeymen, peasants—which found a common objection to the privileges of the nobility in the foreground of their ideas, but which, beyond that, had interests and aims often divergent. So in Northern India in 1857, there were grievances cherished by dispossessed landlords, disbanded native soldiery, dismissed officials, over-assessed peasants, which were disparate: but they were united, in the forefront of their thoughts, by the all-pervading fear of attack upon their religions, examined above in the first chapter. This fear itself was an irrational but uncontrollable obsession which can find its analogies in France both in the panics which coalesced into the *Grande Peur* and also in the unreasoning suspicions of plots directed against the mass of the people by the powerful few, the *complot des nobles* or in prerevolutionary times the *pacte de famine*. With these analogies in mind, it becomes pointless to make any reckoning of how large a proportion of the population openly or secretly joined with the mutineers of 1857, or what proportion preferred the English Government to the anarchical conditions which the mutineers' success would revive: it is sufficient to observe that, however surprisingly and unreasonably, a revolutionary situation had arisen by the end of 1856, with substantial groups nourishing discontents of diverse kinds and a widespread fear of a plot by their rulers against their most intimate well-being, their religious beliefs and customs.

Even the appeal of the mutineers to the impotent King of Delhi is not without its parallel in revolutionary circumstances. There was in 1789 an idea of appeal to the crown against the nobles, a hope of the protection of a benevolent but misguided sovereign against oppressions and innovations introduced by the nobility. Historians, even some of their contemporaries, scorn the mutineers for having turned to the exhausted house of Timur— the aged poetaster, the squalid palace, the futile court, the decrepit elephants, the tinsel robes of honour. Such scorn is justified by the outcome but in this act of the rebel soldiery there is once again an element in common between the eruption of 1789 and the squib of 1857.

The special peculiarity of the outbreak of 1857, in comparison with other cases with which it seems possible to link it as a specimen of a genus, is that the lead was taken by the forces maintained by the Government itself instead of these at first standing by the constituted authorities and being only later drawn into the vortex. The result was a superficially violent commencement, fizzling out into sporadic local outbreaks, as the limits of the discontented or unruly sections of society were reached: the commoner pattern is a slower and apparently less dangerous beginning which works up to an overwhelming crisis as the unsuspected forces behind it are disclosed. This special feature in India is explained by the solidarity of the sepoys with their families and villages, where the suspicions over religious matters and other discontents were rife, the final concentration of the discontent on the cartridge question which was a specifically military problem, and the manoeuvring of the situation over a period of several months and a number of unsuccessful attempts towards an outbreak in a military force which was attained at Meerut.

It is possible that this course of development to some extent frustrated the movement by rousing some degree of moral condemnation among their own countrymen against the mutineers. It is quite untrue to hold that sympathy with them or approval of their acts was widespread or universal. On the contrary, there were a great many of their countrymen who abhorred what they did, apart from those who leant in favour of the English, either because they approved the tranquillity and regularity of the administration, or even because in many directions they desired to see western ideas and methods spread. The English moral condemnation, coloured by ideas of loyalty and allegiance to a national sovereign and her representatives, was beside the point. The Indian moral condemnation was on a different ground—faithlessness to salt. *Yeh badzāt, pājī, nimakharām, bāghī telinge*—'these low-born, base, rebel sepoys, doers of what is forbidden by the salt they have eaten'. Thus Nazīr Ahmad describes the mutineers by the mouth of Ibn-ul-waqt, the 'man of his time'. This was the gravamen of the charge, whether when they slew their officers or defied the *Kampani Bahādur*. The ingenuity of those who seized on the cartridge grievance, and the tragedy of those whom it drove to frenzy, was the suggestion that the hand which nourished the sepoy proffered not only salt, but grease.

NOTES AND REFERENCES

1   This quotation is taken from the *Narrative of Events attending the outbreak of disturbances and the restoration of authority in the Agra Division*, by G. F. Harvey, Commissioner, Agra Division, dated 21 December 1858. This is one of the narratives or reports produced by Commissioners of Divisions or Collectors of Districts in response to a circular letter No. 212 of 1858 from the Government of the North-West Provinces. This narrative will be cited again as *Agra Division Narrative*. There are also separate narratives from the Collectors of various Districts in the Agra Division. In the case of the Meerut Division, there is only one divisional narrative, which is, however, for some reason headed as relating to the Meerut District and will be cited as *Meerut District Narrative*: it was compiled by Fleetwood Williams, who was not Commissioner in May 1857 (H. H. Greathed held the post) and combines in serial order the reports of the Collectors which therefore are not printed separately. Other narratives of the same series will be cited by similar abbreviations, as *Nimach District Narrative*, etc.

2   For these appearances of the chapātīs, see Mark Thornhill, *Personal Adventures etc. during the Indian Mutiny*, p. 2; R. H. W. Dunlop, *Service and Adventures with the Khaki Ressalah*, p. 24; *Depositions taken at Meerut by Major G. W. Williams* (to be cited as *Meerut Depositions*) and his *Memorandum* prefixed thereto (to be cited as Williams, *Memorandum*); Sir J. W. Kaye, *History of the Sepoy War in India 1857–1858* (to be cited as Kaye, *Sepoy War*), vol. I, p. 632; C. T. Metcalfe, *Two Native Narratives of the Mutiny in Delhi* (narrative of Mainodin, properly Mu'inuddin); evidence of Sir John Theophilus Metcalfe, Jat Mull, Chuni, Kishan Singh, Captain Martineau, Rissaldār John Everett and Hakim Ahsanullah printed in *Trial of the ex-King of Delhi* (Selections from the Records of the Government of the Punjab and its Dependencies, n.s. vol. VII); Captain G. Hutchinson, *Narrative of the Mutinies in Oudh*, p. 37; W. Edwards, *Personal Adventures during the Indian Rebellion in Rohilkhand*, p. 15; *The Siege of Delhi*, by an officer who served there (W. W. Ireland), in Kaye, *Sepoy War*, vol. I, p. 636; Sir Syed Ahmed Khan, *The Causes of the Indian Revolt*, p. 3; *Saugor and Nerbudda Territories Narrative, Nimar District Narrative, Nimach District Narrative*. These are the sources not only for the dissemination of the chapātīs described in this paragraph but (unless otherwise stated) for the details of the mode of transmission etc. in the following paragraphs. It is rather surprising that local newspapers such as *The Delhi Gazette* and *The Mofussilite* for the first quarter of 1857 seem to contain no reports about the chapātīs.

3   For the epidemic of 1856, see *Reports on Cholera in the Meerut, Rohilcund and Ajmere Divisions in the year 1856* (Agra, 1857).

4 Mainodin in C. T. Metcalfe, *Two Native Narratives of the Mutiny in Delhi*, p. 41.

5 For the position of the chaukidārs, see B. B. Misra, *Central Administration of the East India Company 1773–1834*; for the cholera pills, the *Reports* cited in note 3 above.

6 For popular uneasiness on the score of religion see Sir Syed Ahmed Khan, *The Causes of the Indian Revolt*; Shaikh Hedayat Ali, *The Causes of the Indian Mutiny* (translated by Captain Rattray in 1858, printed by Government, and most conveniently accessible in M. R. Gubbins, *Mutinies in Oude*; *From Sepoy to Subadār, being the Life and Adventures of a Native Soldier* (passing under the name of Sitaram), translated by Lt.-Col. Norgate and republished by Lt.-Col. D. C. Phillott (still of doubtful authenticity in spite of a valiant defence by the late Sir Patrick Cadell in *Journal of the Society for Army Historical Research*, 1959); M. R. Gubbins, *op. cit.* On the history of Evangelical missionary activity in India, see Arthur Mayhew, *Christianity and the Government of India*; Ingham, *Reformers in India*. For the effects of Utilitarianism, see Eric Stokes, *The English Utilitarians and India*.

7 For the deterioration in the discipline of the Bengal Army, see the standard histories of the Mutiny, namely, Kaye, *Sepoy War*; T. R. E. Holmes (Rice Holmes), *History of the Indian Mutiny*, and (latest and in many ways best) S. N. Sen, *Eighteen fifty-seven*; and now also Mrs Amiya Barat, *The Structure and Organisation of the Bengal Native Infantry, with special reference to problems of discipline, 1796–1852*. This is a thesis of which the original is in the India Office Library under the author's maiden name of A. Sen but which has been printed under her married name in Calcutta: to my mind it shows clearly that all earlier acts of disobedience or mutiny differed *toto caelo* from 1857. For the character of regimental life in the Bengal Army I would like to refer the reader to Lt.-Col. J. S. Hodgson, *Musings on Military Matters* (Meerut, 1851); 2nd edition under title *Opinions on the Indian Army* (London, 1857), a useful work now so forgotten that it does not figure in the bibliography in S. N. Sen, *Eighteen fifty-seven*. A similar work also still worth consulting, but thirty years older, is Captain W. Badenach, *Inquiry into the State of the Indian Army*. There is also the excellent autobiography of Sir Thomas Seaton, *From Cadet to Colonel* and five works of fiction based on experience, namely, *Memoirs of a Cadet by a Bengalee* (Albert Fenton, in India 1818–34); Francis Bellew (in India 1815–30), *Memoirs of a Griffin*; W. D. Arnold, *Oakfield*; R. D. Gibney, *My Escape from the Mutinies in Oude*; John Lang *The Wetherbys–Father and Son*. Gibney's book is sometimes listed as a historical source: it is only a novel, with a Mutiny episode tacked on at the end, but published in 1858 it takes rank as the earliest Mutiny novel, instead of Edward Money's *Wife and Ward* (1859).

8 This is the form of the famous couplet attributed to the King of Delhi as printed in W. Muir, *Indian Mutiny 1857, N.W.P. Intelligence Records*, vol. I, p. 454, from a letter written in August 1857 by H. H. Greathed. Other less convincing forms are in Sir Thomas Seaton, *op. cit.*

vol. II, p. 197 and in Flora Annie Steele, *On the Face of the Waters*, p. 221. It may be that a number of couplets on this theme circulated in Delhi in 1857 and were attributed to the poet-king, without any of them having really been his composition.

CHAPTER 2, pp. 8–20

1 *History of the Delhi Massacre*, etc., by a Lady, the wife of an officer in the Bengal Army and a sufferer during the late tragedy (Liverpool, 1858). Though she conceals her name on the title-page, the writer turns out from the text to be Mrs Peile, the wife of Lieutenant Peile of the 38th N.I. She escaped with Dr and Mrs Wood (he the surgeon of the 38th), enduring many hardships especially because Wood had been badly wounded in the face. Peile, after seeing his wife and the Woods on the road, rather heroically went back with Major Paterson of the 54th N.I. to try and rally their men to duty; it is pleasant to know that both were seen off then by their men uninjured and rejoined Mrs Peile's party just before their ultimate rescue.

2 On the mechanism of firearms, make-up of cartridges, and development of types of weapons, as briefly now described, see H. B. C. Pollard, *History of Firearms* (1926) and W. G. Carman, *History of Firearms* (1955).

3 Young, *Arsenals and Manufactories of the East India Company*. The magazine at Delhi heroically but imperfectly blown up on 11 May 1857 was an expense magazine. The main stock of powder at Delhi was in a storage magazine about four miles up the Jumna which was plundered by mutineers and villagers.

4 Kaye, *Sepoy War*, vol. I, p. 520, footnote.

5 Kaye always so describes it, and borrows the expression from official documents: for instance, it is used in the 1847 order concerning patches which is referred to below.

6 For the use of the Minié rifle on the Peshawar Frontier, see telegram of 28 January 1857 from the Adjutant-General, *Parliamentary Papers*, XXX (1857), p. 47. These will be cited as *P.P.* The volume and page numeration are as in the State Papers Room at the British Museum.

7 H. H. Greathed, *Letters written during the Siege of Delhi*, p. 105, chances to record the capture of a Minié carbine from a mutineer of the 8th Cavalry, meaning the 8th Irregular Cavalry which was one of the Bareli regiments. For the organisation of the skirmishers, see Sir H. Gough, *Old Memories*, p. 10.

8 For an exact description with diagrams of the Minié bullet, see Colonel (Sir G.) Chesney, *Observations on Firearms*, p. 268.

9 The history of this consignment is given in detail by Kaye, *Sepoy War*, vol. I, pp. 516–18. Its return to England is recorded in a document which is unprinted but is in the Military Consultations in the India Office Library: it is headed Military Dept., Separate, Fort William, no. 160 of 1855, dated 13 July 1855. This document will be referred to again.

10 Kaye's account is in *Sepoy War*, vol. I, pp. 512–20: but it is mixed up with the narrative of events and leaves the reader a little confused.

11 Kaye, *Sepoy War*, vol. I, p. 518, and Appendix, pp. 655–6.

12 See above, note 9.

13 Six copies of this revised Platoon Exercise were sent home with the despatch of 8 April 1857 mentioned below, note 31, and one of them will be found attached to the record copy of the despatch in the India Office under the reference below given.

14 Inspector-General of Ordnance to Adjutant-General, 28 January 1857 'the composition used to grease patches of rifle balls is said not to last well but fresh grease can at any time be applied' (*P.P.* xxx, 1857, p. 40): Inspector-General of Ordnance to Secretary to Government of India, 29 January 1857, 'The patch mixture would not answer for bundled cartridges but answers well for patches of detached balls to which it is applied when the balls are about to be used.' Does he mean that it is still being applied in practice, or that, in theory, it answers the purpose when applied in this way? See also Abbott's other note to the Deputy Adjutant-General at Barrackpore in Forrest, *Selections*, vol. I, pp. 3–4 (below, note 17).

15 Kaye, *Sepoy War*, vol. I, p. 656, p. 513 (for the identity of the officer).

16 This again is brought out in the January 1857 correspondence referred to above, note 14.

17 For these Courts of Inquiry, see *P.P.* xxx, 1857 and Sir George W. Forrest, *Selections from the Letters, Despatches and other State Papers preserved by the Military Department of the Government of India 1857–58*, vol. I. Forrest's collection will be cited as Forrest, *Selections*.

18 Telegram from Adjutant-General to Secretary to Government of India 18 January 1857 (*P.P.* xxx, 1857, p. 47).

19 Kaye, *Sepoy War*, vol. I, p. 516, footnote.

20 Lt.-Col. Lewis Butler, *Annals of the King's Royal Rifles*, vol. III, pp. 15, 88. Kaye says the issue was in 1856 (*Sepoy War*, vol. I, p. 518) but this is not quite accurate.

21 Captain Martineau's evidence at the *Trial of the ex-King of Delhi* (*Selections from Records of the Punjab and its Dependencies*, n.s. no. VII), p. 156.

22 Captain Martineau's evidence, *Trial*, p. 157.

23 Lt.-Col. Lewis Butler, *Annals of the King's Royal Rifles*, vol. III, p. 88.

24 Kaye, *Sepoy War*, vol. I, p. 515.

25 *P.P.* xxx, 1857, pp. 35–6; Forrest, *Selections*, vol. I, p. 3; Kaye, *Sepoy War*, vol. I, p. 490.

26 Forrest, *Selections*, p. 25; Letter to Colonel Birch, dated 17 February.

27 Hearsey's report, enclosing Wright's and Bontein's, and Abbott's note to the Deputy Adjutant-General, are the opening documents in Forrest, *Selections*, vol. I, pp. 1–4. Hearsey speaks of ingredients 'for the preparation of the bullet-patch' but this is inconsistent with the drill. Some (older) officers were perhaps using language to which they had grown accustomed earlier, without allowing for the current changes in the make-up of ammunition. Abbot correctly says 'one end of each cartridge (that which contains the ball) is greasy'.

28 *P.P.* xxx, 1857, pp. 35–9, 47; Kaye, *Sepoy War*, vol. 1, pp. 509–15 and see note 18 above.

29 For Bontein's letter, see Forrest, *Selections*, vol. 1, pp. 36–8.

30 For Anson's proceedings at Ambala, see Kaye, *Sepoy War*, vol. 1, pp. 552–9, and his letter to Canning in a footnote on p. 558.

31 The copy despatch of 8 April (Military Letter from Fort William, 8 April 1857, no. 115) and the annexed copy of the Platoon Exercise are in the India Office Records, Bengal Military Letters and Enclosures, vol. 147, 1857, nos. 99–134.

32 Kaye, *Sepoy War*, vol. 1, p. 561. See also note 13 above.

33 The letter of 13 April, as sent to General Hearsey at Dum-Dum, is printed by Kaye, *Sepoy War*, vol. 1, p. 561. As regards the removal of objections by the revised drill, it is somewhat curious that the possibility of pollution by the fingers never seems to be envisaged. Fanny Parkes, *Wanderings of a Pilgrim, etc.*, vol. 1, p. 109 mentions the objection of her servants to *handling* a candle which they thought was composed of pork fat.

34 See Captain Martineau's evidence in *Trial of the ex-King of Delhi*, p. 157.

CHAPTER 3, pp. 21–33

1 The Presidency Division was a military formation, with head-quarters at Barrackpore: the headquarters of the other military divisions east of Delhi were Dinapore, Benares, Cawnpore and Meerut. The Civil Divisions (Agra Division, Meerut Division, etc.) were superior groups of Districts created in 1829. Military and Civil Divisions do not correspond.

2 Kaye, *Sepoy War*, vol. 1, p. 519; T. R. E. Holmes, *History of the Indian Mutiny*, 5th ed., 1898, p. 80.

3 See above, chapter 2, note 27.

4 *Ibid.*

5 Forrest, *Selections*, vol. 1, p. 4.

6 Mainodin in C. T. Metcalfe, *Two Native Narratives, etc.*, p. 38.

7 Forrest, *Selections*, vol. 1, p. 6.

8 For this Court of Inquiry see Forrest, *Selections*, vol. 1, pp. 7–14. The seventh witness mentions the magazine *khalāsis*.

9 Lt.-Col. Wheeler was an intensely Evangelical officer who regarded it as a duty to preach Christianity to his men. See his well-known declaration and defence of his conduct in *P.P.* xxx, 1857.

10 Forrest, *Selections*, vol. 1, pp. 17–24. The four N.I. regiments at Barrackpore were the 2nd, 34th, 43rd and 70th.

11 Major-General J. B. Hearsey had a good command of the language but he was not, as seems sometimes to be suggested, himself of mixed blood. His father, Andrew Wilson Hearsey, was an officer of the Bengal Army: both he and his wife, whom he married in England, seem to have been (pure) English, and Major-General Hearsey was born of this marriage. Previously, it is said that Andrew Wilson Hearsey had had a native connection in India and from this union there was a son, generally known as

Hyder Young (or Jung) Hearsey, the companion of Moorcroft in his Nepalese and Tibetan travels. H. Y. Hearsey, of half-blood, himself married an Indian wife and one of their daughters became the wife of Major-General J. B. Hearsey, so that the latter's sons were of mixed blood. That is the descent as given in Hodson, vol. 2 and vol. 4. It makes J. B. Hearsey marry his niece, which is most extraordinary: in his own memoir, printed fully in Lt.-Col. H. Pearse, *The Hearseys*, J. B. Hearsey always calls H. Y. Hearsey merely 'my kinsman'. Perhaps the true relationship was hidden from him or perhaps it is not so certain as Hodson states.

12 The exact sequence of the following events is probably not without importance but it is not always set out in clear order nor is it easy to disentangle from the documents in *P.P.* xxx, 1857 or Forrest, *Selections*, vol. 1. This is the reason for now setting it out in some detail: the Berhampore affair is of special importance for the purposes of comparison with the Meerut outbreak.

13 For date of arrival at Berhampore and nature of stores cf. Forrest, *Selections*, vol. 1, pp. 43, 63, 70 and 85. Colonel Mitchell records that the escorting guard was of the 65th N.I. *ibid.* Appendix p. xii, but that was not one of the regiments at Barrackpore: one wonders whether it is a mistake for a party of the 63rd, which was with the Sonthal Field Force at Suri, *ibid.* p. 6, and Appendix B, pp. xviiia to xxiv.

14 Forrest, *Selections*, vol. 1, p. 39. A *cossid* (*kāsid*) was a private postrunner, as opposed to the dāk-runners of the Government Post Office.

15 *Ibid.* pp. 39–40.

16 Forrest, *Selections*, vol. 1, Appendix, p. xii.

17 *Ibid.* p. 41.

18 *Ibid.* p. 79.

19 Apart from official records which would establish this, the fact was recalled in D.O. letter of 11 March to Colonel Birch (*Kaye Papers*, HM 724A, no. 2, List of D.O. correspondence connected with the mutiny and disbandment of the 19th N.I.) and it was also remembered by Indians, for it is mentioned by Mainodin (C. T. Metcalfe, *Two Native Narratives*, p. 37).

20 Forrest, *Selections*, vol. 1, pp. 41 and 57. This and the following references are to the evidence of various witnesses at the ensuing Court of Inquiry.

21 *Ibid.* p. 62.

22 *Ibid.* pp. 48, 51, 53, 57.

23 *Ibid.* pp. 53, 57.

24 For the Subadār-Major's detailed and important account, Forrest, *Selections*, vol. 1, pp. 62–5

25 *Ibid.* pp. 52, 58, 67, 69, 71, 79, 81.

26 *Ibid.* pp. 68, 74, 75, 77, 78. The meeting would have been a breach of regulations.

27 *Ibid.* pp. 41, 48.

28 *Ibid.* p. 41.

29 *Ibid.* pp. 53, 63.

30 *Ibid.* p. 53.

31 *Ibid.* p. 41.

32 *Ibid.* p. 48. Mitchell merely says he ordered a general parade, *ibid.* p. 41, but his actual orders as recorded in the Adjutant's evidence have a different significance. The native infantry lines were a mile and a half, the native cavalry lines four miles, from the Square, which comprised the European barracks and parade ground. There is a description of the topography of Berhampore in *Memoirs of a Cadet by a Bengalee* (Albert Fenton) which much helps to understand the incidents of this night.

33 Writing on 28 February to the D.A.A.-G. at Barrackpore, Mitchell himself says that he is not entering his letter in the letter book, 'as the contents would soon be spread over the lines'. The same is undoubtedly true of a verbal order to the Adjutant, which would be overheard or would become known in course of transmission or after its receipt by Alexander : for the latter would have had at once to issue his own orders for his regiment to parade, and even if he did not mention where they were to be taken the object of the message and of his orders would be guessed.

34 For the events of the night of the 26th–27th, the parade of the 27th, the state of things on the night of the 27th–28th, see Forrest, *Selections*, vol. I, pp. 41–4, 48–50, 62–5. For the sepoys' petition, *ibid.* pp. 45–7.

35 The proceedings of the Court of Inquiry are in Forrest, *Selections*, vol. I, pp. 47–81, interspersed with letters from Mitchell defending himself against allegations in the evidence. In his unpublished diary, William Waterfield, B.C.S., then posted at Berhampore, remarks that the Colonel seems to have acted unwisely, taking the cavalry and guns to enforce orders and yet not enforcing them. I am afraid this is too narrow and stringent a view : it is perhaps the case that Mitchell, by yielding, postponed the general outbreak until it was brought on by the events at Meerut in May.

36 It may not be amiss to mention that in Hindustani *do* is two and there is a special word *dhāi* for two and a half.

37 Forrest, *Selections*, vol. I, pp. 43, 63, 77. For size, *ibid.* p. 55. A D.O. letter of 13 February 1857, *Kaye Papers*, HM 724A, no. 2, List of D.O. Correspondence, stated that Dr Macnamara might be right in saying there was no grease in the cartridge paper but 'the other gentlemen' were right in saying that it contained gelatine. For Bontein's evidence and manufacture at Serampore, Forrest, *Selections* App. D, p. lxiii, and *ibid.* p. 91.

38 *Ibid.* pp. 50, 53, 55, 57 and 76.

39 *Ibid.* pp. 87–94 (Minute of G.G. in Council), p. 86 (departure), p. 99 (arrival). In his unpublished diary William Waterfield states that they were replaced by the 63rd N.I. from Suri which refused to march unless all eight companies marched together (two had presumably been detached to Raniganj) and did not arrive until 8 April.

40 The same pattern, or elements of it, appeared in other cases : Nasirabad is a good example (Iltudus Pritchard, *Mutinies in Rajputana*). The panic aspect, understressed in older histories, is well brought out by S. N. Sen, *Eighteen Fifty-seven*, but sometimes (as at Meerut) with too innocent a construction.

41 At Berhampore, it is the alleged panchāyat which comes in question here. At Meerut, the development of events itself betrays the existence of some persons who formed and guided their plan. Perhaps both Mitchell at Berhampore and Carmichael-Smyth at Meerut decided to bring matters to a test.

42 Forrest, *Selections*, vol. I, App. D.

43 *Ibid.* App. C.

44 Forrest, *Selections*, vol. I, pp. 81–3 for Hearsey's second address.

45 *Ibid.* pp. 87–94.

46 *Ibid.* pp. 94–8.

47 *Ibid.* pp. 113–27, 128–31, 132–60 for the proceedings of the court-martial, of a board, and of a court of inquiry, relating to the affair of Mangal Pande.

48 *Ibid.* pp. 109–12 for Hearsey's own account.

49 *Ibid.* pp. 123, 124, 134, 191. The Muhammadan N.C.O. who helped Baugh and Hewson is the main witness for the mutineers' words.

50 *Ibid.* pp. 119–24. His term of abuse, *bhainchutes*, seems to accuse them of incest.

51 *Ibid.* p. 108.

52 *Ibid.* pp. 161–74.

53 See the tables for this regiment, Forrest, *Selections*, vol. I, pp. 176–7. Only about half the regiment was actually at Barrackpore. Most of the right wing was on detachment at Chittagong, whence later on (which does not mean much) they sent professions of loyalty: *ibid.* p. 175.

54 William Waterfield at Berhampore thought that the 34th was much worse than the 19th. George Harvey at Agra had some theory that the 34th were the originators of the whole trouble: they had previously been a local corps, the Bundelkhand Legion, which may account for their mixed composition. As has been seen in chapter 1, Harvey thought the chapātīs had started from Bundelkhand.

55 Forrest, *Selections*, vol. I, pp. 100–2.

56 *Ibid.* p. 100, App. A, pp. i–xviii.

57 Court-martial on Mangal Pande, *ibid.* p. 113; it was the same court as had tried the two men of the 2nd N.I. for the attempt to seduce the Mint guard. Court-martial on Issurī Pande, *ibid.* pp. 177–207. Disbandment of 34th N.I. *ibid.* pp. 212–26. William Waterfield was told by Lieutenant Vallings of the 19th N.I. that these executions had 'a very good effect'.

58 Subadār Sitaram, *op. cit.* p. 113.

59 Sir Syed Ahmed Khan, *op. cit.* p. 51.

60 For the letter of 13 April from Colonel Chester to Major-General Hearsey, see above, chapter 2, note 33.

61 Septimus Harding Becher was the younger brother of the then Quartermaster-General, Colonel A. M. Becher (of whom some contemporaries at the siege of Delhi, as H. H. Greathed, hold an unfavourable opinion). They were members of one of the greatest Anglo-Indian clans: see Sir W. W. Hunter, *The Thackerays in India* and Major V. C. P. Hodson, *List of Officers of the Bengal Army 1758–1834*, vol. I, pp. 114, 118.

Martineau was an officer of the 10th N.I., then stationed at Fatehgarh, where its mutiny produced, directly or indirectly, one of the worst catastrophes in regard to loss of English lives: in his letter next quoted, Martineau mentions his eagerness to get back to his regiment, because he thought he had influence with the men, but fortunately for him he did not do so.

62 Becher's original letters and the copy of Martineau's letter are in the *Kaye Papers*, HM 725, no. 35. They were given to Kaye by Martineau but Kaye could not so soon after the events publish this remarkable letter, which has not hitherto been printed.

CHAPTER 4, pp. 34–46

1 Meerut had been the headquarters of the Bengal Regiment of Horse Artillery for some time; see Thomas Bacon, *First Impressions, etc.*, referring to the middle thirties of the century. The Headquarters of the entire Bengal Corps of Artillery had recently been transferred to Meerut from Dum-Dum.

2 For the 60th Q.R.R. at Meerut, see Lt.-Col. Lewis Butler, *Annals of the K.R.R.*, vol. III, pp. 87–8.

3 Dan O'Callaghan, *Scattered Chapters of the Indian Mutiny: The Fatal Falter at Meerut*, p. 3. O'Callaghan was the Surgeon of the 11th N.I., one of the regiments at Meerut (as to which see below), and it is to be supposed that these figures were obtained by enquiry from the Adjutants of the regiments concerned soon after the outbreak.

4 Captain A. Sprot, *A Continuation of the Historical Records of the Carabiniers (1839–1888)*, pp. 9–11. The spelling 'Carabineers' is used by most writers, but I adopt 'Carabiniers' from Sprot and the regimental badge. This was the regiment in which Roger Tichborne served and Colonel Custance, in command on 10 May, later gave evidence recognising the Claimant: D. Woodruff, *The Tichborne Case*, p. 177.

5 O'Callaghan, *op. cit.* p. 4.

6 Captain H. L. Nevill, *Campaigns on the North-West Frontier*, p. 28.

7 Iltudus Pritchard, *The Mutinies in Rajputana*; O'Callaghan, *op. cit.* p. 3.

8 The 1/5th of 1796 included, if its history is traced, the 5th Battalion of 1764 which had formed part of the 'detachment' that marched across India in the first Mahratta War under Leslie and then under Goddard, and in virtue of this descent the 11th N.I. bore the battle honour 'Guzerat'. The 20th N.I. served in the second Sikh War and bore the battle honour 'Gujpat'. Two similar names but two very different honours.

9 O'Callaghan, *op. cit.* p. 3. An anonymous correspondent in *The Lahore Chronicle* of 22 July 1857 says Hewitt disposed of 1800 men, well short of O'Callaghan's reckoning.

10 Lt.-Col. G. M. Carmichael-Smyth, *Mutiny of the 3rd Light Cavalry at Meerut* in N. A. Chick, *Annals of the Indian Rebellion*, p. 90: this will be referred to in future as 'Smyth's *Account*'.

11 The senior officer present with the 20th N.I. was a Brevet Major with the substantive rank of Captain. The regiments of the Bengal Army were mostly under-officered on account of furlough, local leave, and above all, extra regimental appointments (with the Irregular Cavalry, the contingents maintained by Indian States, the Public Works Department—mainly engineers—the Survey Department, the foreign service at the courts of Indian States, and even the civil administration). The officers scarcely troubled to learn the languages except as a stepping-stone to an extra regimental appointment and communicated with their men through the native officers: the result was blind ignorance of their men's feelings. Regimental service had grown sour and dull though there were many honourable and sound regimental officers such as we meet in the autobiography of Sir Thomas Seaton, *From Cadet to Colonel*. For the most part 'the European subaltern officer looks upon the performance of regimental duty as a task, irksome, if not humiliating', J. S. Hodgson, *Musings on Military Matters* (Meerut, 1851), re-issued as *Opinions on the Indian Army* (London, 1857). Taking only the Native Infantry and Light Cavalry regiments, probably about one third of the officers were absent at any given time on furlough, local leave, and appointments.

12 In the case of every Bengal Army officer mentioned in these pages, the source of the details of age, arrival in India, active service, furlough, and career in general is Major V. C. P. Hodson, *List of Officers of the Bengal Army 1758–1834* cited henceforth as 'Hodson'.

13 Lord Roberts, *Forty-one Years in India*, mentions that his father left Peshawar on 27 November 1853. For Hewitt's feebleness and fondness for the table, O'Callaghan, *Fatal Falter at Meerut*; for his inspections at Moradabad and Delhi, *The Delhi Gazette*, for his bearing at the funeral of the victims, *The Mofussilite*, 15 May 1857.

14 Norman, *Narrative of the Siege of Delhi*, printed separately, and also in Forrest, *Selections*, vol. I and in H. C. Fanshawe, *Delhi Past and Present*. The officers passed over in Wilson's favour were Colonel Congreve, Acting Adjutant-General of Queen's Troops, Colonel Graves (previously station commander at Delhi on 11 May), and Colonel Longfield, of whom the first two left the Delhi Field Force when Wilson was promoted over their heads (see Lord Roberts, *Forty-one Years in India*, vol. I, p. 198).

15 Lord Roberts, *op cit.* pp. 235–40; Griffiths, *Narrative of the Siege of Delhi*, p. 177; Wilberforce, *An Unrecorded Chapter of the Indian Mutiny*, p. 168 (the brandy incident).

16 H. H. Greathed, *Letters Written during the Siege of Delhi*.

17 A copy of Wilson's letter to Hewitt is among the *Kaye Papers* in the India Office, HM 726, no. 21, p. 860.

18 Wilson's explanation in Forrest, *Selections*, vol. I, pp. 260–2.

19 For this incident see the letter from Lt.-Col. Le Champion printed in Kaye, *Sepoy War*, vol. III, App. pp. 679–81. The writer of this letter was in 1857 Lieutenant Henry Möller (thus he is named in the *East India Register*) of the 11th N.I. He bore (or later assumed) the middle name Le Champion, entered the Queen's service, and dropped the Möller, thus ending up as Lt.-Col. Le Champion of H.M. 101st Foot. Colonel A. R. D. Mackenzie, *Mutiny Memoirs*, pp. 44–6, is also unflattering about Wilson.

20 Apart from the notices in Hodson under the various names, most of the details concerning various members of the Carmichael-Smyth family come from the *Scots Peerage*, vol. IV, pp. 568–72, and the articles in the *D.N.B.* on Thomas Carmichael, James Carmichael-Smyth (the elder), and Alexander Monro (*tertius*). The eldest son of James Carmichael-Smyth the elder was another James who had a career in the British Army, obtained a baronetcy, and held two colonial governorships, but his career is irrelevant to the subject of this book.

21 The second son of James Carmichael-Smyth, William Henry, came to India in 1797, had a distinguished and varied career in the Bengal Artillery, returned home in 1820 and was the first Resident Superintendent of Addiscombe College from 1822–24 (Vibart, *History of Addiscombe College*). He married the widowed mother of William Makepeace Thackeray and the novelist became his affectionate stepson. He is perhaps part of Colonel Newcome (cf. Elwin's *Thackeray*). The next son, Charles Montauban dropped the Smyth (and therefore figures in vol. I of Hodson, while G. M. Carmichael-Smyth figures in vol. IV): he had long service in the Irregular Cavalry and finished as a Major-General. The fourth son entered the Bengal Civil Service, and the sixth, doing likewise, became a Judge of the Supreme Court at Calcutta (he again dropped the Smyth). The last-mentioned had three sons, one of whom became Commissioner of Benares, one a Member of Council in Madras, and another entered the British Army (32nd Foot) and is once referred to by his uncle, G. M. Carmichael-Smyth, as 'my nephew, Colonel Carmichael'. The daughter of the Madras Member of Council married Sir Curzon Wyllie (shot by an Indian terrorist outside the Imperial Institute in 1919). G. M. Carmichael-Smyth had also two sisters. The younger of these married Lt.-Col. William Forrest of the Bengal Army, but I have not traced any of her issue who came to India. The elder sister married Alexander Monro, third of his name to hold in succession the Chair of Anatomy at Edinburgh: their grandsons were General Sir Charles Carmichael Monro who conducted the evacuation of the Dardanelles and later became Commander-in-Chief in India and Alexander Monro who did well in the Indian Education Service. This Alexander had a son, also Alexander Monro, who served in the I.C.S. in the United Provinces and retired in 1939. Thus the family's span in India is from 1797 to 1939.

22 For these sets of famous Anglo-Indian families see *In the Company's Service: A Reminiscence* (anonymous but by Octavius Sturges of the Bombay Artillery, 1852–7), p. 88 and Rudyard Kipling, *The Tomb of his Ancestors* in *The Day's Work*. It will be noticed that the Plowdens figure in both lists and a Plowden who signed a letter to *The Times* in the issue of 23 September 1959 was the fourth in his direct male line to serve in India. Sturges' 'Melvilles' should be 'Melvill' without the 'e': the same mistake was made by the late Sir Reginald Coupland in his book on Isandlhwana, where one of them won the V.C. Sir James Cosmo Melvill was the last General Secretary of the H.E.I.C., one of his brothers Canon Henry Melvill the last Principal of old Haileybury College. Another brother, Sir Peter Melvill Melvill (of whom the present writer is a great-grandson) had a long career in the Bombay Army and became Military Secretary to the Governor of Bombay: he was nominated by Lord Falkland to be Commissioner of Sind but this was overruled by the Bombay Council who insisted that the appointment must go to a civilian, whereupon Bartle Frere received the post, which again was resented by the Council because of his junior status (see Martineau, *Life of Sir Bartle Frere*, vol. I, p. 83).

23 Hodson, vol. IV, and *The Scots Peerage, ubi supra*, supply all these details between them.

24 Merivale, *Life of Sir H. Lawrence*, vol. I, p. 441.

25 Gardiner disappeared after the Sikh Wars and re-appeared in 1851 in the service of the last of the Dogra brothers, Gulab Singh, Maharaja of Jammu and Kashmir. He lived on in Kashmir until 1877 and in old age used to purvey to visitors fantastic tales of his early career (perhaps borrowed from the experiences of some of his fellow adventurers in the Punjab). These deceived such listeners as Henry Durand and Richard Temple, who should have known better, and were collected in a later biography by Colonel H. Pearse (author of a useful book on the Hearsey family). Early in his career with the Sikhs, Gardiner made a journey across the Karakoram to Yarkand and back: he may have been the first European to cross the Burzil Pass and he came back by way of Chitral. For his career see C. Grey and H. L. Garrett, *European Adventurers in Northern India*, pp. 265–91. The journal of the Central Asian journey was published in *Journal of the Asiatic Society of Bengal*, vol. XXII, 1853, pp. 284 ff. The name is there spelt Gardner, as by Pearse also. The exploit, however, is ignored both by Pearse as by Grey and Garrett: it is noticed by Prof. Kenneth Mason, *Abode of Snow*, p. 69, who draws on G. Dainelli, *La Esplorazione della regione fra l'Himalaja occidentale e il Caracorum*, pp. 34 ff. (in *Spedizione italiana de Filippi*, Serie II, vol. I). Mason alleges the crossing of the Burzil and does not mention the return via Chitral: Dainelli holds the route to Gilgit to be uncertain and gives the return as via Kafiristan and Chitral.

26 The many-sided activities (at Meerut) of 'the gallant Captain Wetherby', including the composition of a tribute to himself in the local paper on his departure, are amusingly recounted in John Lang, *The Wetherbys—Father and Son* (1853). Sometimes compared to Kipling, Lang is much less sentimental and a fiercer and more amusing writer: they differ rather as *Punch* in 1850 from *Punch* in 1910.

27 This is Smyth's *Account*, see chapter 4, note 10, above.

28 *Memorandum, or, a few words on the Mutiny*, by Lt.-Col. G. Carmichael-Smyth, Bengal Light Cavalry. There are two copies in the British Museum.

29 T. R. E. Holmes, *History of the Indian Mutiny*, 5th edn, 1898, App. W.p. 637.

30 Kaye, *Sepoy War*, vol. II, p. 47.

31 Smyth's *Account* preserves these letters: see chapter 6 below.

32 Forrest, *Selections*, vol. I, pp. 228, 246.

33 The letter chances to be preserved in Charles Ball, *History of the Indian Mutiny* (1858), vol. I, pp. 60 ff.: it is printed with the names blank, but the authorship is not in doubt.

34 See chapter 6 below.

35 *Reports on Cholera in Meerut, Rohilcund and Ajmere Divisions in 1856* (Agra, 1857), p. 23.

36 H. H. Greathed, *Letters written during the Siege of Delhi*; Blunt's retirement is recorded in the *East India Register* for 1858; for Dunlop, Johnston and Turnbull, see Dunlop, *Service and Adventures with the Khaki Ressalah*. The earliest District Officer's report on which the Meerut Section in the *Meerut District Narrative* was based was dated 11 July 1857.

CHAPTER 5, pp. 47–57

1 The descriptions in the standard histories are inadequate: they are in places confused and even inaccurate. Those of Kaye and Forrest, so far as they go, are the better.

2 Mrs Muter, *Travels, etc. in India, China and New Zealand* (1864) and *My Recollections of the Sepoy Revolt* (1911); Surgeon O'Callaghan, *The Fatal Falter at Meerut*; N. A. Chick, *Annals of the Indian Rebellion*, pp. 97–8; *Description of the Cantonment of Meerut*; Minturn, *From New York to Delhi*, pp. 181–2; Thomas Bacon, *First Impressions and Studies from Nature in Hindustan*.

3 This sketch map is among the *Kaye Papers* in the India Office, HM 724A, no. 38, p. 549.

4 A copy of this map is in the India Office, endorsed S.II.C. It is entered on p. 149 of the Map Catalogue of 1878. There is no copy in the British Museum.

5 Copies of both editions of this map are in the India Office and the British Museum: unfortunately, in 1959, the India Office copy of the larger scale edition could not be located. There is a map in Mrs Muter's book of 1911 (above, note 2), marked as of 1857: but it is really (from internal evidence) a map of much later date.

6 The first word is spelt Aboo on old maps and by contemporary writers.

7 This detail comes from Lieutenant Jones' sketch, above, note 3.

8 This word has in Urdu a meaning which is represented in the science of fortification by the word 'Cavalier', an enclosed, isolated structure higher than its neighbours as part of a fortress.

9 Chick, *ubi supra*, p. 98.

10 Cf. the letter in *The Lahore Chronicle*, 22 July 1857, cited above chapter 4, note 9.

11 It is not quite certain that this bridge existed in 1857 but it seems very likely to be the bridge over which Craigie and his party made their escape in the night of 10 May (Colonel A. R. D. Mackenzie, *Mutiny Memoirs*, p. 28).

12 Probably so called because Dragoon regiments had occupied the European cavalry lines through much of their existence: the 8th Light Dragoons before 1820, the 11th Light Dragoons (which became in 1840 the 11th Hussars) from 1820–6 and 1832–7.

13 This bridge is the 'wooden bridge' mentioned in the *Meerut Depositions*, nos. 29 and 44, and the 'plank bridge' marked on the 1867 map. Thornton, *Gazetteer of India*, 1854, vol. IV, p. 449, mentions only the Dragoon Bridge and the Begum's Bridge, which were pukka: but there were certainly some other bridges, of stone or wood, in 1857.

14 To be strictly accurate, there were two roads which forked from the eastern end of the Mall and both led to Garhmukhteshwar, i.e. they reunited later on. The road meant in the text, and which matters for present purposes, is the one nearer to the nullah.

15 The distances given in this and other paragraphs have to be approximate or indefinite because the layout was not regular and one cannot measure from one precise point to another. Moreover, the two western projections did not actually join on to the extremities of the main block or area, but there was a gap at the angle.

16 The New Jail is marked on the 1860 map. For date of construction and capacity, see Murray's *Handbook of India*, 1898, p. 193. For variety of names cf. *Meerut District Narrative*, paras. 159, 168; *Meerut Depositions*, nos. 12 and 21; Williams, *Memorandum* (below, note 18) p. 5.

17 For the probable location of the Old Jail cf. *Meerut District Narrative*, paras. 171, 172; *Meerut Depositions*, nos. 4, 21, 22, 32, 37, 50, 57, 61, 62 and 72. For its capacity, see *Reports on Cholera in the Meerut, Rohilcund and Ajmere Divisions in the Year 1856* (Agra, 1857), p. 20.

18 Major G. W. Williams was the Superintendent of the Cantonment Police as well as being on special duty for dacoity and thagī: on 10 May he was away at Mussoorie writing a report on his latter duties (see his *Narrative* about to be mentioned). After the Mutiny, he was deputed to enquire into the conduct of the police force at Meerut on 10 May. The outcome of this enquiry was the *Meerut Depositions*, frequently mentioned already and many times to be mentioned again: they are the depositions which Williams took from a large number of witnesses as to the events of the evening and night of 10 May. Williams prefixed to the *Meerut Depositions* the *Memorandum* by himself, which is referred to as Williams, *Memorandum*, analysing the *Meerut Depositions* and drawing his conclusions (not to be accepted unreservedly). He also wrote a narrative of his Mutiny experiences (to which I refer as Williams, *Narrative*), dealing mainly with his experiences in the months subsequent to May 1857 but containing one or two points relevant to the Meerut outbreak: a copy of this is in the *Kaye Papers* in the India Office, HM 727, no. 4, p. 735.

19 *Meerut District Narrative*, para. 202; Thomas Bacon, *op. cit.* vol. I, pp. 336, 367; Thornton, *Gazetteer of India*, 1854, vol. IV, p. 450.

20 The absence of a club may come as a surprise, seeing what an essential institution of station life this was later in the nineteenth century. The history of the club among the English in India remains to be written. Clubs seem to have originated in the Presidency towns and then in hill stations: in both cases, they had the advantage over Assembly Rooms of providing quarters for members. The oldest club in Calcutta dated from the late eighteen-twenties, in Bombay from the eighteen-thirties. There seems to have been no club in Mussoorie in Thomas Bacon's time (about 1835) but there was one when John Lang was there in the early or middle eighteen-fifties and he says it had been founded eighteen years before (Thomas Bacon, *op. cit.* vol. II, chapter 4; John Lang, *Wanderings in India*, printed as a collection in 1859 but appearing earlier in *Household Words*, chapter 1). In the plains up-country, the club is perhaps mainly a post-Mutiny phenomenon, which writers of Mutiny novels should remember.

21 I have to thank the Secretary of the Church Missionary Society for answering an enquiry about this church and the clergymen in charge of it; for Mr Medland's narrative, see N. A. Chick, *Annals of the Indian Rebellion*, pp. 110–112.

22 It is so marked on the 1867 map and this position accords with the reference to it in the *Meerut Depositions*, nos. 29, 32, etc.

23 See Smyth's *Account*, p. 95.

24 See Williams, *Narrative* and *Meerut Depositions*, nos. 72 and 73.

25 See below, chapter 7 for the refugees in Carmichael-Smyth's compound; Mackenzie, *Mutiny Memoirs*, for Craigie's and his own and Mrs Chambers' bungalows; below, chapter 7, note 15 as to Whish's; *Meerut Depositions*, no. 32 (Captain Earle) for Eckford's and Surgeon Smith's bungalows.

26 The Rev. Thomas Cartright Smyth's account is in N. A. Chick, *Annals of the Indian Rebellion*, pp. 103–5.

27 Hewitt's despatch of 26 May in Forrest, *Selections*, vol. I, pp. 257–8.

28 For the telegram see *Punjab Historical Records*, vol. VII, part I, *Mutiny Correspondence*, p. 18.

29 The authentic story of the Delhi telegraph clerks is most easily found reprinted in Colonel E. Vibart, *The Sepoy Mutiny*, pp. 247–67. This identifies the location of the telegraph office which till 1856 had been within the city; H. P. Fanshawe, *Delhi Past and Present*, p. 75; Percival Spear, *The Twilight of the Moguls*, p. 147 seems to be in error on the point.

30 *An improved Map of British India and the coast of Burmah: including all...telegraphic...lines etc.* Thacker Spink & Co., 1857.

31 Mrs Muter, *op. cit.* p. 18; the Rev. T. C. Smyth's narrative in Chick, *ubi supra*, p. 103.

32 For information as to these times, I have to thank H.M. Nautical Almanac Office, Greenwich Observatory. Their precise calculation of the hour of sunset is that, taking Meerut at latitude 29° N., the hour was 6.41 p.m. with a possible error of a minute either way. The hours are of course given by the local time.

1 Forrest, *Selections*, vol. I, pp. 228, 242–5.

2 Greathed, among the civilians, was only just back from a tour on 9 May.

3 Forrest, *Selections*, vol. I, p. 228.

4 Smyth's *Account*, pp. 90–1; for the early break-up of the *mela*, Dundas Robertson, *District Duties during the Revolt in the N.W.P. of India*, p. 19.

5 For the fire on the 13th, *Meerut Depositions*, no. 11, footnote; for the fire on the 23rd, Smyth's *Narrative*, p. 91 and his evidence at the Court of Inquiry in Forrest, *Selections*, vol. I, p. 232; Brijmohan's caste, Kaye, *Sepoy War*, vol. II, p. 47. The man is never given the Singh except once in Carmichael-Smyth's evidence at the Court of Inquiry: but Kaye's evidence for his statements is not to be found in the *Kaye Papers* in the India Office.

6 Smyth's *Account*, p. 91 and his evidence at the Court of Inquiry, Forrest, *Selections*, vol. I, pp. 230–2.

7 Smyth's *Account*, p. 91, from which one would gather that the letter was written from Mussoorie: but he recorded in his broadsheet *Memorandum* that he wrote it from Meerut on 23 April. Curzon's reply, anodyne but significantly respectful, is in Chick, *Annals of the Indian Rebellion*, p. iv.

8 See note 6 above.

9 *Meerut Depositions*, nos. 12, 13 and 14.

10 Forrest, *Selections*, vol. I, p. 228.

11 *Ibid.* p. 246.

12 Smyth's *Account*, pp. 92–4; Mackenzie, *op. cit.* p. 33, calls Galway 'Galloway' but Galway was really his name as the *East India Register* shows. There was a famous Bengal officer, Major-General Sir Archibald Galloway, d. 1850, with whom Mackenzie may have confused the name.

13 For what occurred on the firing parade, see Smyth's evidence at the Court of Inquiry, Forrest, *Selections*, vol. I, pp. 230–2, and at the court-martial, *ibid.* vol. I, p. CXLIV, and Smyth's *Account*.

14 *Ibid.* pp. 231 and 239. If these numbers reflect the numbers in the regiment, it was made up of about five Muhammadans to four Hindus.

15 If the carbines were rifled, e.g. Minié carbines such as some regiments had, then the reason why these cartridges were *ungreased* is that they were blank, i.e. unballed.

16 Smyth's report to the Brigade-Major, Forrest, *Selections*, vol. I, p. 228.

17 Hewitt's letter to the Adjutant-General, *ibid.* p. 227.

18 There is a plethora of Joneses in the early story of the Mutiny. Another commanded the 60th at Meerut and a third commanded the 2nd column at the assault on Delhi. For Wilson's absence, see Major Campbell's letter, Forrest, *Selections*, vol. I, p. 241; he was back by 4 May, *ibid.* p. 243.

19 *Ibid.* pp. 227–9.

20 *Ibid.* pp. 230–7.

21 *Ibid.* pp. 237–40.

22 *Ibid.* pp. 240–5.

23 O'Callaghan, *Fatal Falter at Meerut*, p. 5.

24 Smyth's *Account*, p. 91.

25 See a message in *The Delhi Gazette* of 9 May 1857.

26 Forrest, *Selections*, vol. I, appendix E, pp. cxxxix–cxlvi, on which the following account is based. The original proceedings would have been available to Forrest if they had been extant.

27 *Ibid.* pp. cxliv–cxlv.

28 *Ibid.* pp. cxlv–cxlvi.

29 General Sir H. Gough, *Old Memories*, p. 17.

30 Mrs Muter, *My Recollections of the Sepoy Revolt*, p. 47; cf. also a message dated 9 May in *The Mofussilite* of 12 May.

31 Hewitt's letter, Forrest, *Selections*, vol. I, p. 247.

32 See telegram of 9 May from Officiating Magistrate at Meerut to Officiating Secretary to N.W.P. Government at Agra in *Kaye Papers*, HM 724A, p. 33. This also reports sentence. It is rather significant that the *civil* authorities were keeping each other informed: they must have been uneasy. Some writers criticise the use of a native guard: but as already mentioned *all* guard duties were normally undertaken by native troops, not by European, although over the night of 8/9 May the condemned men were under a European guard.

33 General Sir H. Gough, *Old Memories*, p. 19.

34 The document is in Forrest, *Selections*, vol. I, pp. cxlv–cxlvi.

35 Smyth's *Account*, p. 94.

CHAPTER 7, pp. 70–79

1 General Sir H. Gough, *Old Memories*, pp. 21–2; *Meerut Depositions*, nos. 4 and 5; Mrs Greathed's introduction to H. H. Greathed, *Letters written during the Siege of Delhi*, p. xiv. Gough's statement is vitally important. He must have told others at the time; Lord Roberts *Forty-one years in India*, p. 87 has the story before Gough's book appeared, which was only in 1897: Gough's book was therefore unknown to Kaye, but it ought to have been noticed (which it was not) by Rice Holmes, in his 5th edition published in 1898.

2 *Meerut Depositions*, nos. 33–6.

3 The Delhi telegraphists' own story was first published by P. V. Luke in *Macmillan's Magazine* for October 1897 and is reprinted in Colonel E. Vibart, *The Sepoy Mutiny* (1898), pp. 255–6. The Meerut–Aligarh–Agra line remained uncut till the evening.

4 The Rev. J. E. W. Rotton, *Chaplain's Narrative of the Siege of Delhi*, p. 3.

5 *Meerut Depositions*, no. 20.

6 *Ibid.* nos. 15, 18 and 19 for the outcry in the Sudder Bazar at about 5 p.m. and nos. 37 and 38 for Captain Macdonald's servants (nurse and washerman); nos. 30, 31 and 39 for later sound of firing or uproar; nos. 40–5 for the Artillerymen in the bazar, and cf. nos. 51 and 52.

7 *Ibid.* nos. 18, 19, 59, 62. No. 19 mentions the bazar was still quiet.

8 *Ibid.* no. 18.

9 Forrest, *Selections*, vol. I, p. 250.

10 Williams, *Memorandum* (prefixed to *Meerut Depositions*), p. 3.

11 Cook boys were menials employed to cook for, and wait on, European troops: they were no doubt mainly a poor type of Indian (Portuguese) Christian or other Eurasians, or very low caste Hindus.

12 N. A. Chick, *Annals of the Indian Rebellion*, pp. 115–17. The account in the text is based on this source unless some other reference is cited.

13 *Meerut Depositions*, nos. 37 and 38. These two servants of Macdonald did not know exactly what Chambers said to him.

14 *Ibid.* no. 19.

15 *Ibid.* nos. 18 and 19. It is evident from this incident that the Brigade-Major's bungalow or office was somewhere near the 20th N.I. lines: on the 1867 map, it is in quite a different position, up in the European lines.

16 Surgeon O'Callaghan, *A Medical Officer's Description of the outbreak at Meerut* in N. A. Chick, *Annals of the Indian Rebellion*, pp. 99–103. References to his movements in this and the following paragraphs are from this source unless otherwise stated.

17 *Meerut Depositions*, no. 15.

18 *Ibid.* no. 16.

19 *Ibid.* no. 17.

20 *Ibid.* no. 17.

21 *Ibid.* nos. 15 and 17.

22 *Ibid.* no. 17.

23 O'Callaghan, *ubi supra*, p. 100 and *Fatal Falter at Meerut*, pp. 22 for the officer's name.

24 O'Callaghan says by a sepoy of the 11th but he certainly means the 20th: the 11th had not yet seized their arms.

25 *Meerut Depositions*, nos. 15, 16 and 17.

26 Smyth's *Account*, p. 95; Le Champion's (Möller's) letter, Kaye, *Sepoy War*, vol. III, p. 680, for Warde's and Möller's actions.

27 *Meerut Depositions*, no. 19. Tregear's position is given by F. M. Sir Donald Stewart who mentions his bungalow was near the jail, probably the Old Jail; G. R. Elsmie, *F. M. Sir Donald Stewart*, p. 37.

28 *Ibid.* no. 19.

29 These details and the subsequent particulars of the officers' fates are taken from the account in Chick, *op. cit.* pp. 116–17, unless otherwise stated.

30 *Meerut Depositions*, no. 18.

31 *Ibid.* no. 19. These *Depositions* make it appear that the wounding of Henderson and Taylor happened before the officers left the lines, but the narrative in Chick shows that they were both among the six who got to Smyth's compound, and so they must have returned to the lines.

32 *Ibid.* no. 32. Captain Earle after describing his own adventures mentions where Taylor's body was found.

33 *Meerut District Narrative,* paras. 235, 236.

CHAPTER 8, pp. 80–87

1 *Meerut Depositions,* nos. 12 and 14. It is confirmed by Sir Donald Stewart, G. R. Elsmie, *F. M. Sir Donald Stewart,* p. 38.

2 *Ibid.* nos. 15–19. This order of events accords with the warning given to Gough the previous evening.

3 Colonel A. R. D. Mackenzie, *Mutiny Memoirs,* p. 12. In addition to swords, the men had pistols and carbines (the skirmishers, carbines), but whether these were not kept in bells of arms like infantry muskets is not clear. They may have been kept in the regimental magazine.

4 Smyth's *Account,* p. 94.

5 *Ibid.* pp. 94–5; Sir Hugh Gough, *Old Memories,* p. 42. The rum godown was probably the new rum godown in Clement Street behind the Artillery Mess.

6 O'Callaghan, *Fatal Falter at Meerut,* p. 20.

7 *Meerut Depositions,* nos. 12 and 14.

8 *Ibid.* nos. 5 and 73.

9 *Ibid.* no. 73.

10 *Ibid.* nos. 56 and 57. *Kambohs* are a good class agricultural caste in the North-West Provinces and there was a quarter where they lived to which this gate no doubt gave access.

11 The important evidence of the head jailer is in *Meerut Depositions,* no. 21. The '70 or 80 convicts in prison dress' of *Deposition* no. 56 seem to be the rescued sowars returning with their rescuers; cf. also *Deposition* no. 57. The story of the release of the other prisoners is undoubtedly due to confusion with the release by sepoys of the convicts in the *Old* Jail, mentioned in the next chapter.

12 Sir Hugh Gough, *Old Memories,* p. 25.

13 *Ibid.* pp. 28–9. He says his troop lines were the first on the right 'according to the number': but the letters of 27 April in Smyth's *Account* (above, chapter 6) show that his troop was the 2nd, Plowden's being the 1st. Perhaps Gough's own normal troop was the 1st (Plowden was a Major) and he was for some reason temporarily commanding the 2nd on 27 April.

14 *Ibid.* p. 31. Gough's memory for names is not always accurate. He calls Veterinary Surgeon Philips 'Parry' (*ibid.* p. 51). I think the true story of the Quartermaster-Sergeant is given by Mackenzie, see note 18 below: the N.C.O. in Gough's story was perhaps the Regimental Sergeant-Major.

15 *Ibid.* pp. 32–3, p. 38; Mrs Greathed's accounts in N. A. Chick, *Annals of the Indian Rebellion,* pp. 105–8, and in her introduction to H. H. Greathed, *Letters written during the Siege of Delhi.*

16 Colonel A. R. D. Mackenzie, *Mutiny Memoirs,* p. 8.

17 *Ibid.* p. 31.

18 *Ibid.* pp. 9–10, 29–30. Seeing that it was the bungalow of the Quartermaster-Sergeant which had been burnt down early in May (chapter 6, note 25 above), I think he must be the N.C.O. whom the sowars intended to kill and hence Mackenzie's account is here correct as against Gough's (note 14 above).

19 For the adventures of Craigie and Mackenzie, Mrs Craigie and Miss Mackenzie, see Mackenzie, *op. cit.* pp. 10–29 and the letter from Mrs Craigie which is printed in Charles Ball, *History of the Indian Mutiny*, vol. I, pp. 60–4.

20 The letter from Mrs Craigie says this incident occurred on the return journey: Mackenzie gives testimony that it happened on the way to the jail, which must be accepted. Mrs Craigie and also the Rev. A. Medland in N. A. Chick, *Annals of the Indian Rebellion*, p. 114, say that the woman was Mrs Courtney: but this does not square with the evidence about her death in *Meerut Depositions*, nos. 39 and 62, and Mackenzie does not state that it was she.

21 *Meerut Depositions*, no. 62, refers to the telegraph line being cut before 7 p.m. The matter will be further discussed in the next chapter.

22 *Meerut Depositions*, no. 14.

23 It happens that Fanny Parkes saw this regiment at the *Rām Līla* festival at Cawnpore about 1830 just after they had performed their annual *pūja* to their colours *Wanderings of a Pilgrim*, etc., vol. I, p. 109: whether the colours in 1857 were the same set as in 1829 or a later set, we do not know.

24 Mackenzie, *op. cit.* p. 33.

25 On this party, see below, chapter 10, note 26.

26 *Meerut District Narrative*, para. 170.

CHAPTER 9, pp. 88–96

1 *Meerut Depositions*, nos. 18 and 19.

2 N. A. Chick, *Annals of the Indian Rebellion*, p. 115.

3 The castes mentioned in this connection are butchers, *pulladars*, *khaticks*, weavers, *chamars*, *kahars*, *lodhas*, *duriewalas*, *koonjras*: servants (*khansamas*, *khidmutgars*, grass-cutters, *syces*) are also mentioned and sometimes Muhammadans generally. See *Meerut Depositions*, nos. 3, 5, 18, 19, 32, 55, 61, 67, 69. The deponents generally give pride of place to butchers and *pulladars*. For the various castes, see W. Crooke, *Tribes and Castes of the N.W.P. of India*. *Pulladars* are porters, *khaticks* cultivators and vegetable sellers connected with the strange Pāsī tribe, *chamars* leather workers, *kahars* palki-bearers, *lodhas* field labourers said to be of an uncouth type with aboriginal admixture, *duriewalas* weavers, *koonjras* greengrocers.

4 Colonel A. R. D. Mackenzie, *Mutiny Memoirs*, p. 22; *Meerut District Narrative*, para. 223; letter from Colonel Le Champion (Le Champion Möller), Kaye, *Sepoy War*, vol. III, p. 680.

5 For Mrs Macdonald's adventures and fate see *Meerut Depositions*, nos. 37 and 38.

6 For the Dawsons, see Mackenzie, *op. cit.* p. 23: he was serving with the Artillery, but their bungalow must have been in the native lines.

7 *Meerut Depositions*, no. 39.

8 Further account in N. A. Chick, *Annals of the Indian Rebellion*, p. 114.

9 *Meerut Depositions*, nos. 69 and 70.

10 *Ibid.* nos. 2 and 3.

11 *Ibid.* nos. 67 and 68.

12 *Ibid.* nos. 42 and 45.

13 Williams, *Memorandum*, p. 1.

14 On the Kotwal being a Gujar and on these episodes, *Meerut Depositions*, nos. 67 and 68.

15 For the 'pop shop' *Meerut Depositions*, nos. 41 and 45 and Lt.-Col. Lewis Butler, *Annals of the K.R.R.*, vol. III, p. 16.

16 *Meerut Depositions*, nos. 42 and 43. One group was warned by a Christian drummer from a native regiment, *ibid.* no. 45.

17 *Ibid.* nos. 43 and 44; for the wooden or plank bridge, above, chapter 5.

18 *Ibid.* no. 18.

19 Colonel A. R. D. Mackenzie, *Mutiny Memoirs*, p. 16.

20 Stubbs, *History of the Bengal Artillery*, vol. III, p. 250.

21 *Meerut Depositions*, no. 30 (Eckford), 31 (Chapman), 46 (Mrs Markoe), 47 (Mrs Cahill). Surgeon Smith was retired on the Veteran Establishment. The location of the bungalow is established by Eckford's deposition and by the fact that Captain Earle of the 20th N.I. passed Smith's bungalow after travelling some way up towards the Dragoon Bridge (*Meerut Depositions*, no. 32).

22 *Ibid.* no. 22; Colonel A. R. D. Mackenzie, *Mutiny Memoirs*, p. 23.

23 Sir Hugh Gough, *Old Memories*, p. 45.

24 *Meerut District Narrative*, para. 171; *Meerut Depositions*, no. 22.

25 M. B. Thornhill, *Personal Adventures, etc. during the Indian Mutiny*, pp. 145 ff. Thornhill, with Sherer, was the best writer of those who have left their Mutiny experiences on record.

26 *Meerut Depositions*, no. 52.

27 *Ibid.* nos. 53 and 54.

28 Letters from H. H. Greathed's brother, Lieutenant Wilberforce Greathed in H. H. Greathed's, *Letters written during the Siege of Delhi*, Appendix, pp. 289 ff.

29 The Greatheds' adventure, so creditable to their servants, is mentioned in a number of sources: *Meerut Depositions*, no. 71; Mrs Greathed's *Account* in N. A. Chick, *Annals of the Indian Rebellion*, pp. 105–8; the letter from Lieutenant W. Greathed, *ibid.* pp. 108–10, mentioned in the previous note; and Sir Hugh Gough, *Old Memories*, pp. 33–7. Jan Fishan Khan was an Afghan Sirdar who sided with Shah Shuja and the British, and is often referred to in Kaye's *War in Afghanistan* and in Mrs Colin Mackenzie's *Six Years in India*: his nephew's name is given in the letter from W. Greathed as Sirdar Bahadur Peer Mohamed Khan and he is doubtless the person called 'Syed Meer (sc. Peer) Khan known as the Sirdar Bahadur', whose magniloquent account of his exploit is contained in *Meerut Depositions*, no. 28.

30 *Meerut Depositions*, no. 29. Somewhere perhaps in the National Archives of India are lying the original *Depositions* and with them possibly the map marked by Furnell, a pre-1857 cantonment map which would be of the greatest interest. It is to be wished that a search might be made.

31 *Meerut District Narrative*, paras. 187–90, where the name of the Conductor is not given and the time of his murder is put at midnight. Obviously, he was Sergeant Law whose death and the sufferings of whose family are recorded in *Meerut Depositions*, nos. 48 and 49, where the time is given by Mrs Law herself as soon after 10 p.m. and confirmed by Sergeant Foster. The case recorded by Furnell is much earlier, but he may have been present when she really was brought in later.

32 *Meerut Depositions*, no. 21, by the head jailer; *Meerut District Narrative*, para. 191. It must be repeated that there is no doubt at all about this: contrary to what was thought at the time, even by an eye-witness of the rescue, as Mackenzie was, the prisoners were *not* released at the same time as the sowars. For the flight of the jail guards, see *Meerut Depositions*, no. 23.

33 *Meerut Depositions*, nos. 59–69. Gujars are a caste with a somewhat mysterious and perhaps not ignoble origin. They are agriculturalists but they have a propensity, apparently long practised, for cattle-thieving, from which follows a tendency to violence in general: they thus form a peculiarly lawless element in the countryside, are accustomed to keep weapons hidden, to plunder their neighbours when opportunity occurs, and to defend their villages even against military forces. See W. Crooke, *Tribes and Castes of the N.W.P. of India*.

34 On the 1867 map the (or a) Telegraph Office is marked in the rear of the Carabiniers' lines: it cannot have been from there that these messages were despatched.

35 The telegram (or rather Colvin's telegram relaying it to Calcutta) was printed in the *Parliamentary Papers*, 1857, but can more easily be found in Kaye, *Sepoy War*, vol. I, p. 595.

36 *Meerut District Narrative*, para. 200; *Agra Division Narrative*, para. 9.

CHAPTER 10, pp. 97–105

1 For Hewitt's escape, see the letter from Lt.-Col. Le Champion, who in 1857 was Lieutenant Möller of the 11th N.I., printed in Kaye, *Sepoy War*, vol. III, p. 679: Le Champion says that Hewitt was 'half-dressed', probably meaning he had put on part of his uniform over the common hot-weather housewear of loose shirt and pyjamas. Le Champion claims that three times between 6 p.m. and 7.30 he applied to Hewitt for permission to ride with a warning to Delhi: this was after Le Champion had been back to Mrs Chambers' bungalow. On each occasion, Hewitt told him to get Wilson's permission, so Wilson and Hewitt were not then together. It may be doubted whether the last application was as late as 7.30 p.m. For Wilson's claim about the presence of the divisional commander, see his explanation in Forrest, *Selections*, vol. I, p. 261.

2 O'Callaghan, *Fatal Falter at Meerut*, p. 22, for Captain Dennys' mission; Wilson's explanation in Forrest, *loc. cit.* for Whish's arrival; Mrs Muter, *My Recollections of the Sepoy Revolt*, p. 27, for his guard firing on Wilson and cf. the Rev. T. C. Smyth's account in Chick, *Annals of the Indian Rebellion*, pp. 103–5 for other firing by Wilson's guard: see above, chapter 7, note 1, for Gough's encounter with Wilson on the evening of 9 May.

3 For Möller's escape, see his (Le Champion's) letter, note 1, above; for O'Callaghan's escape, *Fatal Falter at Meerut*, p. 22.

4 Möller (Le Champion) and O'Callaghan as in note 3; Kaye's final comment in his *Sepoy War*, vol. III, p. 682; for Lieutenant Furnell and the party of Carabiniers, see above, chapter 9, note 30.

5 Surgeon O'Callaghan's two accounts are in N. A. Chick, *Annals of the Indian Rebellion*, pp. 99–103 (*A Medical Officer's description of the outbreak at Meerut*, anonymous, but certainly by him) and his pamphlet, *Fatal Falter at Meerut*; the former was written not later than 1858, the latter not later than 1864. Apart from comments or discussion, I use so far as possible O'Callaghan's own words about the Carabiniers' movements (the pages in *Fatal Falter*, etc., are 22–24).

6 Le Champion's statement in his letter already quoted. It seems a possibility that he saw the party move off with Furnell and thought this was a general move.

7 Smyth's *Account*, p. 95.

8 O'Callaghan, *Fatal Falter at Meerut*, p. 25; the Rev. T. C. Smyth and A. Medland in Chick, *op. cit.* pp. 103–5 and 110–12.

9 On the time, see chapter 5 above.

10 For the two messengers, see Lt.-Col. Lewis Butler, *Annals of the K.R.R.*, vol. III, p. 96; his account is mainly drawn from Mrs Muter, with some unfortunate embellishments of his own, but he has also some interesting details. Captain Muter, in a chapter appearing in his wife's book, mentions how the men seemed to melt away without orders. When they reassembled, they included large numbers of those who are described by Mrs Muter, in the prim language of the orderly room, as 'the excused', that is the Roman Catholics and Presbyterians who had not turned out for the Anglican church parade and may even have outnumbered the Church of England men.

11 Mrs Muter, *op. cit.* p. 24; Butler, *op. cit.* p. 95.

12 Butler's picture (*op. cit.* p. 95) of the Rifles moving 'flanked on the left by some troops of the Carabiniers and on the right by a Battery H.A.' is fanciful.

13 See the account of Earle's escape, chapter 7 above.

14 Mrs Muter, *op. cit.* p. 28.

15 O'Callaghan, *Fatal Falter at Meerut*, p. 25. His topography here is uncertain: he speaks of crossing the parade ground to where the Delhi road leads off, but no sense can be made of this: even the road to Baghput was a long way off to the south, beyond the native cavalry lines.

16 *Ibid.* p. 26.

17 *Ibid.* p. 26.

18 *Ibid.* p. 26.

19 These are the Brigadier's words as recorded by Muter himself, Mrs Muter, *op. cit.* p. 101; Butler, *op. cit.* embellishes, as too often, and makes Wilson say 'Yes, shoot them like dogs.' Note there is no mention even of Hewitt.

20 Mrs Muter, *op. cit.* p. 29.

21 For the Artillery's performance, see O'Callaghan, *Fatal Falter at Meerut*, p. 26; Mrs Muter, *op. cit.* p. 29; Mackenzie, *Mutiny Memoirs*, p. 33.

22 O'Callaghan, *op. cit.* p. 27, for the retirement of the European troops. He cannot, however, be right in saying that they re-entered the burning station from the southward: the evidence about the Craigie party never hearing them precludes this. Their point of entry may have been slightly south of the centre of the main block but not much. At this point O'Callaghan lost the Carabiniers and attached himself to the Artillery; see his narrative in Chick, *op. cit.* p. 101.

23 O'Callaghan, *Fatal Falter at Meerut*, p. 27, says they went by the 'main street' and Mrs Muter, *op. cit.* p. 32, says they 'passed through the bazars'. This means, I think, that they went by Sudder Street which was certainly the main street in the area of the native lines and ran for a good distance along the edge of the Sudder Bazar. Gough, *Old Memories*, p. 45, says 'through the bazar and the cantonments lately occupied by the officers'.

24 For these various survivors, see chapters 7 and 9 above.

25 O'Callaghan, *Fatal Falter at Meerut*, p. 27.

26 Mackenzie, *Mutiny Memoirs*, p. 25, says that his (the Craigie) party heard nothing, but learned afterwards that 'a strong mounted party had been sent to clear the cantonments and rescue any survivors of the massacre; but—incredible to relate—it had been misled by the Staff Officer who was detailed to guide it, and never reached its destination'. He is here (writing thirty-five years later) confusing his account with some memory of the supposed deviation of the whole of the Carabiniers when they left their parade ground. Chapman, moreover, says he was rescued by the arrival of the Carabiniers (not of the European troops, as do the officers of the 20th N.I.). I think these two passages are traces of a party of Carabiniers having been sent round the side roads during the retirement. It cannot have been sent at any other time, for O'Callaghan would have mentioned it, but at this stage he had parted from the Carabiniers and joined the Artillery (see his narrative in Chick, *op. cit.* p. 101).

27 O'Callaghan, *Fatal Falter at Meerut*, p. 28, 'on the course close to the Dragoon lines'. The Course means the Mall and Mrs Muter says they bivouacked on the Mall. For the guns at the bridges (or some of them) see Mackenzie, *Mutiny Memoirs*, p. 28, and for the picquets in the Artillery lines, the Rev. T. C. Smyth in Chick, *op. cit.* p. 104.

28 Mrs Muter, *op. cit.* p. 19.

29 The Rev. T. C. Smyth in Chick, *op. cit.* p. 104.

30 For the various native guards, see the Rev. T. C. Smyth *ubi supra*, and *Meerut District Narrative*, paras. 174–8.

31 Gough, *Old Memories*, p. 46; *Meerut District Narrative*, para. 201.

32 *Meerut District Narrative, ibid.*; Smyth's *Account*, p. 96.

33 Colonel Carmichael-Smyth was with it and returned when it struck the *pukka* (surfaced) road, two miles from the cantonment: this may mean either the Baghput or the Delhi road, probably the latter. See Smyth's *Account*, p. 95.

34 *Meerut District Narrative*, para. 202.

35 General Hewitt's telegram of 18 May 1857; Forrest, *Selections*, vol. I, p. 255; the Rev. T. C. Smyth's *Account* in Chick, *op. cit.* p. 105.

36 *Meerut Depositions*, nos. 46, 48 and 52. The Rev. T. C. Smyth, *loc. cit.* says three of Law's children were killed, but from Mrs Law's deposition (no. 48) there seem to have been only two.

37 *Meerut Depositions*, no. 31.

38 *Ibid.* nos. 44 and 45.

39 The next morning, the Brigadier told Carmichael-Smyth that there were ten or twelve (Smyth's *Account*, p. 95). Earle says there were fourteen or fifteen and that they were European soldiers and their wives (*Meerut Depositions*, no. 32). Sergeant Harwood gives the number as eight (*ibid.* no. 50).

40 *Meerut Depositions*, no. 50.

41 *Ibid.* no. 52.

42 *Ibid.* nos. 69 and 70.

CHAPTER 11, pp. 106–118

1 Kaye, *Sepoy War*, vol. III, p. 678. Kaye actually printed this correspondence in the last issue of vol. II, but it is simpler to give the reference to vol. III where he printed it as an Addendum to vol. II.

2 For Le Champion's letter, see Kaye, *Sepoy War*, vol. III, p. 679, and for the reference in the *Meerut District Narrative*, see the footnote to para. 181.

3 Kaye–Malleson, vol. II, p. 49.

4 T. R. E. Holmes, *History of the Indian Mutiny*, 5th ed. p. 102.

5 For the Rosser episode, see O'Callaghan, *Fatal Falter at Meerut*, pp. 29–30; a letter from Charles Raikes quoted by Kaye, *Sepoy War*, vol. II, p. 663; Mackenzie, *Mutiny Memoirs*, pp. 33–4; Gough, *Old Memories*, p. 43; T. R. E. Holmes, *op. cit.* p. 103; Kaye, *op. cit.* vol. II, pp. 67, 663–4.

6 See a letter from Wilson to Kaye in 1868, *Sepoy War*, vol. II, p. 663.

7 Le Champion's letter in Kaye, *Sepoy War*, vol. III, p. 680.

8 Forrest, *Selections*, vol. I, p. 23, footnote. On 10 May, Grant was Commander-in-Chief in Madras, 1500 miles away: his opinion was expressed when he reached Calcutta to succeed Anson.

9 Lord Roberts, *Forty-one Years in India*, vol. I, pp. 89–90. Rice Holmes in his sometimes schoolmasterish way overrules Lord Roberts but one should not accept that.

10 As Kaye, *Sepoy War*, vol. II, p. 107.

11 For the Vellore affair, see Wilson, *History of the Madras Army*, vol. III, p. 185.

1   There is a copy of this map in the British Museum. When it was made, the direct road link from Mooradnagar to Ghaziuddinnagar had not been constructed. The Meerut–Delhi road took a more northerly slant from Mooradnagar and crossed the Hindan by a ford a good deal higher up than in 1857. On the western bank, it went through a place called Farrukhnagar, which does not always appear on modern maps but was a little south-east of Rajpur. This was the road which Thomas Bacon (*First Impressions, etc. of India*) followed in 1835. The route was altered after 1835.

2   *Meerut Depositions*, no. 26. This deposition is said to be made by Bidhee Singh, chaukidār of Mulleeana, Luchminger and Khosiallee and other residents of Keshunpoor. It is uncertain who said what.

3   For the assembly at Rethanee, see *Meerut Depositions*, no. 4: the place appears as Rutanee on Brown's map and Rithani on later maps.

4   Munshi Mohanlal's testimony, his *Memorandum on the causes of the Mutiny*, of which there is a copy in the *Kaye Papers*, HM 725, p. 359 (no. 10 in Hill's *Catalogue*). There is no reason to doubt Mohanlal's report of the conversation and no reason either to suppose that the sowar, in a chance conversation in those circumstances, distorted the truth. Rice Holmes, *History of the Indian Mutiny*, 5th ed. (revised and enlarged) 1898, p. 102, inserted in his text a new statement that the majority were for taking refuge in Rohilkhand but one pointed out that the best course would be to make for Delhi and his counsel prevailed; for this, he gives as references *P.P.* XVIII, 1859, p. 335, para. 15, and *Depositions*, no. 8, but both these references are wrong, and he had got them somehow mixed. His mention of Rohilkhand probably depends on Mohanlal: his reference to one single speaker in favour of Delhi remains untraceable. He missed the reference in the *Depositions* to Rethanee. For Möller's statement, Kaye, *Sepoy War*, vol. III, p. 680.

5   *Meerut Depositions*, no. 27.

6   *Ibid.* nos. 23 and 24.

7   *Meerut Depositions*, no. 26 (Mulleeana chaukidār); *Meerut District Narrative*, para. 184 and Williams, *Memorandum*, p. 8, also reflect the idea of this party having gone down the Grand Trunk Road.

8   *Meerut District Narrative*, para. 184 and Williams, *Memorandum*, p. 8, speak of disorganised flight in small parties along by-roads but the evidence in the *Meerut Depositions* does not by any means support this.

9   Hewitt's despatch is in Forrest, *Selections*, vol. I, pp. 249–50; Waterfield's telegram from Umballa is in *Selections from the Records of the Government of the Punjab*, vol. VII, part I, *Mutiny Correspondence*, p. 18, no. 12. A fantastic story about defending the line of the Hindan is in N. A. Chick, *Annals of the Indian Rebellion*, in the Red Pamphlet (*History of the Indian Mutiny by an officer who has served under Sir Charles Napier*, sc. G. B. Malleson) and in Charles Ball, *History of the Indian*

Mutiny. There are some writers who say that Graves received a message but they probably confuse despatch from Meerut to Delhi with receipt at Delhi; they go on to give fantastic accounts (as in the *Red Pamphlet*) of the Mutineers advancing from the Hindan 10 or 12 miles away, Graves leading the Delhi troops to meet them *out of* the Kashmir Gate (when he was three miles or so away on the Ridge), and the whole mass being forced back through that gate into the city. People were oddly ignorant about topography in those days: William Waterfield in his diary complains of such ignorance in the newspapers, citing a case of a newspaper which described the view from Delhi of the mountains round Kabul, doubtless because Delhi had a Kabul Gate.

10 *Meerut District Narrative*, para. 200.

11 *Trial of the ex-King of Delhi* (*Selections from the Records of the Government of the Punjab, etc.*, n.s. no. VII), p. 158, diary of Chuni Lal, newswriter; Mainodin in C. T. Metcalfe, *Two Native Narratives etc.*, p. 42. The suggestion of Mrs F. A. Steel, *On the Face of the Waters*, pp. 196–7, footnote, that Fraser received a *telegram* from Meerut is impossible because the Delhi–Meerut wire was cut before 4 p.m. on 10 May.

12 Mrs Peile (anonymously), *History of the Delhi Massacre, etc.*; Marshall escaped with Colonel Knyvett of the 38th N.I. and joined Vibart's party (Colonel E. Vibart, *The Sepoy Mutiny*); Knyvett was at the Flagstaff Tower, so then was Marshall. From the Meerut end the times do not fit. Any messenger from the civil authorities would not have been sent off until hope had been lost that Greathed would appear in the European lines. That would postulate a despatch at around 9.30 p.m. after moonrise or more probably about 11 p.m. when the European troops returned. Whether the messenger went by the main road, dodging the mutineers down by-roads, or by the longer Baghput road, he could not possibly have reached Ludlow Castle before Fraser went to bed. Fraser appeared at the Red Fort rather earlier than might have been expected but this can be explained either by a message from the Calcutta Gate or by the swift spread of a report even as far as Marshall's. A rumour may have preceded the mutineers' arrival. Forty years later, Mrs Flora Annie Steel, *On the Face of the Waters*, p. 189, was told by an eyewitness of a Muslim fanatic who crossed at dawn on camel-back, a tale one does not easily forget.

13 See H. C. Fanshawe, *Delhi Past and Present* (1902), pp. 33–4, 96, who elucidates this movement of the sowars, misunderstood by most writers, who make them get *into* the Fort and appear below a veranda or balcony *within*. It may be recalled that Aurangzīb's first care after a grave illness early in his reign was to drag himself from bed and appear at this jharokha.

14 *Trial of the ex-King of Delhi*, pp. 118, 125, 136, 251.

15 *Ibid.* pp. 136–8.

16 *Ibid.* pp. 38–40; Fanshawe, *op. cit.* p. 96. Douglas wanted to go out by the postern and speak to the men but the King forbade this.

17 *Trial of the ex-King of Delhi*, p. 119.

18 *Ibid.* pp. 118, 125, 127 (evidence of Bakhtawar Singh chaprāsī and

Makhan chobdar); C. T. Metcalfe, *Two Native Narratives, etc.,* pp. 41–2, 76–80, 236–38.

19 C. T. Metcalfe, *op. cit.* pp. 41–3, 78. Mainodin was told or thought that Hutchinson, when he set off for the Kashmir Gate, was going to Fraser's house.

20 His full name was Sir John Theophilus Metcalfe and he is sometimes referred to as Sir John, sometimes as Sir Theophilus. He was the son of Sir Thomas and the nephew of Sir Charles (Lord Metcalfe). He lived at Metcalfe House on the bank of the Jumna about two miles from the Kashmir Gate, which had been built by his father during his long tenure of the Residency at Delhi. There are two printed accounts of his escape, one by Mainodin in C. T. Metcalfe, *Two Native Narratives of the Mutiny in Delhi* and one in an appendix to Colonel Keith Young, *Delhi, 1857;* there are also two brief unprinted accounts in the India Office Library, one among the Ricketts papers (Reel 576/11) and one among the Hardcastle papers (Photo Eur. 31/18): these unprinted accounts substantially agree. All the accounts printed or unprinted are really accounts of the escape of Metcalfe and there does not appear to exist any written record by him of the events of the early morning, except a brief mention that he saw the mutineers crossing the bridge of boats, a fact mentioned (without giving Metcalfe's name) in Mr Perceval Spear's, *Twilight of the Moguls.*

21 Forrest was one of those awarded the V.C. for the blowing up of the Magazine and was the father of Sir George Forrest, the historian, and of R. E. T. Forrest, who wrote as R. E. Forrest, *Eight Days,* a novel which describes the outbreak in Delhi, the blowing up of the Magazine, and the escape of the party (which included Lieutenant George Forrest and his wife) whose adventures are recorded in Colonel E. Vibart, *The Sepoy Mutiny.* The novel *Eight Days* contains many things which obviously the author derived from his father or mother and it describes the escape of an English family from a bungalow in the area adjacent to the Kashmir Gate Main Guard: this must have been Forrest's own bungalow. It is not so probable that this bungalow was behind or around St James's Church, or behind (to the west) of Skinner's house. By 1857 that area had become mainly occupied by prominent Eurasians while the European officials had moved out to the cantonment on the Ridge. As shown on a map of Delhi in the India Office Library with lettering in Urdu which dates from after 1835 (because it shows William Fraser's tomb on the edge of the churchyard west of the church) there was Skinner's house across the open space outside the Main Guard: a large bungalow at the north-west angle of the churchyard was occupied by Major Forster, another Eurasian, who raised and commanded the Shekawati Brigade; cf. the above map and Vibart *op. cit.* In the novel of Nazīr Ahmad, *Ibn-ul-waqt,* when the hero decides to become a reformer in his own community, his first step is to acquire a bungalow in the cantonment.

22 Forrest's written report to the Inspector-General of Ordnance is in Forrest, *Selections,* vol. I, pp. 272–75, his verbal evidence in *Trial of the ex-King of Delhi,* pp. 115–18.

23 For Mrs Aldwell's account, see *Trial of the ex-King of Delhi*, p. 273; for the position of her house Fanshawe, *Delhi Past and Present*, p. 104, note 1. She and her children escaped, as the sole survivors, from the massacre of the prisoners in the palace: she claimed they were Muhammadans and no doubt she was a dark Eurasian. They got away to Meerut.

24 For the presence of the Jhajjar sowars at the Calcutta Gate see *Trial of the ex-King of Delhi*, p. 127. Perhaps however there were only the few orderlies present: the evidence is not clear.

25 C. T. Metcalfe, *Two Native Narratives*, etc., pp. 43 ff. The editor was a younger brother of Sir Theophilus, who served in the Police.

26 The rumour at the Calcutta Gate was that the mutineers had entered by the Zīnat-ul-masājid Gate which is another name for the Rajghat Gate. That is true of the earlier small party but not, it seems, of the later, larger party who were seen going down past the Khairati Gate, south of the Rajghat Gate.

27 *Trial of the ex-King of Delhi*, pp. 109, 119, 125, 127; C. T. Metcalfe, *Two Native Narratives*, etc., pp. 41–5, 78, 235–45.

28 Major Abbott's report, Forrest, *Selections*, vol. I, p. 263; Major Patterson's evidence, *Trial of the ex-King of Delhi*, p. 146; Fanshawe, *Delhi Past and Present*, p. 101. The Main Guard was a twelve-sided enclosure on the inner side of the Gate. The map referred to in note 21 above, marks it as *Kiranchi Gard*, which was presumably its native name. Kiranchi is not in Forbes' *Hindustani Dictionary*, but Platts gives it and translates 'a superior description of goods' cart (made of wood instead of bamboo)'. *Hobson-Jobson* gives it s.v. *Cranchee* as a kind of rickety and sordid carriage standing for native hire in Calcutta but also has a quotation from Augustus Prinsep's *The Baboo* where it figures as 'hackney coach'. An addition by W. Crooke, the later editor, says the word was used in Northern India as well as in Calcutta. It seems thus that to the natives of Delhi, the Main Guard figured as an enclosure for baggage wagons or officers' coaches. However, Nazīr Ahmad in his novel of the Mutiny period, *Ibn-ul-Waqt*, calls it simply *Kashmiri darwaze ka gard*.

29 *Trial of the ex-King of Delhi*, p. 138.

INDEX

Abbott, Colonel Augustus (Inspector-General of Ordnance), 13; suggests committee on greasing, 16

Abū Nullah, the, character and course of, 48–50; 87, 91, 94, 101

Account, Smyth's, troop commanders' reports (23 April), 61

Adley, Assistant Surgeon(20th N.I.),78

Agra, 93, 120; telegraph-line 55–6; cutting of, 96

Agra Division Narrative, 96, 136 n. 1

Ahsanullah (physician), 124

Aldwell, Mrs, evidence of, 126–7

Alexander, Lt.-Col. F. (Executive Engineer), his map, 47

Alexander, Captain W. C. (11th Irregular Cavalry), at Berhampore, 25; presides at Court of Inquiry, 26

Allen, Lieutenant (34th N.I.), 22

Ambala, Musketry Depot, 14, 56; first use of new cartridges, 15; new greasing order received, 16; revised firing practice, at, 19, 31; incendiarism at, 58; telegraph line from Meerut, 56

Ammunition, *see* Cartridges

Anderson, Major G. F. (Deputy Superintendent), his maps, 48

Anson, the Hon .George (Commander-in-Chief), 37, 63; at Ambala, 17; orders court-martial at Meerut, 64; deplores public shackling, 69

Arot, John, 93

Arsenals and magazines, 10

Artillerymen, depositions of, 91

Ashburnham, Lieutenant (Q.R.R.), 101

Austin, Lieutenant (Q.R.R.), secures Treasury, 101

Bacon, Thomas, account of Meerut in 1837, 47, 53

Badaon District, chapātīs in, 1

Baghput, 119

Bajenghur, chapātīs at, 1

Bakhtawar Singh (chaprāsī), 124

Baksh Ali, Havildār-Major (3rd L.C.), 66; obeys order to fire, 62–3

Barnard, Sir Henry, 37

Barrackpore, 21; incident of rumoured plot, 22–3; uneasiness at, 28, 132

Baugh, Lieutenant (34th N.I.), 29

Bazars (Meerut)
  Artillery, 50
  Cavalry, 52
  Dragoon, 49, 94
  European Infantry, 49
  Sudder, 50, 52; *see also under* Sudder Bazar

Becher, Captain S. H. (First Assistant Adjutant-General), 17; his correspondence with Martineau, 32

Begumabad, 119

Bengal Army, nature of grievances of, 6; cohesion of, 7; Government awakes to fears of, 15; mutinous state alleged, 58–9; state and outlook of European officers, 147 n. 11

Bengal Artillery, 68, 100; at Berhampore, 23; at Meerut, 34, 49; depositions of men, 91; alerted by Wilson, 97; route of (10 May), 101; at native parade ground, 102; cause of delay, 107

Berhampore, 4; serious incidents at, 23–6, 58, 132; causal factors in episode, 27, 115; parallels with Meerut, 130; psychological features, 134–5

Berners, Captain (Brunswick Army), suggests improvement of rifle, 10

Bessokur, sowars at, 121

Bhorboral, 119; mutineers at, 121

Blunt, George (Judge), 46

Bontein, Major J. (Musketry Depot), 15, 26, 32; suggest revision of loading-drill, 16–17; suggestion adopted, 18

Bridges (Meerut)
  Begum's, 49, 50, 79, 93, 116, 119
  Dragoon, 49, 50, 77, 79, 97, 100, 102, 116
  Plank or wooden, 50, 91, 64
  Terminus Road, 50, 87
  Others (including Sūrajkund), 52, 85

Brijmohan, 44, 81; his hut burned, 58–9, 61; fires and reports on cartridges, 59–60, 66, 67

Brown, Captain W., his map of Meerut District (1831), 119

'Brown Bess' smooth-bore musket, 10

Brunswick rifle, 10, 11

Buksh, Elahi, shop of, 54, 78, 94, 116

Bungalows (Meerut), burning of, 85
Men's, 49
Officers', 47, 49, 51, 91; of named owners, 54, 92, 94

Cahill, —, 116
Mrs, escapes, 92

Calcutta, 106

Canning, Lord (Governor-General), writes to Anson, 18; minutes case of 19th N.I., 28; attempts to subdue cartridge agitation, 31; receives Colvin's message, 96

Caps, percussion, use of, 9; withholding of, 10; acceptance refused by 19th N.I., 24

Carabiniers, the, *see* Dragoon Guards, 6th

Carbine, used by cavalry, 10

Carmichael-Smyth, Colonel G. M. (3rd L.C.), 86, 145 n. 41; origins and career, 38–41; relationship with Gardiner, 41–3; his documents on Meerut outbreak, 43, 61; alleged unpopularity of, 44–5; summary of character, 45–6; bungalow of, 54; absence and return of, 58–9; his actions on 23 April, 59, 62; ambivalence of, 59–60; questions troop commanders, 61; cajoles and dismisses firing parade, 63; at court-martial (6 May), 65; abused by prisoners, 68; reproves Gough, 70; dinner party (10 May), 80–1; conduct during evening of 10 May, 81–2; at native lines (11 May), 104; a claim unsupported, 133; his behaviour assessed, 134

Cartridges, types of, 8, 11–12; manufacture of, 10; loading of (balled), 13; service and practice, 13–14, 153 n. 15; greasing of, 21; paper called in question, 22, 26, 67; fired by Brijmohan, 59–60; examined by Court of Inquiry, 64; subject of evidence, 65–6

'Balled', 17; general introduction of, 13, 18

Casualties at Meerut, extent of, 104–5

Cavalry, Irregular
8th, at Bareli, 140 n. 7
11th, at Berhampore, 23, 25

Cavalry, Light, 10–11
3rd, 13, 112; suspicion of cartridge paper, 14; at Meerut, 35, 52; shares guard with 20th N.I., 36; ordered to firing parade, 39, 59; skirmishers refuse cartridges, 61–2; skirmishers condemned, 67; and publicly shackled, 68; rumoured appeal of, 71; outbreak subsequent to infantry's, 80; party release imprisoned sowars, 82–3; another party follows Craigie, 85–7; protection of Mrs Courtney, 89; no wholesale attack, 103; reach Delhi, 123, 126, 127; near Kashmir Gate, 128

Chambers, Captain (11th N.I.), bungalow of, 54; visits Macdonald, 72, 75
Mrs, body found, 86; murder of, 88

Chandni Chauk (Delhi), 125

Chapātīs, extent of distribution, 1–2; significance of, 2–4, 133; background of, 5–7

Chapman, — (pensioner), 102, 116; experiences of 10 May, 92

Chaprāsīs, mission of, 4

Chaukidars, as chapātī-bearers, 1–2, 3

Chester, Colonel (Adjutant-General), 63; questions new greasing-order, 16; orders target-practice, 18; fears refusal, 19; false sense of security, 32

Chick, N. A. (*Annals of Indian Rebellion*), 43, 47, 98, 111

Chittagong, 31

Cholera, epidemic of 2; pills, 3, 45

Christianity, suspected threat of, 5–6, 23

Christians, disperse *badmashes*, 75, 88; as object of attack in church, 133

Christie, Surgeon-Major (3rd L.C.), 80–1, 100; wounded, 103

Chuppattees, *see* Chapātīs

Index

Churches (Meerut)
  Protestant, 49, 54; service time on
    10 May, 56
  Roman Catholic (chapel), 54, 91
Civil Station (Meerut), 52
Clubs, English, in India, 152 n. 20
Colvin, Mr, message to Canning, 96
Cook boy, doubtful existence of, 73,
  129
Court-martial, proceedings at Meerut,
  65–7
Courtney, Mrs, death of, 89–90,
  157 n. 20
Courts of Inquiry, 14, 45; hears 2nd
  N.I., 22; significant factors at
  Berhampore, 26–7; hears officers
  of 34th N.I., 30; at Meerut, 63–4
Craigie, Captain H. C. (3rd L.C.), 45,
  66, 112, 116; bungalow of, 54;
  sends note to Melville-Clarke, 60,
  61; actions on 10 May, 85–6, 151
  n. 11
  Mrs, 79, 84, 85; rescues carabinier,
    86, 91; escapes, 87
Cunninghame, RQMS (or RSM), two
  versions of behaviour of, 83, 84
Curzon, Colonel (Military Secretary
  to Commander-in-Chief), 59
Custance, Lt.-Col. W. N. (Carabiniers), 58, 70, 77, 146 n. 4; dis-
  putes fact of roll call, 98, 107,
  109–10, 113; failure to pursue
  justified, 114–15; failure to secure
  bridge criticized, 116
Cutcherries (Meerut)
  Collector and Magistrate's, 53, 101
  Judges, 53

Dacoits, at Meerut, 53
Dam-damma (Artillery School,
  Meerut), 47, 89, 100, 103; position
  of, 49; recruits dismissed, 64
Dareean, musician or bandsman, 73
Daryaganj, 126; Metcalfe at, 127
Dawson, Veterinary Surgeon (Bengal
  Artillery), murder of, 88–9
Delhi, chapātīs in, 1; fighting at, 37;
  mutineers make for, 114; arrival,
  123–6; as planned objective, 120–
  1, 132
  Court of, 132
  Field Force, commanders of, 37, 74
  Gates of, see under Gates

King of, 120, 124, 128; the appeal
  to, 136
Dennys, Captain (11th N.I.), 76, 97, 116
Dhunna Singh (Kotwal), justification of, 91
Dhurma Sabha, the, 21
Dildar Khan (of royal bodyguard,
  Delhi), 125
Divisions, military and civil, defined,
  142 n. 1
Doab, suspicions and fears in, 5;
  cholera in, 2, 45; mutineers' homes
  in 114
Douglas, Captain (of royal bodyguard,
  Delhi), actions on 11 May, 123–5;
  murder of, 127
Dragoon Guards, 6th (Carabiniers),
  68, 94; stationed at Meerut, 34–5,
  49; alerted by Wilson, 97; roll
  call of, 89; move off in darkness,
  99; route of, 99–100; at native
  parade-ground, 101–2; rescue
  party, 103; movements analysed,
  107–13, 116–17; alternative suggested, 115–16; see also Troops,
  European
Dum-Dum Musketry Depot, 14, 19;
  incident of khalāsi's warning, 15;
  new greasing order received, 16
Dunlop, R. H. W. (Collector and
  Magistrate), 46

Earle, Captain (20th N.I.), 63, 101;
  joins exodus, 78–9
Eckford, Lieutenant J. (Executive
  Engineer), 102, 116; bungalow
  of, 54; experiences on 10 May, 92
Enfield, 11
  Enfield Rifle, 11, 18; introduction
    causes crisis, 14–15; cartridges
    shown, 22
European troops, see under Troops
Evangelicism, influence in India, 5–6

Fairlie, Major (3rd L.C.), 81, 82, 86
Fatehgarh, 146 n. 61
Faujki Bheera, in Bengal Army
  (Gubbins), 7
Finnis, Colonel (11th N.I.), 97; shot, 76
Fire arms, types of, 10–11; see also
  Small-arms
Firuz Shah, Kotla of, 124, 127
Flagstaff Tower (Delhi), 56, 123

Forrest, Lieutenant George (Assistant Commissary of Ordnance), actions and evidence of, 125–6; awarded V.C., 165 n. 21

Fraser, Simon (Lieutenant-Governor, N.W.P.), alleged receipt of message, 122–3; at Lahore Gate of Fort, 124; at Calcutta Gate, 125; murder of, 127

Fraser, William (Resident of Delhi, 1830–5), 127

French Revolution, the, crowd behaviour in, 134–6

Furnell, Lieutenant (Mounted Police), 91, 99; account of 10 May evening, 94–5

Galway, Captain G. A. (3rd L.C.), 66, 86, 102; warned of trouble, 62

Ganges, river, 23, 121

Gaols, *see* Jails

Gardiner, A. H., relations with Carmichael-Smyth, 41–3; further details of, 149 n. 25

Gates (Delhi)
Calcutta, 119, 123, 124–5, 127
Delhi, 127
Kashmir, 119, 125
Khairati, 126–7
Lahore, 123, 124
Rajghat, 124, 127

Gates (Meerut)
Kamboh, 82
Shahrah, 82

Ghaziuddinnagar (Ghaziabad), 119; engagements at, 37

Ghulam Abbas (Delhi Court), 124

Gillespie, Colonel, actions at Vellore (1806), 117–18

Goolaothee, 121

Gough, Lieutenant Hugh (3rd L.C.), 7, 81, 86, 93, 104; denies being warned of cartridge refusal, 61, 62; reports intention of mutiny, 70, 74, 107, 129; actions on 10 May, 83–4, 112; basis of his report assessed, 129–30

Government of India, the, receives Wright's report, 15; issues new greasing order, 16; reports to Court of Directors, 18; orders disbandment of 19th N.I., 27; dismisses Hewitt, 106

Grant, Sir Patrick (Commander-in-Chief), dismisses Hewitt, 106; judgment upon 10 May, 114–15

Grant, Brigadier (Station Commander, Barrackpore), 22

Graves, Brigadier (Commander at Delhi), 56, 128, 147 n. 14; first news from Meerut, 122

Greasing materials, at Enfield, 11; on Peshawar frontier, 14; committee suggested, 16; Anson's view of, 17

Greathed, H. H. (Commissioner), 46, 70, 153 n. 2; bungalow of, 54; concealed on roof, 81, 83–4, 93; reaches safety, 93

Group behind outbreak, suspected existence of, 27, 30, 129–31

Guard duties, 154 n. 32; briefly shared by cavalry, 36

Gubbins, Martin, 7

Gujars, arson and plunder by, 95; release New Jail convicts, 95; defined, 159 n. 33

Gulab Jan, 70–1

Gulab Singh, Maharajah, 28

Gurgaon, chapātīs in, 1

Hardwar, 58

Harriott, Major J. F. (Deputy Judge Advocate-General), 38, 63; possible proposer of public ironing, 69; sent away by Carmichael-Smyth, 81; evidence of, 106, 130

Harvey, George (Commissioner, Agra Division), 1–2

Hauper, 121

Havildārs, depositions of, 72, 73

Hearsey, Major-General J. B. (commanding Presidency Division), 15, 36; receives new greasing order, 16; forwards Bontein's letter, 17; reports to Government, 21; orders Court of Inquiry, 22; addresses brigade at Barrackpore, 23, 28; courageous act of, 29; cheered by 19th N.I., 31; origins of, 142 n. 11

Hearsey, Lieutenant J., explains Enfield rifle, 22

Henderson, Lieutenant (20th N.I.), killed, 78

Hewitt, Major-General W. H. (commanding Meerut Division), 58,

Index

Hewitt (*cont.*)
107, 159 n. 1; career and character, 36; censures Wilson, 38; dwelling of, 54; orders Court of Inquiry, 63; confirms sentence with qualification, 67; reports to Anson, 68–9; first report after outbreak, 73, 74; goes to European lines, 77, 97; relieved of command, 106; comparison with Gillespie false, 117; differences at Mian Mir, 118

Hewson, Regt. Sergeant-Major (34th N.I.), 29

Hindan, river, 119, 121, 122

Hindus, religious fears of, 5–6; as sepoys and sowars, 6; judged untrustworthy, 30; witnesses to oath at Meerut, 60; on firing parade, 63; at court-martial, 65

Holkar, Jaswant Rao, campaign of 1804, 3

Holmes, T. R. E. (Rice-Holmes), 36, 73, 113; on greasing of cartridges, 21; on Carmichael-Smyth, 44; on nature of outbreak, 129

Hughes, – (pensioner), 93

Humphrey, Lieutenant (20th N.I.), escape of, 78

Hutchinson, J. R. (Delhi Magistrate), movements of, 125, murder of, 127

India Office records, 11, 12, 44; sketch-map of Meerut, 47

Indians, shopkeepers attacked, 95; moral condemnation of sepoys, 137

Jails (Meerut), 52
New, 53, 55, 72; imprisonment of condemned sowars, 68; release by fellow-sowars, 82–3, 131; Gujars release convicts, 95; as alleged objective of Carabiniers, 109–13
Old, 53, 105; convicts released by sepoys, 93

Jhajjar, 127

Johnston, Alexander (Deputy Collector and Magistrate), 46

Jones, Lieutenant E. (Bengal Artillery), his sketch map, 47

Jones, Colonel H. R. (Carabiniers), 58, 63

Jones, J. H., 93

Jumna, river, 115, 119, 124

Kaye, Sir J. W., 36, 98, 146 n. 62; on ammunition, 11–12, 21; on Carmichael-Smyth, 44; on movements of Carabiniers, 110, 113, 117

Kinly, — (pensioner), killed 92

Knyvett, Colonel (38th N.I.), 164 n. 12

Kotwal at Meerut, behaviour of, 91, 95

Kudrat Ali (naik, 3rd L.C.), 60, 65; refuses cartridge, 63; not a ringleader, 131–2

Lahore, History of Reigning Family at, Carmichael-Smyth's editorship of, 42–4

Lane, Bibi, 93

Larke, — (pensioner), 94

Law, Sergeant (conductor), killed, 95
Mrs, wounded, 94; escapes, 95

Lawrence, Henry, disparaged by Carmichael-Smyth, 42–4

Lawrence, John, 118

Le Bas, Judge, 125

Le Champion, *see* Möller

Lefebvre, G., his study of revolutionary crowds, 134–5

Lewis, Ensign (20th N.I.), escape of, 78, 79

Lines (Meerut), 103
European, position and area of, 49–50, 55; unmolested after midnight (10 May), 95
Native, position and area of, 51–2, 55; uproar in, 72, 74, 78

Ludlow Castle (Delhi), 122–3, 125

MacAndrew, Lieutenant (Adjutant, 19th N.I.), 25

Macdonald, Captain (20th N.I.), 63, 72, 75, 81; shot, 77, 89
Mrs, murder of, 88–9

Mackenzie, Lieutenant A.R.D. (3rd L.C.), 44, 83, 96; bungalow of, 54; account of actions on 10 May, 84–6
Miss, 79, 84; rescues Carabinier, 86, 91; escapes, 87

Macnabb, Cornet (3rd L.C.), 116; death of, 92–3

Magazines
expense, 10; blown up at Delhi, 140 n. 3
storage, 10, 140 n. 3

Index

Main Guard (Kashmir Gate, Delhi), 128, 166 n. 28

Mainodin (Mu'inuddin), 122, 125, 127

Malleson, G. B., 113

Mangal Pande (sepoy, 34th N.I.), incident at Barrackpore, 29–30, 132; hanged, 31

Markoe, — (pensioner), 116; killed, 92 Mrs, escapes, 92

Marshall, — (merchant, Delhi), 123; 164 n. 11

Martineau, Captain E. M. (Musketry Depot, Ambala), 17; prescience of, 32–3

Matadeen, evidence at court-martial, 66–7

Maun Singh, Jemadār (Havildār-Major, 3rd L.C.), 81

Medland, Rev. A., 100

Meerut, issue of ammunition at, 15; comparison with Berhampore, 27; new drill introduced, 32; British and native troops at, 34–6; officers and officials at, 36–46; topography of cantonment, 47–55; extent of cantonment, 55; telegraphic communications, 55–6; ascertainable times, 56–7; incendiarism at, 58–9, 64–5; parade of all troops, 67–8; signs of discontent, 70–1; synthesis of events on 10 May, 71–9, 80–7, 88–96, 97–105; casualties at, 104–5; handling of troops at, 106–18; the essential questions reviewed, 129–35; historical analogies, 134–6; a special peculiarity, 136–7; *for topography, see* Bazars, Bridges, Bungalows, Churches, Jails, Lines, Roads, Streets *and* Theatres

Meerut Depositions, 71–2, 90, 129; origin of, 151 n. 18

Meerut District Narrative, 46, 96, 104, 110, 113, 138 n.

Meerut Division, chapātīs in, 1; cholera at, 2

Mehree (mother of Sophie), 70–1

Melville-Clarke, Lieutenant (3rd L.C.) 59, 81, 82; receives note from Craigie, 60; warned by men, 61–2; accompanies Craigie, 85

Metcalfe, Sir Theophilus (Joint Magi-strate, Delhi), 125; encounters mutineers, 127

Mian Mir, factors at, 118

Minié rifle, 10, 11

Minturn, — (American traveller), 47

Missionaries, suspected government support of, 5–6

Mitchell, Lt.-Col. W. St L. (19th N.I.), 45, 145 n. 41; handling of regiment, 23–6, 144 n. 35; an order distorted, 27

Mob (*badmashes*), 75; plunders and murders, 88–95; joined by villagers, 95; composition of, 157 n. 3

Möller, Lieutenant (subsequently Le Champion) (11th N.I.), 77, 110, 113; sees Mrs Chambers and catches her murderer, 88–9; actions and evidence of 97–9, 114, 120–1, 159 n. 1; name and career, 148 n. 19

Montgomery, R. (chief civil officer at Lahore), 118

Mooradnagar, 119, 121

Mooree, 121

Moradabad, Hewitt visits, 36

Mouza Bessokur, 119

Muhammadans, religious fears of, 5–6; as sepoys and sowars, 6; judged trustworthy in 34th N.I., 30; refuse cartridges at Meerut, 60; on firing parade, 63; at court-martial, 65

Mulleeana, 119

Munshi Mohanlal, evidence of, 120

Murshidabad, spinning wheels episode, 4

Mussoorie, 58

Muter, Captain (Q.R.R.), 101, 103; sends party to secure treasury; orders a volley, 102

Mutineers, decide on objective, 119–21; character of journey, 122; reach and enter Delhi, 123–4; 125–6; at Daryaganj, 127; merged in turmoil, 128

Mutiny, suspicion of a planning group, 27, 30, 129–31

Muttra District, chapātīs in, 1

Native Infantry
2nd, 31; suspicion of cartridge

Index

Native Infantry (*cont.*)
  paper, 14; at Raniganj and Bar-
    rackpore, 21; sepoys court-mar-
    tialled at Barrackpore, 28
  7th, Oude irregular, 33
  10th, at Fatehgarh, 146 n. 61
  11th, at Meerut, 35, 52; connection
    with 20th N.I., 35; hear of
    skirmishers' action, 64; hear
    rumours of disarming, 72–3; out
    of control, 76; partially loyal, 79;
    dutiful guards of, 100, 103;
    alleged 'Delhi' cry, 120–1; reach
    Delhi, 126
  15th, leave Meerut, 35
  19th, disbandment of, 19, 27, 30–1;
    unrest at Berhampore, 23–7
  20th, at Meerut, 35, 52; connection
    with 20th N.I., 35; share guard
    with 3rd L.C., 36; senior officers
    absent, 58; supply guard for
    prisoners, 68; hear rumours, 72–
    3; first disobedience and disorder,
    74–6; casualties among officers,
    77–9; entirely mutinous, 79; res-
    pite of six officers, 81–2, 102;
    reach Delhi, 126; leading part of,
    131
  34th, plot rumoured, 22; escort-
    parties, 23–4; case of Mangal
    Pande, 28–9; partially disbanded,
    31
  36th, native officers taunted, 17
  38th, guard at Delhi, 123, 128
  43rd, 31
  54th, at Delhi, 128, 140 n. 1
  63rd, 22
  65th, 23
  70th, 28, 31
Nazīr Ahmad, 165 n. 21; on faithlessness to salt, 137
Nerbudda territory, chapātīs in, 1
Newspapers, publication of incident
  suggested, 66–7
Nimach, chapātīs at, 1
Nimar, chapātīs at, 1, cholera at; 2
North-West Provinces, background
  of Bengal Army, 6, 7

Oath, at Berhampore, 24; at Meerut,
  27, 60, 66
O'Callaghan, Surgeon D. (11th N.I.),
  45, 47; on troop-strengths at

Meerut, 34–6; gets to Carabiniers
  lines, 76–7; accusation against
  Carmichael-Smyth, 82; criticism
  of roll-call, 98; account of Carabiniers' movements, 99–10, 107–
  11, 116–17
Ostracism, social, as factor in discontents, 6
Oudh, chapātīs in, 1; suspicion and
  fears in, 5; background of Bengal
  Army, 6, 7; mutineers' homes in,
  114, 120

Paharganj, 127
Panchāyat, at Berhampore, 24, 27, 145
  n. 41
Pande, Issurī (Ishwari), hanged, 31
Pande, Mangal (sepoy, 34th N.I.),
  incident at Barrackpore, 29–30;
  hanged, 31
'Pandy', origin of term, 29
Parkes, Fanny, 142 n. 33
Parliamentary Papers, 12; Craigie's
  note, 61
'Patch', use of, 8; greasing of, 12;
  obsolete, 18
Paterson, Major (54th N.I.), 140 n. 1
Pattle, Lieutenant (20th, N.I.) 75;
  killed, 78
Peile, Lieutenant (38th N.I.), 140 n. 1
  Mrs, 8, 123
Philips, Veterinary Surgeon (3rd
  L. C.), 80–1, 100, 103; body
  found, 94
Pīr Ali, 60; refuses cartridge, 62–3;
  not a ringleader, 131–2
Platoon Exercise manual, revision of
  loading-drill, 12–13, 17–18; re-
  vised manuals in Upper Pro-
  vinces, 19; shown to Carmichael-
  Smyth, 59; applied by him, 62
Plowden, Major (3rd L.C.), warned of
  trouble, 61, 62
Police, failure in duty, 90–1, 96; attack
  Furnell, 94; a message to Delhi,
  122
Presidency Division, 21, 132, 133

Queen Victoria, birthday of, 133
Queen's Royal Rifles (60th), 57, 68;
  issued with Enfield rifle, 14–15;
  at Meerut, 34, 49; church parade
  of, 73–4; preparations of, 100–1;

Index

Queen's Royal Rifles (*cont.*)
at native parade ground, 102;
cause of delay, 107; parade
ground, 97, 108, 115

Raman Singh, 45
Raniganj, incendiarism at, 21
Reed, Major-General Thomas, 37
Religion, native fears, 5–6, 135–7;
cited as ground for plot, 22; in-
voked by Pande, 30; invoked by
sowars, 82
Report to Gough, 70; assessed, 129–30
Rethanee, 119; mutineers assembly
at, 120, 132
Richardson, Major (3rd L.C.), warned
of trouble, 61, 62
Rifles, 60th, *see* Queen's Royal Rifles
Rifles
Brunswick, 10, 11
Enfield, 11; introduction causes
crisis, 14–15
Minié, 10, 11, 14
Ripley, Colonel (54th N.I.), at Delhi
(11 May), 128
Roads (Meerut)
Abū Lane, 50
Bulandshahr (Grand Trunk), 50,
51, 52, 85, 96, 121
Cemetery, 108–9, 112
Delhi, 50, 52, 79, 119
Garmukhteshwar, 51, 52, 112
Mall, the, 49, 53, 94, 101, 112, 114
Roorkee, 108–9
Sardhana, 108
Terminus, 50, 87, 99
see also Streets
Roberts, Field-Marshal Lord, opinion
of Wilson, 37; judgment on
feasibility of pursuit, 115
Roberts, Major-General Abraham, 36
Rohilkand, chapātīs in, 1; cholera in,
2; suspicion and fears in, 5;
mutineers' homes in, 114, 120
Roll call, of Carabiniers, 98, 107
Rosser, Captain (Carabiniers), offer to
pursue mutineers, 113–14
Rotton, Rev. J. E. W., 104
Mrs, 71
Rudé, G., 134

Saligram (jemadār, 70th N.I.), court-
martialled, 28

Sati (suttee), abolition of, 5
Saugor Territory, chapātīs in, 1
Sekree, 119; sowars at, 121–2
Selimgarh (Fort, Delhi), 119, 123
Sen, S. N., 73; on nature of Meerut
episode, 129
Sepoys, drawn from N.W. Provinces
and Oudh, raise first outcry in
bazar, 88, 130; swell mob, 92;
release Old Jail convicts, 93;
looting by, 95
Serampore (paper factory), 26, 28
Shahjehanpur, attack on Christians,
133
District, chapātīs in, 1
Shaikh Murad Baksh, Subadār-Major
(19th N.I.), 24
Shuldham, Lieutenant (20th N.I.), 78
Sialkot Musketry Depot, 14, 19; new
greasing order received, 16
Sikhs (of 34th N.I.), judged trust-
worthy at Barrackpore, 30; Car-
michael-Smyth's interest in, 41–4
Simla, 32
Small-arms, method of loading, 8–9;
method of discharge, 9; *see also*
Firearms
Smith, Surgeon (Veteran Establish-
ment), 70, 116; bungalow of, 54;
death of, 92
Smyth, Rev. T. C., evidence of, 54,
57, 100, 103, 104
Sophie (prostitute), spreads a rumour,
70–1
Sowars, rescue of imprisoned, 82–3,
131
Spinning wheels, episode of, 4, 133
Streets (Meerut)
Baker, 50
Bridge, 50, 100, 108, 116
Chapel, 50, 54, 94
Church, 50, 101, 103
Clement, 50, 54
Cross, 108–9, 112
Hill, 50, 108
School, 50, 112
Sudder, 50, 51, 79, 91, 102
see also Roads
Sudder Bazar, 50, 52; rumours in,
70–1, 73; first outcry, 72, 74, 80,
88; outbreak of violence, 90; sig-
nificance of outcry assessed, 130
Sūrajkund, 51, 52, 82

Index

Taylor, Major (20th N.I.), 116; commanding regiment, 75; killed, 78

Telegrams (10 May), text of, 96

Telegraphic communications, lines from Meerut, 55–6; line to Delhi cut, 71, 96; line to Agra cut, 96; significance of cutting, 129–30, 132

Theatres (Meerut), 53
Royal, 53
Station, 53

Thornhill, Mark B., 93

Treasury (Meerut), 53, 103; secured by Austin, 101

Tregear, — (Inspector of Education), 77

Troops, relative strengths at Meerut, 35–6; on full parade, 67–8
European, rumoured intervention of, 71, 72, 76; rumour confirmed by sowar, 77; rescue party ineffective, 86; at native parade ground, 102; return to Mall, 102–3; reconnoitring force, 104; handling of, 106–18; planned distraction of, 130–1
see also Bengal Artillery, Dragoon Guards and Queen's Royal Rifles

Turnbull, D. G. (ex-Collector, Bulandshahr), 46

Tytler, Lieutenant (20th N.I.), 78

Umballa, messenger reaches, 122

Utilitarianism, influence of in India, 5–6

Vellore, false parallel of, 117–18

Vibart, Colonel E., 126, 164 n. 12

Warde, Lieutenant (11th N.I.), escorts Hewitt, 77, 97

Waterfield, Major John (38th N.I.: Deputy Assistant Adjutant-General), 38, 69, 122; guides Carabiniers, 99, 109; not responsible for divagation, 116–17

Waterfield, William (B.C.S.), 4, 144 nn. 35, 39, 145 n. 54

Waterfield, Ensign W., death of, 128

Wazir Ali Khan (Deputy Collector), 90

Wheeler, Lt.-Col. S. G. (34th N.I.), 22, 29, 36

Whish, Captain G. P. (60th N.I.), 38, 54, 63, 69, 97, 116; probable course of action (10 May), 76–7

Williams, Fleetwood (later Commissioner, Meerut), 46, 113

Williams, Major G. W., 73; bungalow of, 54; as court registrar, 70; his judgment of police, 90–1

Williams, Captain H. F., 101

Willoughby, — (commanding Magazine, Delhi), 125

Wilson, Brigadier Archdale (Bengal Artillery), 40, 58, 69, 106, 107; career and character of, 36–8; quarrels with Hewitt, 38; bungalow of, 54–5; incredulous of warning, 70; account of outbreak suspect, 74; alerts Artillery and Carabiniers, 97; at Artillery parade ground, 100; at native parade ground, 102; at native lines (11 May), 104; explanation of actions, 111–12; failure to pursue justified, 114–15; order to Carabiniers criticized, 115–16; comparison with Gillespie false, 117; differences at Mian Mir, 118; culpability of, 134

Wilson, J. Cracroft (Judge), his version of outbreak, 133

Wood, Dr and Mrs, 140 n. 1

Wright, Captain (Rifle Instruction Depot), 15

Young, Colonel K. (Judge Advocate-General), 69; recommends court-martial, 64; memorandum, 65

Zeenut, 70

Zer Jharokha (Delhi), 3rd L.C. reach, 123–4